ASSIGNMENT: ZAIRE

BY

Dorothy Louise Kopper

EDITED BY

David R. Enlow

AUTHOR, EDITOR, ORLANDO, FLORIDA

AND

Gary Hardaway

WITH

MENNONITE BRETHREN MISSIONS AND SERVICES

COVER DESIGN BY KENT SULLIVAN

Assignment: Zaire

ISBN 0-9658068-0-4

Library of Congress Catalog No. 97-68851

Cover design by Kent R. Sullivan

Most photographs, some from slides, were taken by Dorothy Kopper. She thanks the other unknown photographers for their contributions.

Printed in U.S.A. by Mennonite Press, Inc., Newton, KS 67114

DEDICATION

Dedicated to my parents:
PETER AND SUSIE BOESE KOPPER
and
to all their descendants

Father said he too had wanted to be a missionary but with a large family he couldn't afford to go back to school. The Lord led him to raise his family so that some of us would become missionaries.

To all missionaries and Christian workers who served on our Congo-Zairian, African Mennonite Brethren field between 1912 and 1996

To all who prayed and gave that made it possible for Mennonite Brethren Missions and Services to keep us on the field.

ACKNOWLEDGMENTS

Thanks for words of encouragement from: family; friends and neighbors; Michael Brago, writing college professor; Joanne Frantz, for introduction to interested people; Ron Newfield's interest and suggestions; Paul Toews, Mennonite Brethren Archives Executive Director.

Missionaries serving in the Belgian Congo in the late 1950s.
Names listed in Appendix A, page 303.

CONTENTS

PART THREE: God Has Done It for Zairian Women, 1970-1987

FOREWORD

IRVIN L. FRIESEN

In the fall of 1996, the poverty-stricken nation of Zaire made daily headlines with stories originating in the Eastern Zaire cities of Goma and Bukavu. Formerly called Belgian Congo, this mid-Africa nation ranges from the thriving capital city of Kinshasa in the far West to the eastern border refugee havens now making the headlines. Dramatic background on this exciting nation has been presented in this significant book by a long-time missionary to Zaire, Dorothy Louise Kopper

The women of Zaire, historically, have been shackled to a life of providing food, sex and the rearing of offspring. Their life through the years has been one of toil, hardship and pain. Furthermore their animistic religion offers them no comfort or hope, but only fear and misery. This is the way it has always been and, according to their way of thinking, this is the way it must continue to be.

When our mission first started to enroll girls in school, their mothers would protest vigorously, wailing and throwing dirt into the air. They needed their daughters to assist them with their work, and to baby-sit the smaller children while they themselves were gone to cultivate their fields, harvest their crops, and to get water from the spring or stream and wood from the forest for their household. One can easily understand their situation and sympathize with them. This does not mean, however, that some women have not progressed beyond this point. In societies where women are permitted to hold positions of responsibility, some have proven to be powerful leaders, and those who have been given the opportunity to receive an education have shown themselves very capable in their chosen fields.

Culturally, the advancement of women has been almost an insurmountable struggle, but with government-supported education and new opportunities for educated girls, and with the pressure of educated men upon their families to provide them with educated wives, tremendous changes have taken place. Now, there are not enough openings for the girls who apply for entrance into secondary-level schools. Many mothers, who once kept their daughters from going to school, now sit in the principal's office saying that they will stay there until their daughters have been accepted. Many obstacles hinder the normal development of civilization in Zaire. First and foremost, leaders seek to provide qualified staff for all its institutions. A limited number of expatriates may be brought in, but the majority must be trained locally. This takes time - much time! The same holds true for the transfer of responsibility for the administration of institutions.

Then there has been the political battle for independence, followed by coups, rebellions on a national scale and mutinies with the military, with jealousies and tribal animosities. Yet, in spite of it all, progress has been made, and women are a part of it. The conflict among traditional tribal culture, an unstable democratic system, the fluctuating economy, and a changing world-view concerning God and His place in their personal lives and in the development of nations - forms the background of this book.

Miss Kopper takes time to describe these cultural, political, geographical, economic and religious influences upon her work in Zaire. It is clearly evident that her chief concern is for the women, but this concern is tangled up with all the other pressures present in a new and developing society, which is Zaire. This book gives a kaleidoscopic view of thirty-five years of the advancement in the civilization of a people, and in particular, the struggle of the women. Miss Kopper sees the hand of God in this struggle.

PART ONE
BUILDING ON MY ROOTS
1878–1962

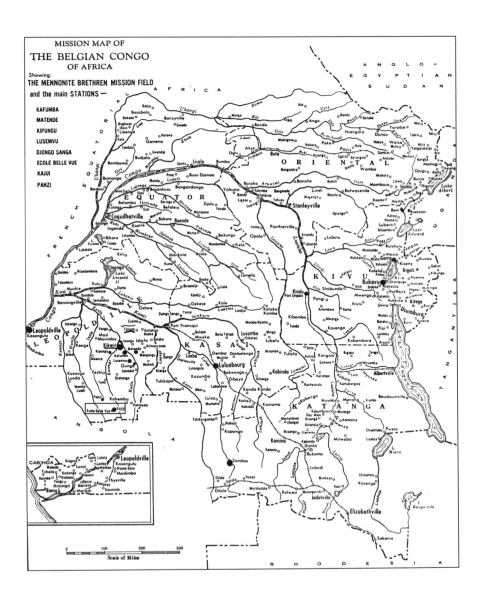

MISSION MAP OF
THE BELGIAN CONGO
OF AFRICA
Showing:
THE MENNONITE BRETHREN MISSION FIELD
and the main STATIONS —

KAFUMBA

MATENDE

KIPUNGU

LUSEMVU

DJONGO SANGA

ECOLE BELLE VUE

KAJIJI

PANZI

Grandparents: Elizabeth (Fast) Boese, John H. Boese

Back Row: Ruth Newfield, Art and Alice (Kopper) Newfield, J.C. and Frances (Kopper) Krause, Dennis Krause, Edwin and Margaret (Hofer) Kopper, Lorraine (Kopper) and Clifford Young, Ronald Newfield.

2nd Row: E. Arthur and Margie (Pickel) Kopper, and Timothy, Mother, Mrs. Susie (Boese) Kopper, Darrel Krause, Florence (Kopper) and Lee Siebert.

3rd Row: Larry Newfield, Steven Siebert, Carol Siebert, Pam. Kopper, Richard Kopper, Donald Krause, my father, Peter Kopper.

Born Later: Denise Krause, Sharon Siebert, and Daniel Krause.

CHAPTER 1

A SLEEPER'S MESSAGE FROM GOD

Today's headlines from Eastern Zaire tell only a small part of the dramatic story of this African nation. Many warm memories flood my heart and mind as I recall exciting and memorable experiences from my past in that troubled land. To get the full impact of that period of my life, I must begin at the beginning.

We were normal children growing up on a farm in Shafter, California. While I, the fourth child, was still in a high chair, we moved to Bakersfield. Many of our Mennonite Brethren members were our neighbors. Soon we moved from Niles Street to California Avenue, where Dad had bought property to start a dairy.

To supplement his meager income, my father drove the school bus. He would often amuse the children by moving the top of his head in such a way as to cause the students to think his cap would fall off. The children, in turn, would hold out their hands to prevent the cap from falling. Both Dad and his riders enjoyed the play-acting.

My father's brothers, Uncle John from White Water, Kansas, and Uncle Dietrich from Aberdeen, Idaho, would roll over in laughter as they recalled some of the harmless tricks they played in their youth.

At times, Dad would gather all six of us children around the dining room table for a Bible sword drill. Other evenings he spent preparing for his young people's Sunday school class. Often after milking and bottling, he would hurry off to a deacon's meeting at the church.

Mother, Aunt Katy (Boese) Kopper and Grandfather John Kopper found Bakersfield's 100-degree heat unbearable. Often, while sitting on the screened front porch, I would watch the thermometer and hoped it would climb so that we would leave for the beach or the mountains.

When we camped in the Breckenridge mountains, our mattress was pine needles covered with a tarp. We cooked in an outdoor barbecue pit.

One day my cousins and I built a "wall" around some trees with a large, wide roll of white paper. One evening, I started telling ghost stories. Suddenly someone saw a white rag hanging on a fence. All of us got scared, broke through our precious walls and ran a stone's throw away to our parents. My mother forbade me to tell any more ghost stories.

Later, three Kopper families bought property in Green Horn mountains, California, and erected a log cabin. My delight was to view the moss that covered evergreens on one side, while hiking, picking up pine cones, wading in the small stream, and at the same time picking gooseberries with a fork. God created these beauties as a small witness of His greatness.

I loved camping with a wood-burning, cooking stove. The aroma of mother's bread baking in her home-made Dutch oven was out of this world. We hauled water from the store in a ten-gallon milk can. I loved roughing it here, which surely prepared me for my later missionary life in the Belgian Congo, now called Zaire. Meanwhile, my days of preparation continued - all a part of God's training program.

Soon after I started school, a physician diagnosed me as having a heart condition. He ordered me not to exert myself. Instead of continuing German lessons at our Mennonite Brethren Church on Wednesday evenings and various activities on other days, I had to go to bed at 7:00 o'clock. According to the doctor, it was either that or take me out of school. Thankfully, my parents kept me in school.

With nearsightedness and stigmatism, I had difficulty with my school work. Mother took me to an optometrist who said I was switching numbers around. When a thoughtful teacher wrote the arithmetic problems in large numbers on the blackboard, it was much easier for me. After hearing about dyslexia, I thought maybe that was my problem, but I have never been diagnosed as such.

Though we were normal children, mother had to scold us quite often. I even felt guilty at times for not keeping my shoestrings tied properly.

One day when I was outside, my oldest sister called me to come in. "Did mother say so?" I asked.

Without answering, she simply repeated, "Dorothy, come in."

"Did mother say so?" I asked again. I didn't feel obligated to obey my oldest sister. But mother had said so, for she gave me the only spanking I remember.

Mother, however, was a fair disciplinarian. She sent us to corners when we got into each other's hair. Sometimes, she just had to look at us and we knew we had done wrong. She loved us and taught us how to pray. I don't remember father ever having to discipline us.

One evening after retiring, I started to cry. Alice, my oldest sister, who was sleeping in the same bed with me, asked what was the matter. I told her how guilty I felt because mother had to scold us so often. I remember hearing that "all have sinned and come short of the glory of God." That verse became real to me.

In evangelistic meetings, first at the age of six and again at 8, I went forward and asked Jesus to forgive me and enter my heart. The verse given to me was Acts 16:31, "Believe on the Lord Jesus Christ and you shall be saved."

Even after making the most important decision of my life, something still bothered me. I had told my teacher I had read all the books listed on a coveted library certificate. All my peers were reading books. I too wanted to impress my teacher as a reader, even though I was having trouble with my eyes. Finally, I wrote and asked her pardon. She gladly forgave me. When I read 1 John 1:9, "If we confess our sins He is faithful and just to forgive us our sins, and to cleanse us from all unrighteousness," peace and joy filled my heart. My sins had been forgiven.

On a momentous May 22, 1932, at the age of 10, the Mennonite Brethren Church, now Heritage Bible Church, in Bakersfield, heard my faltering testimony. It was in German. They baptized me in a nearby canal. It deeply impressed me that all the members came and shook my hand, welcoming me as the youngest member of the church.

When my sister Alice heard a message from Acts on the Macedonian call, she invented a game which she called Macedonia. We drew connecting paths on the vacant lot next to our home. Some led to dead ends, while others guided us to all the other puzzling options. The one who was "it" would call "Macedonia," then all of us would scatter. The first one caught then became "it."

Although at that time I didn't understand what this Macedonian call meant, later Alice and (husband) Arthur Newfield's call was to raise a Christian family. That included entertaining children and peers around their outdoor swimming pool. Their daughter Ruth once said, "My grandfather George Newfield liked your father, for they came from the same village abroad. He changed the spelling of their name from Neufeld to Newfield because he was tired of spelling it out!"

This same call - to raise a Christ-centered family - was true of my oldest brother Arthur and (wife) Margie Kopper; my younger sister, Frances and (husband) James Curtis Krause, and my youngest sister Florence and (husband) Lee Siebert, as well.

My brother, Edwin's (wife Margaret Kopper), calling was to be an ordained minister, while I hoped mine would be as a missionary. I especially remember missionaries who came from China, India and Africa. They told such exciting stories. They were nurses, teachers, medical doctors and church planters. They stressed the great need; they had more to do than they could possibly do.

From the age of 10, I had a deep desire to be a missionary. My only question: did God want me to be one? As a teenager I taught in the Wednesday night Bible classes at our home church. At our Mission church, I taught a Sunday School class. Serving the Lord in this way gave me much joy.

Five years after graduating from Kern County Union (now Bakersfield) High School, the Lord gave me a deep burden for lost men and women. I wept as I asked Him to either take this burden from me or to show me what I should do. When the burden became heavier, I went to my room and read my Bible. The Lord showed me through Scripture that He would lead the way. My first clear direction: I should attend Bible School.

I will never forget my first day at Pacific Bible Institute (now Fresno Pacific College). Our 1944 class was the first ever to enroll at the school. Twenty-six of us stood outside the building at 1095 North Van Ness Avenue for the dedicatory prayer, then entered to begin our course of studies.

Our first student fellowship night was memorable. We had so anticipated the event that we dressed up for the occasion. During the evening, we were asked to give our names, home towns, and why we had come. I shared the verses that had led me there: Romans 12:1-2, ("...present your bodies a living sacrifice...")and James 1:5. (I wanted to study God's Word to know His will).

Acting principal Sam Goosen called me into his office for an interview. "You are one of the students who will really do something in your life for God," he said.

"How do you know?" I asked.

"I can tell," was the simple reply.

A couple of months later, the Lord spoke to me in a special way. A student chapel speaker had just made clear our obligation to a lost and dying world. As I considered his challenge, I heard an inner voice: "Dorothy, are you willing to go to Africa alone?"

"Yes!" I responded.

After that experience, God filled me with such joy that it was hard to explain. I hadn't heard an audible voice, but the message was even more convincing and definite than if it had been audible. On that decisive November 30, 1944, each time the subject of missions was mentioned in the classroom, I thought I would burst. I kept moving back and forth in my chair until I knew the people around me wondered what was wrong. Finally, I wrote a note to my girl-friend, Ann Fast (Enns), telling her about being led toward Africa.

Though our church forbade dancing at that time, when I got to my room, I just had to jump up and down. The Lord wanted me to be a missionary for Him! I had to share this experience with someone who would understand. I went downstairs and told one of the ministerial students of my decision. With tears in his eyes, Henry Heinrichs gave me some Bible verses to stand on in times of testing.

After the newness of school wore off, we had to buckle down to our studies. It was wartime, 1944. To get food, we had to use government-issued ration cards. The cook had to cut costs as much as possible in order to make ends meet, so there was grumbling about the food.

When the chapel committee put me in charge of an upcoming chapel service, I asked Henry, "What can I do?"

"The Lord will show you," he replied.

Later, I asked him, "Would it be all right to share my testimony?"

"As soon as I heard your story," he said, "I knew that the Lord wanted you to give it in chapel."

When the morning finally came for me to give my testimony, the students were not in the proper frame of mind to receive it, I felt. Satan knew how to work hard, even in a Bible School. In our group of lively young people, some had come only after much persuasion. Some simply wanted to get away from home. Others enrolled in spite of their parents' refusal to help financially. Happily, most of us earnestly desired to learn at the feet of Jesus.

Faced with a dilemma, I went to Ann Fast. I knew she had dedicated her life to the Lord, and she would have some words of wisdom. Her fiance, David Enns, was in the Marines and wanted to serve the Lord together with her when he was discharged. Even though he contracted polio, Ann stayed true to him knowing that her mission in life was beside him. They married, had two children and two lovely granddaughters. "Ann," I said, "I was going to give my testimony this morning, but the students are in no mood to receive it."

"Let's pray," she said.

We fell to our knees and called to the Lord for wisdom.

"Dorothy," Ann said, " give your testimony and make it live."

After sharing my story in chapel that day, I noticed some students reaching for their handkerchiefs. After the service, many wept and confessed a need for reconciliation with God and with other students. The evidence of the Holy Spirit at work was a revival.

An outstanding event in the Pacific Bible Institute year was Bible Emphasis week, a time between semesters set aside for special meetings - mornings, afternoons and evenings. Daytime topics included such themes as the missionary call and the work of the

FIRST YEAR STUDENT BODY AND FACULTY
L. to R.—Row 1: T. Quiring, J. Becker, H. Rogalsky, L. Fachner, C. Wall, A. Fast, D. Beier. Row 2: W. Ulsh, E. Epp, R. Huebert, B. Thiesen, O. Dick, E. Berg. Row 3: M. Wall, R. Nord, A. Thiessen, D. Kopper, M. Funk, L. Hodelm, V. Krause, L. Berg, V. Goossen, R. Bartell. Row 4: W. Funk, E. Kopper, H. Warkentin, B. Wall, D. Hoff, A. Goossen. Row 5: A. Klassen, A. Heinrichs, E. Hofer, Rev. S.W. Goossen,, Rev. J.J. Toews, Rev. S. Wiens.

Holy Spirit. Evening services were evangelistic.

During this time I was assigned to help with breakfast preparation, requiring earlier rising than my roommates.

Then I had time to ponder my missionary call, *Was it truly God calling?*

One morning I awakened earlier than usual. "Millie Wall, what time is it?" I asked one of my roommates. (A vibrant teenager, Millie later was courted by Walter Funk, whom she married. A few years ago she was called home to glory after a long siege with cancer.)

When Millie answered, "It's only 3:30," I went back to sleep.

A little later I asked the same question, "What time is it?" but didn't mention any name. Another roommate, Tena Quiring Fischer, responded. "Second Peter 1:12," she said, obviously not fully awake.

"Second Peter 1:12?" I questioned.

"Yes," she said, in her sleep.

Tena was a shy, hard-working, practical girl who did not assert

herself. She was not the kind to spout Bible verses indiscriminate-
ly. Her present response seemed completely out of character.
(Tena and Floyd Fisher married and had two lovely children, who
are now married. A dietitian for 16 years she worked as a self-
employed caterer.)

Now puzzled by the turn of events, I picked up my Bible. Finding Second Peter 1:12, I read the verse, then the chapter, then the
verse again.

After breakfast, upon returning to our room, Tena looked at me.
"What did I say to you this morning?" she asked.

You said "Second Peter 1:12." When I looked up that verse, I
read this, "Wherefore I will not be negligent to put you always in
remembrance of these things, though ye know them, and be established in the present truth."

Checking her notes, she could find no mention of that verse.
Finally Tena said, "That verse means nothing to me. In fact, I did-
n't know it existed."

"But that verse means all the world to me," I said. "Now I know
that Jesus Christ has called me into full-time service in Africa."

If the Lord wanted me to stand in the "gap" (Ezekiel 22:30) I
would obey His calling and leading. God does indeed work in mysterious ways, using a sleeping roommate to send me a clear message of confirmation.

CHAPTER 2

MY FOREFATHERS' MIGRATION

My family's Mennonite heritage, which goes back more than a hundred years, has substantially shaped my identity and spiritual values. The courage of my ancestors has often inspired me to keep on with the task, rather than quit and leave a good work undone.

To begin at the very beginning of the Mennonite movement, Menno Simon, born in 1496, assumed the duties of the priesthood at the age of 28. When he saw the hypocrisy, and false teachings and the executions of the Anabaptists, done by his church, he wrote, "O how shall their shed blood though in error rise against me in judgment of the almighty, and pronounce sentence against my poor miserable soul, if I do not tell them the truth."

In January of 1536, he laid down his priestly office, renounced the Catholic church and deliberately chose the way of the cross. For the rest of his days he remained an outlaw and, with his wife and children, a wanderer upon the face of the earth - with a reward upon his head. Followers of Menno, soon called Mennonites, had to flee because of religious persecution.

The influx of non-Dutch Anabaptists into Prussia began as early as 1535, when they were expelled from Moravia. These constituted the main core of the Montau (now called Matawy in the Polish language) Mennonite churches in Poland for more than 400 years.

One name listed among others in the Montau, a Friesan Mennonite settlement, was that of Kopper. Existing records, dating back to 1661, make it and the Danzig church the congregation with the oldest of all existing records of all the Mennonite churches.

Historian Adalbert Goertz surmises that the names ending in er were not Dutch, but Silesian, Bavarian, or Swiss who spoke the High German, according to the California Mennonite Historical Society. (My father said when they as children spoke the Low German at home, they were punished. My grandparents wanted their children to understand the church services, which were always in the High German.)

In 1764, Catherine the Great gave the first of several newspaper invitations to different European countries to settle in Russia. Because she had guaranteed them religious freedom, many Mennonites migrated to Russia. The Koppers settled in Chortitza's old colony. Grandfather John Kopper was born in Saratof, Ukraine, in 1856, married Justine Hamm in Koeppental, and died in Bakersfield, California, in 1937.

In 1881, when their first son Jake was 6 weeks old, my grandparents started on the great trek led by Klaus Epp, who had predicted that Christ would appear on the earth in the year 1889 somewhere in middle Asia. An exodus of five groups traveled to a wild, unknown, barren land in the heart of a Mohammedan population to meet the Lord and inaugurate the Millennium.

Epp's followers sold their property and started out in their quest for Utopia. The last of 70 wagons carrying 25 families from Saratov got a late start. They experienced extreme suffering. Wagons breaking down, sickness, births, deaths and even a wedding delayed their progress. They did not reach Turkestan until after Christmas,

The Kopper family, deciding that they had had enough of the great trek, stayed at Auli Ata, where my father was born in 1885. Grandpa John Kopper cobbled shoes to support his growing family.

Satan so deceived Epp that he claimed to be the son of Christ, just as Christ was the Son of God, according to C, Henry Smith in his book, *Story of the Mennonites.*

In 1892, when my father Peter Kopper was only seven years old,

Baby Found Under Weed Clump

My great-great-great-grandfather, when a tiny baby, was left under a clump of weeds in Prussia for anyone to find and rear. The people who found him named him Boese as a last name. That was the name of the weed he was found near.

I don't know what the weed looks like or what it would be called in our good old American language. The name is pronounced "Baze." Some have changed the spelling a little or the pronunciation to Bose. Still they are descendants of the same man. I have a family tree that stems from this baby boy.

He was never given the last name of the people who reared him, so we don't know who they were or their names. All of his descendants live in America. I am thankful he came to America and proud to be an American. Most important, he was a Christian and reared in a Christian family.

You say strange? Yes, but it's TRUE.

Oklahoma

my grandparents, John and Justine (Hamm) Kopper, left Auli Ata Turkestan, with their entire family in search of religious freedom. He did not want his sons to have to take up arms. He found it hard to say good-bye to Uncle Yerot, who told the departing Koppers, "I will join you in a year." But the doors closed before the year passed.

Meanwhile, the Koppers migrated with their 6 children to Brenery, Kansas, near White Water, where their son John farmed until his death. Their daughter, Anna, married Henry Fast. Two more children were born to them in Kansas.

Grandfather worked hard to pay the debt he incurred by coming to the United States, and to support his family. Later, he and his three daughters, (Helen, the seamstress, and cook; Justine, an R. N., and Marie, a school teacher, in Kansas, who later married my Uncle Ike Boese,) moved to Bakersfield.

One day while visiting in their home, I heard my aged grandfather ask my youngest sister, Florence, to get out all his shoes. A cobbler by trade, he wanted no doubt to have any necessary repairs done. He also loved geography. He would have Florence sit on his lap while he paged through the maps of countries through which he had traveled.

My great, great grandfather on my mother's side as a tiny baby in Prussia, was left under a clump of weeds. The people who found him were Christians, gave him the last name of Boese, the name of the weed he was found under. My family tree, numbering more than 2,100 names, all living in the United states, stems from that baby boy.

Some years later, a man posing as a good Mennonite circulated among Mennonite Brethren communities in Colorado, Oklahoma and Kansas promoting land sales in California's San Joaquin Valley. He told of winters so mild that one could keep warm simply by burning several newspapers each day.

Since he carried a big Bible under his arm and attended prayer meetings wherever he went, surely he could be trusted. Many farmers sold out and paid this salesman for land in the San Joaquin Valley. Upon arriving, however, my grandfather John Boese and the others soon learned that the property actually belonged not to them but to the Kern County Land Company.

Pastor John H. Boese, born in 1844 in Halbstadt, Moloschna, S. Russia married Susie Warkentine in 1867.She bore him two children, but died in 1875. Later, he married Elizabeth Fast. They migrated from Russia to Peabody, Kansas, in 1879. They moved to Granada, Colorado, in 1889. Mother was born in Colorado on February 7, 1891, the youngest of 13 children. They later moved to Martensdale, California.

My grandparents did manage to make the culprit deed them a small farm on Snow Road outside of Bakersfield, but that was not nearly the amount of real estate they had been promised. Most of the farmers stayed in California and made the best of a bad deal. Grandfather Boese served the Rosedale Church, now Rosedale Bible Church, as its first pastor, taking no pay while helping people in need. When they died, the sale of the property just paid for their funeral.

As a young man of 18, my father learned the Catechism. He was baptized and accepted into the Emmaus Mennonite church in White Water, Kansas. That very afternoon, while reading a book, my father trusted Christ as his personal Savior, saying that neither baptism, nor Catechism saves. He received assurance from Isaiah 43:1, "Do not fear, for I have redeemed you. I have called you by name. You are mine." My mother and father were married on March 25, 1915, in Bakersfield California. From Kansas, they moved to Idaho where father took up homesteading. Soon after their first child, E. Arthur was born, they moved to Bakersfield where their second, son, Edwin was born. Later, they moved to the

Parting wasn't easy. These people tugged at my heartstrings.

THE KOPPERS
Back Row: Jake, minister and dr. magnetic treatments; Marie, (Kopper) Boese, teacher and secretary; my father Peter, dairy farmer and maintenance man; Justine, RN.
Front Row: Grandma Justine Hamm Kopper; John, farmer; Grandpa John Kopper, farmer and shoe cobbler; Helen, seamstress and cook; Dietrich, farmer and clerk; Ann (Kopper) Fast, housewife and mother, deceased.
Inset: Grandmother Justine Kopper

farming community of Shafter, a pleasant town with numerous Mennonites. The Shafter Mennonite Brethren church soon became the center of their religious and social life.

On November 2, 1921, they welcomed me into their home as their fourth child and second daughter. By the time I entered Pacific Bible Institute, my father was bedridden and Mother was his faithful nurse. When I told them that the Lord had called me into His service in Africa, Father wept.

"After I was married and had a family," he said, "I too wanted to be a missionary. Financially, it was impossible to go back to school, for we had a large family of six children. The Lord showed me that I should raise my family and some of my children would become missionaries. Now you are going."

Tearfully, he continued. "But now, since I'm in bed, I can't help cover the cost of your schooling." My decision had blessed my mission-minded father, endearing me to him all the more.

A Zairian village.

CHAPTER 3

EN ROUTE

Walking into the Post Oak Comanche church in Inia-homa, Oklahoma, I noticed cinnamon-colored grand-fathers taking off their ten-gallon hats. Their long, braided, black hair conveyed a sense of identity and dignity. Grandmothers with their long, flowing dresses, shoulders covered with colorful India shawls, blended in with their children and young people dressed in western style clothes. All worshiped the true and living God together as they sang their hymns in the Comanche language.

Before sending me to Africa, Mennonite Brethren Missions and Services assigned me to teach for one year in a Christian grade school at Post Oak Mission, a school for Comanche Indian children.

Seldom does a missionary simply pack up and go overseas to the appointed work. Practical experience at home - especially cross-cultural ministry - helps equip the candidate for the challenges of other continents and cultures. As a new Bible School graduate with only a B.A. in Missionary Anthropology, I needed that kind of stretching.

At the Post Oak Church, members and friends truly worshiped God while some of their neighbors and relatives still gathered in tepees to carry out their heathen religious rituals, including the peyote drug.

In the classroom, two of my students were Harold and Jaquetta Parker, the great, great grandchildren of the last famous Comanche chief, Quana Parker. Teaching them and the other children was a great privilege, and I loved it.

One night Harold Parker took some of us teachers out on a lonely country road. In the darkness, we could hear pounding drums and sounds of wailing coming from one of the tepees. We didn't dare go any closer for fear of angering the heathen, who worshipped the Peyote ritual. We wanted to win them to the Lord.

By the end of the year, I felt very much a part of the community. Parting was not easy. Those dear people tugged at my heartstrings as we exchanged good-byes. Forty-five years later, on the 100th anniversary of the start of that mission work, some of my former students sent me a scroll in recognition of my service there.

On September 9, 1951 the Mennonite Brethren Church on Miller and Monterey in Bakersfield, ordained me for foreign mission service. For the next 30 some years, their continued prayers strengthened me in the Lord's work in the Belgian Congo, now called the Republic of Zaire.

A teenager who grew up in the church once confessed to me that at one time she thought my name was Dorothy Kopper Zaire, because that was the way they called for prayer on my behalf every Sunday morning.

In May, 1952, friends and relatives gathered at the Santa Fe railroad station in Bakersfield to see me off. Saying goodbye to family and friends was a traumatic experience, but even the farewell to my ailing father was not without hope. I knew I would again see him in heaven.

Rev. B. Richard gave me a few words of comfort from Isaiah 52:7 before I stepped onto the train. "How beautiful upon the mountain are the feet of him that bringeth good tidings, that publishes peace; that bringeth good tidings of good, that publisheth salvation..."

Whose peace? Whose tidings? My works? In my own strength? No, a thousand times no! Tidings for the whole world come from our Prince of Peace, our Lord and Savior, Jesus Christ.

The sorrow of parting was softened somewhat by the excitement of visiting with many people on the scenic trip across the United States. From the dome car, I had a splendid view of the green hillsides in San Joaquin Valley covered with poppies, lupines and other wild flowers. Then the climb began. We went through many tunnels as the train gained higher and higher ground. Slowly we wound our way up the slopes of the Sierra Nevada, around count-less horseshoe turns called loop-the-loops.

When it was time to go to my sleeper, a young man asked me whether I was alone. I was frightened. Hesitating just for a minute, I said, "No, I am not alone." After all, God was my constant companion.

Other "companions" along for the ride included two suitcases and an old trunk. The trunk and I had already experienced some adventures together. For four months in 1950-51 I lived in Montreal, studying French. In preparation for that trip, I had purchased this particular second-hand trunk. When I arrived in Montreal, my landlord noticed its somewhat frazzled condition. She offered to repaper the inside of the trunk.

"Where shall I leave it so that you can get to it?" I asked.

"Just leave it in the fenced-in back yard," she replied.

Five months later, my time of departure from Montreal came. I looked for the trunk. It was right where I had left it, yet still in one piece after four months of rain, wind and snow. Now this aging trunk would render its final service. Once I got to New York, I planned to buy filing cabinets there, then repack everything from the trunk into them to sail on a freighter to Africa.

Only one stop was scheduled on my way to New York, a visit to our Foreign Board of Missions office located in the small town of Hillsboro, Kansas. From New York I was to board the *Bastogne*, a Belgian freighter, headed for the Belgian Congo.

Arriving in New York for the first time, I looked for the address of a mission home our mission board had given me. A cab driver helped to unload my luggage at the home. In the process my trunk broke and my things were scattered all over the entrance hall. The clerk, not enthused about providing housing for workers from other missions, asked me to look for another place to stay.

"Look," the taxi driver told him, "she's a stranger here. It's late and her trunk just broke. Can't she stay at least tonight?"

The clerk agreed but told me I had to vacate the room the next day. Others were coming and they needed the room. After cleaning up the mess and getting to my room, I felt like crying. Opening my Bible to the book of Job, I started to laugh. After all, my troubles were minor compared to his.

The next day I moved to Hephzibah ("The Lord delighteth in thee," Isaiah 62:4) House. An important ministry of the house was to provide comfortable rooms at modest rates for missionaries and other Christian workers in transit. It is a peaceful oasis in New York City.

Meanwhile, filing cabinets were bought and packed, and the old broken trunk was discarded. My departure was delayed for several days, providentially, as one of my shots had laid me low.

Finally, on May 24, 1952, I called the docks to see when the *Bastogne* would be ready to leave for the Congo. I was told to board as soon as I had eaten my evening meal. Mrs. Brand from Hephzibah House took me to supper, then snapped my picture and wished me God's speed.

On May 24, 1952, I boarded a ship called the Bastogne, a Belgian freighter, headed for the Belgian Congo.

As I boarded the ship, the sailors were still loading cargo. "Look how she walks!" one sailor said. "One thing is sure, she's never been on a ship before!"

Another said, "You're going to the Congo? You'll rot out there!" Two families, the Rockes and the Burkettes, and I were the only passengers on the freighter. After they put their children to bed, we stood looking out the port-hole windows. Finally, the news came that we weren't leaving until the next day.

Shortly after sunrise on May 25, we pulled away from the New York shoreline, past the imposing Statue of Liberty. Gray clouds cast their dim shadow over the vast sea, as they met together on the far horizon.

When the glorious homeland - the United States - vanished completely from our view, we stood breathless with damp fog etched upon our faces. We could hardly believe we were on our way - God's messengers to a strange land.

Our daily devotions, right after a sumptuous breakfast, gave me needed fellowship with the two families and an opportunity for communion with our Lord. We wanted to honor Him for the great privilege of going as His ambassadors to the Belgian Congo, now known as Zaire.

Waters of the sea proved enchanting, with a variety of color and form - sometimes, like glass; others like a large piece of dark sandpaper. We saw fish jump out of the water, hang in the air for a moment, then plunge into the deep. These curious creatures seemed like sightseers who wanted to look us over as intruders into their world.

Meanwhile, our meals proved adventurous. One day they brought us what they called "Americani." It turned out to be raw hamburger. I sent mine back to be cooked. Between bites of food, I watched the gently rolling landscape. Gliding behind fluffy white clouds, the sun turned them to silver. Streams of light pouring from the edges of the clouds displayed the incomparable artistry of our Heavenly Father.

Our next course of food consisted of assorted cuts of cold meat, sliced cucumbers, potatoes, sliced tomatoes and dressing. That day everyone seemed to take their dessert, an orange, to their rooms, so that they could continue to watch the sun's fading rays glimmering and dancing on the rippling waves. Sailors kept busy painting the vessel to keep it free from rust. As they painted, they too watched the mysterious waters with admiration. Whenever another ship was sighted, the crew buzzed with excitement. When the fog lifted, we gladly joined them on deck to gaze at the ocean. Mile upon mile stretched endlessly before us.

Crew members lifted stabilizers, which were ballast - weight to provide or improve a vessel's stability. This helped to gain time we had lost. When the ship rolled badly as a result and tilted downward, my body felt light. When the ship pitched upward, I felt the sensation of a great weight pressing against my whole being. In those moments, I leaned all the more on God, more conscious than ever of my humanness, my unworthiness.

Coming to the breakfast table one day, I noticed that side boards partitioned off each plate separately. I had to maneuver into my chair without pulling it away from the table, because both were chained down. Such were the perils of the sea.

Sitting on deck one time, I noticed that the sea now rolled in great swells without the white breakers. Luminous phosphorus lights of soft blues and radiant pinks appeared on the waves beating against the ship. It seemed that whales were searching for their home, with flashlights to direct their way. Actually, I learned, a secretion from jelly-fish and other sea-dwellers emits light through oxidization when the surface of the sea is broken - another of God's remarkable provisions for His creatures.

During the voyage, I had the privilege of talking to two mechanics. One, a hefty fellow with a smelly pipe, showed only brief interest. The other, Joe, planned to be married as soon as he reached Belgium. He listened intently as I told him about the best Friend anyone could ever have.

Sometimes, Joe became embarrassed as I explained Scripture to him in front of his sailor friends. Whenever we went into a room for further discussion, I would take Mr. Burkette with us. We had many 3-way talks together.

Meanwhile, we made a stop at Cape Verde Islands, off the coast of Africa - the first land we had seen in weeks. Many small boats met us, with island people selling their wares. I did my Christmas shopping for my companions' children, trading old clothes for fancy sea shells made into ornate shapes. My own nieces and nephews were far away, so these precious missionary children took their place.

After the ship refueled we were on our way, but not without sheer drama that lasted for anxious minutes. Three of the refuelers, still aboard our ship, desperately needed to get off and back to their small boat. One of the men tried a suspended rope, but the rope broke as he tried to maneuver the distance. He slipped, but somehow managed to land safely in his boat. The others also finally made it across.

On June 11, we first saw the mountains, a few trees, houses and then the port of Lobito, Angola, Africa. This large country borders Congo. Black citizens, wearing gunny sacks for loin cloths, unloaded coal from our ship. A tyrannical foreman whipped them with a belt or threw a piece of coal at them if they didn't work to his satisfaction. Sometimes singing in rhythmic harmony with the shovel proved to lighten their drudgery.

The Congo port on the Atlantic Ocean has but 40 kilometers of coastline, leading to a very short navigable waterway, that is narrow and dangerous. Since the heavy vessels cannot enter until they have complied with the allotted weight, preventing their getting stuck between Banana and Matadi in the Belgian Congo, they had to unload coal until all requirements were met.

Joe continued to show interest in the Word of God. One day when the three of us were studying together, I left the room to allow Mr. Burkette to show him how he could ask Jesus into his heart. That was an exciting time for both of them as Joe responded to the good news of the gospel.

After having been on the *Bastogne* from May 24 to June 21, we finally saw where the colorful Congo river entered into the Atlantic Ocean. Although the invisible shore was miles away, a large stream of cocoa-colored foam marked the point where the river ceased its flow into the blue waters of the measureless Atlantic.

Sailing up the mouth of the Congo river, we stopped at one of the small islands to take on the captain who would guide us safely through Congo's treacherous, rocky passageway. As we laid anchor for the night, a full moon stood as a sentinel over the tranquil setting. Silvery moonbeams reflected on the pathway ahead, reminding us that God, the captain of our lives, who was present with us, would guide us into our newly adopted land.

The pathway reflected dancing moonbeams from it to our ship reminding us of God the captain of our lives who was present with us, guiding us to this our adopted land of Africa.

CHAPTER 4

BELGIAN CONGO AT LAST

O n the 22nd of June we proceeded with caution up the Congo river. With growing excitement, we fastened our eyes on the African life on the shores of Congo's river.

Was it all a dream, or was I actually arriving? It seemed like a dream. What would the administrators give me to do? Would I be working with someone special? I knew almost no one there. God had led me thus far; why should I worry now? He promised that He would show me the way; that He would be with me.

We soon docked at Matadi's sea-like port, on the banks of the Congo. This river circled the northern part of the Congo, forming a natural boundary for hundreds of miles inland. It was a country rich in resources, but undeveloped.

Around the city's one luxurious hotel, where we spent our first night, blooming flowers and colorful tropical bushes flourished - a small but delightful sample of the vast variety of tropical vegetation that marked God's creation. From this moment on, we would enjoy the handiwork of our great Creator.

We soon arranged lodging with the Swedish Mission. Our Bible study continued with Joe in the office of the Mission in charge of this guest home. This inexhaustible book of knowledge provided a rich feast for him - and for all of us.

After saying goodbye to Mrs. Rocke and her sons, and Mrs. Burkette and her three daughters, the men and I had to stay on to see our things through customs. While doing this, we continued to take our meals at the hotel.

This surprisingly modern hotel was built around a spacious patio. An elevator took us to the large dining room on the second floor. A picture window gave us a magnificent view of Congo's busy trading port where we had landed. On the opposite side, we saw some of the prosperous colonial homes with artfully manicured gardens. Further up on the rocky hills stood many small Congo huts.

Sitting at the table with the two missionary men, I was trying hard to remember my manners. Mr. Burkette asked me if the napkin was the same one the waiters had given me that morning. To my utter dismay, I learned that the waiter would give out slightly used napkins to anyone. I had been wiping my mouth on a napkin that had been used!

While waiting for the Belgian officials to pass our things through customs, we visited Matadi's market to survey the wood carvings, basketry and many brightly painted gourds. Finally, our paper work was done, with all copies delivered to the right offices. Baggage was sent inland to our respective destinations. We were now ready to travel inland by rail.

The railroad had been cut through rocks to bypass the Congo river's massive boulders that created rapids which no man was able to navigate. It stretched across the country, reaching the river's famous Stanley Pool in Leopoldville. The Belgians, called *Bula-Matadi* ("hit a rock,") forced many Congolese to work on this back-breaking project where many a man met his death. Eventually, the railroad became one of the main ways of transportation inland.

On July 5, 1952, the three of us climbed aboard a dusty railroad car, along with a number of Congolese. At almost every small village, mothers with babies tied to their backs boarded the train. On their heads they carried large parcels wrapped in colorful, ragged clothes.

The train reeked of human sweat, palm oil and dried *makiabu* (fish). It sounded like a barnyard, as most of the passengers carried a chicken with them. These poor creatures, jostled by the pushing crowd, cackled in protest.

With windows open for fresh air, dust and cinders from the dry-season fires started to cover us. Not wanting to appear half black and half white by the time we reached Leopoldville, we closed the window and endured the heat.

On arrival, we went directly to the historic Union Mission Guest House, built by the Congo Continuation Committee in 1922 for the accommodation of missionaries in transit. Many famous missionaries shared with each other as they stayed there over the years: Dr. Clyde Taylor, Archie Graber, Vernon Sprunger, Dr. Merlin Schwartz, Arthur Lundblad, Aaron A. Janzen, Martha Mantz, Martha Janzen, Dr. Helen Rosevere, Joseph Tucker, Hector McMillan, Dr. Paul Carlson and others.

After climbing the wooden steps to my assigned room, I found someone else already there. Quickly, I got acquainted with my unexpected roommate. She too was a missionary, so I was not lonesome for long. Soon I fell into a peaceful sleep.

Other missionaries who lived in town often stopped at the guest house to chat with missionaries passing through. In this way, they kept up with news from other places and the comings and goings of many missionaries.

On the grounds was a church that had two worship services every Sunday morning, one in French, the other in English. Protestant missionaries from many denominations worshipped the Lord together. Mission work in the Congo was divided up among the various missions to avoid overlap.

On May 27,1943, the Mennonite Brethren General Conference at Buhler, Kansas, had officially decided to accept the mission field in the Belgian Congo, where from 1912 a number of Mennonite Brethren missionaries had been laboring. They had established two mission stations - Kafumba and Bololo - that gained some 4,500 believers. By 1953, we carried the responsibility for more than a half million people.

As churches multiplied among the diverse tribes, and as many rural people migrated to the cities, each group wanted a church of the same denomination they had known in their village or inland mission station. This caused no problem, as the missions continually enjoyed a spirit of cooperation and mutual respect.

Belgians had colonized Congo and chose Leopoldville as the capital. Their influence could be seen in their homes, government offices and public places. They erected statues of historic figures; Leopold II, Henry Stanley and others.

Congolese too made their presence known in the capital. On a vacant lot in the middle of town they exhibited their carvings of ivory and wood and their oil paintings. It was evident that my adopted people had great talent; they needed only an opportunity to express themselves.

With great anticipation, I looked forward to meeting representatives from our mission. Soon I met Rev. John Toews, a member of our Mission Board, visiting the Congo. John Ratzlaff, a missionary from Ecole Belle Vue at Kajiji, also met me. He and his wife, Edna, taught and served as house parents to missionary children. When I told them about my year at the Mennonite Brethren Post Oak Mission school, serving the Comanche Indian children, at Indiahoma, Oklahoma, they rejoiced.

"Would you be willing to spend one year teaching the missionary children in the mornings while studying the trade language of the area in the afternoons?" they asked.

After only a moment's hesitation, I agreed. After one year of studying a Congolese trade language, it would be much easier to direct and teach in a primary school.

En route to Ecole Belle Vue, Kajiji, from Leopoldville, my first experience on a plane, the flight took us to Kikwit. While I drank in Congo's lush expanse of vegetation, interlaced with rivers and dotted with small villages below, Mr. Ratzlaff told me more about where I would be teaching.

After enjoying Christian fellowship around the table at a Baptist Mid-Missions guest house at Kikwit, we had to say good-by to our new-found friends, climb into a pickup waiting for us and head out to our mission stations in the Kwilu area.

As we arrived at these mission stations for the first time, I observed that the surroundings of each one was different. Kafumba (elephant's nest) had many palm trees among the rolling lawns. Neat, well-swept paths led from clusters of huts to their coffee plantation, print shop, dispensary, maternity center, primary school, Bible school and church.

In back of the simple missionary dwellings was a thick tropical for-

After lunch in Kikwit we had to say goodbye to our new-found friends and get into our pickup already loaded for the trip inland. Dorothy Kopper, Edna and John Ratzlaff.

est bordering a rushing river. Weather was hot and humid. When Aaron Janzen built the station, one night elephants trampled down his day's handiwork. As I walked into the mud-and-stick church for the first time, a lizard fell from the grass roof onto my head and slid down my back. Though it made me shiver, no permanent harm was done.

Soon we traveled through newly planted groves of palm nut trees. After three hours on dirt roads, we put our pickup into low gear to climb the steep, twisting mountain road to Kipungu Station.

While we visited in the home of a missionary couple, John and Ruth Kliewer, we heard coughing just outside the door. A group of girls stood there; this was their way of knocking.

"This mademoiselle who just came, is she going to stay here to teach us?" one of the girls asked.

"No," Ruth replied, " not now."

"But mademoiselle must stay here and help us," the girls insisted. "We have no one to teach us. Please don't let her go away! We need her."

In the villages surrounding Kipungu, many echoed the plea. "We also want schools. We need you to teach us. Why do you not stay? Our children must learn to read and to write."

We saw the need firsthand. Someone must teach the Congolese the fundamentals of reading so they could eventually read the Bible for themselves. Thus they could verify the truth of what they were being taught.

Our next stop, Matendi, was an arid-looking mission station. Except for the area around the missionary dwellings, the grounds seemed like a pile of white sand glistening brightly under the hot sun. When rain fell, the sand just seemed to swallow it up.

As I wandered around the station, grade school and dorms were empty. Abe Esau and his wife, Sarah, faithfully gave out the Word of God to the workmen and their wives, school teachers and others living on the grounds.

On the verandah of the primitive but well-run dispensary, Congolese of all ages displayed tropical ulcers as they unwrapped their bandages, made of torn sheets. Inside the two-roomed dispensary, lines of ragged, brightly dressed women and men with crying children waited for a pinprick from the attendant. Drops of blood would be tested for malaria. Malaria and worms caused many Congolese to have a dangerously low hemoglobin.

When I too gave my blood, a child exclaimed in amazement, "Why they are just like we are." That reminded me: Christ became like me. A missionary must become like the people she seeks to win. Christ's blood purified me, and that same cure is available to all.

Chapter 5

Missionary Kids

After I had studied one of the trade languages, Kituba, for about a month, my pupils began to arrive. Missionaries from various stations brought their children to Ecole Belle Vue, Kajiji. Since neither trains nor buses ran to this remote mission station, they had to come by four-wheel drive or a truck. No small car was safe on these treacherous mud roads.

Parents seemed happy to find a Christian dorm and school for their grade school children. Attending Congolese schools was out of the question. American children needed to study in English and to be educated in a system comparable to their native land, so they could be integrated back into their culture eventually.

John and Edna Ratzlaff joined me in greeting the parents and children. We led them into the spacious living room with its homemade davenports. They looked out the large picture window, past the verandah to the mountains below. Further down they saw thick foliage and small clearings on the mountainsides where the Congolese women had cut out the trees and bushes to make their small gardens. Walking down the hall, they carried their suitcases to the different bedrooms with their homemade bunk beds attractively arranged for each student.

Congolese bush stores, two-room mud and stick huts, had either a grass roof or a tin roof. As we approached one store to buy groceries for our expected guests, a salesman wearing a loin cloth greeted us. He was heating a large barrel over an open fire. We presented him with our bottle and he filled it with the freshly heated bright-orange oil. Rarely did the Congolese eat any greens or meat without this rich, tasty palm oil.

Walking in, we almost stumbled on the red, uneven dirt floor. After our eyes became accustomed to the dark, we saw a bamboo counter separating us from the storekeeper and his merchandise. High up against the back wall was a row of brightly colored, large, designed material. It was cut in four-to-six-meter pieces for the Congolese women to have a blouse made, then they used the rest for two wrap-around skirts, called *pan*.

Bars of laundry and hand soap in cartons lay on the floor directly in back of the bamboo counter. Sometimes they had notebooks for the school children, but more often the truck driver brought in cases of beer instead, for this brought larger profits. To our left were sacks of dried caterpillars, in season, called *mingolos*.

No refrigeration could be found here. Dried fish were sold piece by piece from cartons hauled into the region. Sometimes canned fish came in. Rarely was sugar or dried milk available. When they were, foreigners felt guilty buying them, for the Congolese too needed a way to buy some of these things.

Our "meat market" or "butcher shop" - the Congolese hunter - often came to the door with venison (bambi), often the entire animal. Other times they would come with a leg of a wild pig, or a leg of beef that someone had just slaughtered.

Fresh fruits and vegetables usually came from our own gardens. If not, they had to be ordered well in advance for the truckers to bring in. Flour, sugar, vegetables, soups and meats were stored for a year at a time.

We were glad when a Congolese hunter came with venison the day before the children arrived. After the cook soaked it in salt water overnight, parents, pupils and teachers all enjoyed the feast of venison, with walnut-sized potatoes bought at the door. The usual tropical salad was served - paipai, bananas, mangos and fresh pineapple. The guavas weren't quite ripe.

After the meal, we all gathered in the living room. Fire in the hand-cut, sandstone brick fireplace licked up the wood while spreading its homey atmosphere. Though it really wasn't cold enough to have a fire, we all enjoyed its dancing flames as we compared notes about our different mission stations. After Uncle John

Ratzlaff led in devotions, we prayed that this year would be one when the seed of the Word of God would penetrate the darkness of many Congolese hearts. John seemed to feel the heartache of each parent and child. Separation wasn't easy for either the child or parent. After prayer for God's grace and strength, the children were shown their individual rooms. Primitive accommodations for the parents were gladly accepted. With flashlights, they walked across the dark campus. Behind the school building, the trail led to individual cabins. Mostly one-bedroom huts with grass roofs, they had no electricity or running water. Parents crawled under the mosquito netting above their beds, tucking it under the mattress to keep out cockroaches, scorpions, centipedes and mosquitoes. The parents soon blew out the candle and fell asleep to the sound of the distant drums, beating out Congolese messages.

After breakfast, they accepted fresh homemade bread for their trip home. It was heart-rending to see second-through-eighth-graders saying goodbye to their parents for the next four months. One girl started to run after the moving van. She was quickly brought back and comforted by her older brother and the house parents.

In their separate classrooms, students and their teachers bowed their heads and prayed for their parents' safety as they traveled to their mission stations. They knew each curve in the one-way, rutted, dirt road and remembered how many hand-drawn ferries and log bridges they would have to cross.

A couple of years before I came to the field, Congolese workers had dug a big hole near the dorm's outside kitchen, a homemade swimming pool. Water from kitchen and dorm roofs would fill it. Obedient students could swim in the pool after school.

One day Uncle John made a platform of hand-cut planks.

"We are making a basketball court, Aunt Dorothy," one of the boys said to me. "Won't that be fun?"

They suddenly stopped work, for young Jack Shannon spied his father walking across the school grounds. The Shannons headed the mission station at Kajiji, a mile and a half from the school. Mrs. Shannon served as principal of the Congolese grade school, while her husband pastored the church and directed evangelism efforts in nearby villages.

"Dad, where are you going? How long will you stay?" asked daughter Joy as she flung herself into her father's arms.

"Don't you remember," Mr. Shannon said, a sun helmet on his head and galoshes over his shoes, accompanied by Congolese porters, "I told you this morning I must go into the far villages and share God's word. This time we're going near the Angolan border."

In a homemade, waterproof bag, porters carried a sleeping bag, mosquito net and DDT. Tick fever had taken the lives of many in the area. Medicines, water pills, food, literature, a flashlight, candles and a hurricane lamp filled a small chest.

As the children waved good-by, they knew that Tshimika Isaac, the tall, wiry head Congolese guide would protect Joy and Jack's father while he led them to remote villages. Mr. Shannon was training him in leading other Congolese to Christ, then forming a centrally located compound to build a church. This would double as a school until villagers saw the need of building a mud-and-stick school.

After school the next day, the kids again started to level the basketball court. Suddenly Johnny Bower left and headed towards a young eucalyptus tree. Before anyone could stop him, he began to climb the tree. When the limb started to bend, I held my breath. Surely, the tree would snap and cause a terrible accident. When the sapling bowed closer and closer to the ground, at about six feet he jumped down. All the children yelled and clapped, then took turns doing the same thing.

On Saturday, Uncle John took the pupils on a hike to a branch of the Kambululu river that boasted a waterfall. The children wanted to pretend they were pioneer missionaries, going into unknown jungles like their Dads. After trekking through thick underbrush, they spied the falls. Some children skidded on the seat of their pants to where the falls dropped into a natural basin for swimming.

They pretended that crocodiles were after them, forgetting for a moment they had actually seen Congolese carried to the mission station after having been bitten by them. They tried to catch insects, birds and butterflies. They hid sacks and flashlights so they wouldn't be stopped from getting what they wanted - bats from the cave underneath the waterfalls.

What fun the boys had later as they let the bats loose in their rooms - after the house parents thought that they were sleeping.

Front Row: Glenn and Donnie Ratzlaff.
Second Row: David and John Bowers.
Third Row: Nancy Chambers, Joy Shannon, Jack Schmidt.
Fourth Row: Lois and Ruth Chambers, Edna Ratzlaff.

Bats would swoop down and scare the younger boys, who were sworn to secrecy. Covering their heads with sheets, they finally fell asleep. Next morning, those who cleaned the rooms unknowingly freed the bats by opening the windows.

Jack Shannon had been in the area for a long time, so he knew the sports of the Congolese children. With the help of natural erosion, they had made a clearing down a steep mountain to the stream of water, just a 15-minute walk away. With a toboggan-like palm tree branch, they maneuvered the slippery dirt slope.

Later, Aunt Edna Ratzlaff inspected their clothes for possible mending. "What happened to the new jeans your folks bought you?" she asked. "How come they have holes in the bottom of them?" Finally, the truth came out.

After teaching second-through-fourth graders in the morning, which I thoroughly enjoyed, I studied Kituba in the afternoons. Experts from our Mission formed a committee to work on improving the Kituba language. They sought to coin words that would add to its vocabulary.

Knowing that I was now studying the language for the first time, they invented a word for "in," (*mu*), "over"(*va*) and "it" (*yau*). The actual word for "in," "over," and "it" was simply *na*. Because I used the three words constantly, the Congolese secretly called me "*va, mu, yau*". The kids got a big laugh and teased me about it. I laughed along with them.

Often on Saturdays the children would climb in the pickup for a bumpy ride to see the Shannons and Congolese cows. They watched the Congolese workers herd the cows to and from the corrals, and saw them lasso some of them.

"How come there were fewer cows today than last week, Uncle John?" one of the boys asked.

"I thought you boys heard," came the reply. "Last night a lion jumped the fence and dragged off several cows before the night watchman got a shot at it."

Upon returning to their dorms, the younger boys soon began playing cowboy. They became either a cow or a herder. After capturing the human "cow," the herder would lead the cow off to a makeshift corral.

One day when the girls - including me in that group, please! - came back from a hike, Uncle John was in the process of buying a lion's skin. That night he told the children that the Congolese believed the large lions were real animals but the smaller ones were people. Actually, some witch doctors had roamed around the villages in lion skins to scare the people. They quit this when some were wounded.

A gardener was hired to keep fresh vegetables and fruits on the table. A cook had been trained to give the children and staff balanced meals. To keep us in clean clothes, without either washing machines or dryers, we had several Congolese washing by hand. Housekeepers swept our rooms so that John and Edna and I could prepare our lessons, teach and correct papers, and still have time with each child in our care.

Before the day's work began and after roll call, Uncle John had morning services with all our Congolese friends, including our workmen. He was their spiritual leader. Just before Christmas, the Ratzlaffs took a 12-hour trip for medical help. I was asked to lead the morning services for the workmen. The Orville Wiebes had just arrived, so they didn't yet know the trade language. With the help of flannelgraph, I told them the Christmas story. Smiles on their black faces for the Christmas card were thanks enough.

Just before our pupils were due back to school after Christmas vacation, word came from Nkara that Dr. Leben Schmidt, the only dentist in Congo, had died. He had been building a home for his wife and two sons, Jack and Jim. Working up in the rafters, he accidentally stepped on a beam that was not securely nailed down. He fell, hitting his head on the cement floor below, and never regained consciousness.

Why he had been promoted to heaven while so young and promising, we don't know. Mrs. Schmidt chose to stay on in spite of her great loss. No one was available to take her place at Nkara. It was hard for the two boys to leave their grieving mother, so Jim and Jack came back to school late.

When the main building became overcrowded, it was decided that the girls - including me - should live separately from the house parents and the boys. This was a delight to me, for I loved the girls. My nieces and nephews were far away, so these precious girls became my family.

A larger cabin than the other 29 was being remodeled for us. Because of a leaking roof, the work took so long that we finally decided to move into a smaller cabin. It had a grass roof but no ceiling nor glass for the windows, and no running water, or electricity. An empty barrel, conveniently placed, was filled with water daily by faithful Congolese carriers.

With no clothes closets, we found bamboo and attached it to the rafters. Now at least the girls could place their clothes across this bar. Since the hut had no ceiling, night winds swirled through the space between the walls and the grass roof. Congolese would have solved the draft problem by building a fire in the middle of the hut. The extra space became their chimney for the smoke to escape.

Finished or not, we soon chose to move into the cabin being remodeled for us. At least, I hoped, the carpenters surely would have succeeded in fixing the leaking roof.

One evening, after we were all settled in bed, a tropical storm suddenly lit up the Congo night.

"Aunt Dorothy," one of the girls exclaimed, "we're getting drenched!" The carpenters hadn't succeeded in stopping the leak after all. Therefore, a plastic sheet was kept handy to be placed over the beds.

Our dyed, unbleached, yellow muslin drapes often blew in the Congo breezes. With a small front room looking so empty, I longed for a davenport. No furniture store could be found for many miles. Suddenly I got an idea.

"Girls," I said, " go out and gather the soft, fuzzy heads of that plant you see all over the fields. Take a large bag, for we need lots of it. Get your Congolese friends to gather some for us as well. I will pay them according to the amount they gather."

Before coming to Congo, while packing, I realized I didn't have enough barrels in which to ship my things. My girlfriend's mother heard about the need.

"If I send you a big box that a casket came in, would you take it?" she asked.

"Yes!" I said, not knowing how large it was and how heavy it would become when fully packed. Filling it was a joy, for it was neatly lined with watertight, rustproof tin.

About three months after my arrival in Congo, the huge box came. As a crew of men brought it into the house, they called it "the man killer." Now, not much later, I was asking the men to move it into our tiny front room. My girls and I worked hard to cover it with unbleached muslin, dyed yellow to match the drapes.

For a back, cushions were stuffed with straw. The seat was filled with the soft feather-like plants the girls had gathered. Even though it was too large for the tiny room, the makeshift davenport looked cheery and blended well with the yellow drapes. We had just completed the sofa when it was our time to have the Sunday evening missionary service.

After we greeted our guests at the door, many found a place to sit among the borrowed chairs. When the evening service had already begun, I looked over to our prize covered casket box. Six-

We named our school Ecole Belle Vue because of its gorgeous scenery. Here the full moon shines brightly through the clouds, giving a fairy-like view of God's creation at night.

foot Orville was one of its occupants. His feet dangled in mid-air, his legs not even long enough to touch the floor. When I came down with the giggles, others became amused and we all had a good laugh before we could continue.

One day, just before our evening devotions, the girls asked me to retell the story of how Ecole Belle Vue became ours. These were precious minutes, spent in a family-like atmosphere, where we shared our love for one another.

"But," I said, "you've heard it over and over again. Why repeat it?"

"Please, Aunt Dorothy, just one more time. Okay?"

"Before we came to Congo," I began, "the Belgium colonizers heard of a man from their country who wanted to start a silk-worm industry. He bought this piece of land that you and I are now living on. We called it Ecole Belle Vue. Can you tell me why we named it this?"

"Because it is beautiful," Lois Dolby said. "Just look outside right now. The full moon is shining so brightly, giving us a fairy-like view of God's creation."

"Yes, Lois, you are right," I said.

Joy, the book-worm, then spoke up, "Do you know that the other evening the moon was so bright I could even read outside?"

"One day," I continued, "the silk-worm specialists were relaxing on the verandah, the same one where you play when it's raining. As the sun sank quickly, Congolese women came from their fields of manioc, corn, peanuts and sweet potatoes.

"Baskets were piled high with produce and firewood for their evening meals. The setting sun was just behind a cloud. The rays spread across the west, turning from silvery rays to pinks, then to brilliant roses, fading to blues, orchids and then to gray.

"Belgians and Congolese had worked hard to finish the building for their conference rooms, dining area and kitchen. Thirty small cabins for the workers had been built with stones laid up in red mud. Elephant grass, cut just before dry season, had been brought to roof these huts. The main conference rooms were covered with corrugated iron.

"The owner of this project, their boss, came out to join them. They all stood up at once. After shaking hands with each one, he sat down. 'You have done well,' he said. 'The buildings are now complete. We are comfortable here, *n'est-ce-pas*? Isn't it beautiful to see the sunset? You have laid out the plans for the mulberry groves. In fact, many rows are now ready for the silkworms.

" 'They are to arrive tomorrow. We will raise them for the silk they spin. They will grow well in this tropical climate. We will be rich; you will see.' Of course, the children knew better.

"Children, let me tell you again how God had them erect these buildings, not really for them but for us."

"For who?" they asked. with no thought of proper grammar.

"For us," I replied.

"Please, go on with the story, Aunt Dorothy," they said.

"Citizen Lubambu, who today is our gardener, was to be laid off," I continued. "He had finished his job as a mason, having learned his trade well. When the Belgians told him he was finished, Lubambu asked for a job as a gardener. They offered him a job as the foreman on the crew that brought up compost for the mulberry plants.

"Citizen readily agreed, for he felt he had to work to support his growing family. He wasn't afraid to try something other than masonry. Even though his wife raised the food for their table, he was the man of the house and should supply the protein for the meals. Told to be at work when the first cock crowed the next morning, the 45-year-old Lubambu came with his torn shirt and bare feet.

"Monsieur Guillaume called him to the front of the line of men who were to work. 'Citizen Lubambu, here are the 15 shovels, 12 baskets, and 12 short-handled hoes. You are to see that all this is given back to me at the end of the day. Only you are responsible.'"

"'*Aaaa*, (yes) I will give them back.' came the response.

"Twelve Congolese with baskets on their heads filed by. In each basket was a hatchet. They sang in a chant-like song as they marched, hidden behind the steep mountain path they were following:

" 'The white man wants lots of dirt;/ Light dirt from under the trees./He will pay us for carrying dirt./In the basket we bring much dirt!' "

"Coming back with their baskets full of compost for the long trenches where the new mulberry sticks were to be planted, they dumped it in turn while Lubambu marked each trip by their names.

" 'But your basket isn't full,' he said to some. 'For that you will have to make extra trips.'

"*Monsieur* Guillaume came to look at the mulberry bushes already growing. Many silkworms were placed on these lush green leaves. The Congolese looked on, shaking their heads in disbelief. 'What is this?' They asked. 'They plant *mingolos* called silkworms?'

"*Mingolos* were a type of caterpillar they gathered to eat. About three inches long, they are fat - about the size of a finger. They are a good source of rich protein for their meager diet. (Almost all the girls said they had eaten *mingolos*.)

"The Congolese said that they didn't have to place their *mingolos* on bushes. They only had to pick them when they were ready. 'Can we eat these silkworms, too?' they asked, in their tribal languages.

Mingolos in Zaire feed on leaves. They are considered better protein than beef.

"The Belgians could understand the Kituba trade language of the region and French, but Chokwe and Lunda were beyond them," Citizen Lubambu interpreted, saying that, "The Congolese were surprised they had to place silkworms here on these plants.

"*Mingolo* season would start in a month's time. Even the Congolese school children were allowed two weeks vacation to gather them for money to buy school clothes. After being gathered, they were cleaned by popping them open, draining them and placing them on hot coals to dry. Then they were sacked and sold to truckers for distribution all over Congo.

"When the silkworms got a little fatter, Lubambu took one, cleaned it and tasted it.

"'Truly, this is delicious.' he said to himself, 'Maybe they won't miss just a handfull of these, for there are so many. Some day I will take a few for my wife and children. They have need of them.'

"After work, Lubambu counted the tools with each basket. When he got home, his wife asked, 'Husband of mine, what have you brought me from the house of the white man today?'

"'Nothing yet,' he replied.

"'No meat with our luku tonight? I have no greens.'

"'I will go and get something now.'

"Citizen Lubambu went back to Ecole Belle Vue. He picked a banana leaf on the way. He brought a piece of vine string to tie up his package, placing a generous handful of silkworms in the leaf. Then he took it to his wife and children. 'Nobody will miss a few,' he thought.

"The next morning, he surveyed his workers as usual. He noticed that after they dumped their compost in the trenches, they each took a few of the silkworms. He told them plainly not to take them now, but to get them at night when he could not see them.

"The next morning, *Monsieur* Guillaume looked at his precious mulberry rows. 'This astounds me.' he said. 'Where are the silkworms? Yesterday there were many fat ones. They just lacked a week before they would spin their cocoons. Now I see very few. I do not see any dead ones on the ground. The ones I see seem healthy.'

" 'Citizen Lubambu,' he called, 'where are the silkworms?'

"'Do I know the way of silkworms?' came the response. 'How can I know?'

"The next evening, he again took some of the white man's silkworms to his wife and family. His family loved them. 'If I don't take them, everyone else will,' he said to himself. 'What would my wife say then?'

"That evening, pickers came with sacks of dried *mingolos* (not silkworms) they wanted to sell. They asked *Monsieur* Guillaume whether he wanted to buy some.

"'What do you do with them?' he asked.

"'We eat them with palm fat.' they replied. 'They are fresh. They are exquisite.' " 'OOh!' he exclaimed, slamming the door in the *mingolo* picker's face. He had suddenly caught on.

"*Monsieur* Guillaume called his night watchman. 'Please call all my Belgian workers. Call my foreman, Lubambu, too.' "'Do you know where our silkworms are going?" he said to his Belgian workers in

Flemish. 'Have you seen and been observant? *Kaput*! (ruined) Why had I not studied the Congolese eating habits before spending all this money on this great adventure? What is there left for me to do?'

"'What is wrong?' asked the Belgian workers. 'The buildings are good. The mulberry bushes are growing well. Please, *Monsieur*, what is the matter?'

"'Did Congolese come to your home to sell you *mingolos*, dried caterpillars?' he asked.

"*Oui, oui,* but what has that to do with this silkworm industry?' they responded.

"'The silkworms are gone. They were just days from spinning their cocoons, but there are only a few left. The Congolese have eaten them. We cannot produce silk like this! We are ruined! Ruined I say.'

"Foreman Lubambu came. He had heard the usually calm white man a block away. He became fearful. Clapping both hands together and bowing slightly, he asked: 'You called for me, *Monsieur*?'

"'Citizen Lubambu, what happened to the silkworms? Just day before yesterday there were many. Where are they, Lubambu?'

"'But Monsieur, silkworms were eating up all your precious plants. They needed picking off. Now that silkworms are fewer, the plants will bear fruit. Is that not so? Why should we let the silkworms go to sleep? We cannot eat sleeping silkworms.'

"'Citizen Lubambu, call all the Congolese workers. Tell them to come with their contract books.'

"The Congolese came with their oiled loin cloths and bare feet. They squatted down on their haunches, talking among themselves in both Chokwe and Lunda.

"'Why did our Monsieur call us now?' they asked one another. 'Is he going to give us something?'

"Foreman Lubambu asked for quiet. He wanted them to know that the white man was very angry. 'Listen only with your ears, not with your mouth,' he suggested.

"Obviously distraught, Monsieur Guillaume began, 'Congolese, you ate up your salaries. I cannot pay you for this week. You must look for work some other place. You ate up our silkworm factory. Lay your contract books here and get out of sight. I don't want to see any of you again, ever!'

"With that, he broke down and cried. 'Who will buy these beautiful stone buildings from us?' he asked. 'What a fool I was not to have studied the eating habits of these Africans before I went to all this trouble.'

"Girls," I continued, "Mennonite Brethren Missions and Services heard about this place way off in the Belgian Congo. It was sold to us - a place was higher in elevation than most of the Congo and cooler than the mission stations you came from. Missionaries and executives looked into it and decided it was ideal for you children. Aren't you happy that God provided these buildings for us in this scenic place?

"Thank you, Aunt Dorothy, for telling the story again," they said.

Now it was time to do something with the outside of our home. Seeing plants in the forest I desired to have, I borrowed the Ratzlaff's red wagon. Some Congolese dug up the plants and loaded them in the wagon.

Suddenly, the cook's wife, a slim well-dressed Congolese, was at my side. She looked at me with pity . I couldn't speak to her since she spoke neither Kituba nor French. In sign language, she indicated she wanted to pick up the wagon and carry it on her head. When I objected, she looked puzzled. She was still convinced that carrying it on her head would be easier than pulling it. The modern use of the wheel hadn't reached her culture yet.

In school, meanwhile, we were studying *Pilgrim's Progress*. One of the boys told me why their rooms were so messy. They were acting out the story where Giant Despair came and gave the Pilgrim a good beating. In doing this, their clothes were placed in piles on the floor as bones. They decided that Giant Despair knew how to whip well.

Though all claimed to be children of the Heavenly Father, we never lacked for excitement. Punishment had to be dealt out quite frequently to the boys, but I don't remember ever having to punish the girls.

Occasionally, the boys and girls worked up a flannelgraph story and had a service with the Congolese children. As Jack Schmidt took his turn to tell the children of Congo the story he had prepared, his listeners sat on the grass in front of our home.

Speaking in Kituba and filled with emotion, he put up the figures relating to his story. He remembered that his father, before his death, told all his dental patients about His Lord and Savior Jesus Christ. Jack was now doing likewise.

Isaac Kilabi the head teacher (left), and Tata Elie, speaker at the Kipungu church dedication .

CHAPTER 6

KIPUNGU STATION'S MOUNTAIN TOP MISSION

It was hard for me to forget the dorm girls of the primary school at Kipungu Mission Station, who insisted that they too needed my help. All year, while teaching our missionaries' children at Ecole Belle Vue, Kajiji, that request kept ringing in my ears.

At our conference in 1953, the missionaries decided I could answer Kipungu's request. Their plea for help intensified in my heart and mind as we neared Kipungu's steep mountain. Throwing the carryall into low gear, we slowly climbed up to the summit where the mission station was located. The Lord had answered their request - and mine.

As director of the primary school, I soon found myself registering 110 students, grades one through five, mostly in rags. Some wore shirts so shredded that I wondered how the children's arms finally found where the sleeves had been.

Five teachers had come back for another year of teaching. In checking their qualifications, I found that the fifth-grade teacher, Isaac Kilabi, had only fourth-grade education. He was an exception, however. He did manage to keep ahead of his pupils. He later furthered his education, including theology school in France. For a time he became legal representative for our Mennonite Brethren mission before the Congolese government. Later, he was placed in charge of the Bible school in Kikwit. In 1996 he was promoted to heaven.

At the early hour of six o'clock each morning, all the school children and staff attended chapel. After chapel Susie Brucks, a medical missionary in charge of the dispensary, and I entered our home to the smell of steaming hot coffee. It had been brewed by our help over a wood burning-stove. By 7:15 a.m., Susie had returned to her dispensary, and I was at school watching as our children saluted their Congolese flag outside. Then they marched into their crumbling, grass-covered, mud-and-stick classrooms.

After opening prayers, math was taught. Each student had been given a slate to work out daily problems. Some students erased their work by spitting on the slate, then drying it by sliding the slate across their full head of hair.

First-graders began with the alphabet. Students then received a small Kituba book, from which they all read together. Many memorized the story, and I found it challenging to weed out those who were not really reading. In dry weather, I took them outside under a tree where a fallen log gave us good enough seats for an extra "classroom."

In the last class of the morning, music, it was a delight to hear Isaac Kilabi leading the third, fourth, and fifth grade students in a mass choir. Singing in beautiful harmony, they brought life to the meaningful words of "Christ Returneth."

In the lower grades, one single Bible lesson was presented all week. On the first day, the teacher told the story; second day, she retold it; the third day, the children told it to her; fourth day, they dramatized it.

This crude row of classrooms, built with temporary materials from the forest, lacked a school office. My "office" was a chair placed under the overhanging grass roof of a classroom. Our teachers had no formal training. Sometimes I caught a teacher skipping to the back of a book. When asked why, he said that he had to prove to the pupils how much he knew.

Finally, I collected all the books and marked where the teacher should be each week. That made it easier for me to check up on the progress of both teacher and student.

We encouraged the use of visual aid materials, even though we had few to utilize. One day, teacher Mupepe's class suddenly erupted into an uproar, heard from blocks away. I hurried to the scene and found that some children were ready to run out of the classroom. Looking closer, I saw the cause of it all. Mupepe, deciding to employ visual aid, had brought a frog to class. Unfortunately, the Congolese believed frogs were their ancestors, reincarnated to check up on them. The incident had frightened them and brought on the turmoil.

Sitting outside another classroom one day, I listened while Citizen Kilabi tried to explain the scientific origin of tropical storms. Lightning had killed many in the region, so the students really sat up and listened. This older group of students felt that their ancestors had told them the truth.

If they wanted to curse someone, they would throw an egg while cursing their enemy. The egg turned into a full-grown chicken, cackling (thunder) and would strike the one cursed (lightning).

Some years later, in another part of Congo, I asked some Congolese how they could distinguish between normal thunder-and-lightning and a curse. They said that if there were only few clouds in the sky and the lightning suddenly strikes out of a clear sky, that was a curse.

I was reminded of Ephesians 6:12, "Our struggle is not against flesh and blood...but against spiritual forces of wickedness in the heavenly places."

Meanwhile, at Kipungu, I learned that there was an exceptional child, Akadiko, roaming aimlessly on the mission station grounds. Some had marked him as a thief.

"How can he be so considered," I asked, "when he is completely blind? How did he become this way?"

They explained that Akadiko was very mischievous as a small boy. Because of this, his parents consulted the local medicine man. He put red pepper in the boy's eyes to burn out the evil spirits. No matter how many times his parents washed out their son's eyes, they soon realized he was blind. His eyes had been burned out.

At the time Kipungu mission station was built, Akadiko's parents came to listen to the good news of Jesus Christ. They asked God to forgive them for what they had done, then asked Jesus to live in their hearts. They were baptized and joined the church.

Akadiko's eyes had been burned out by putting red pepper into them to burn out the evil spirits.

When Citizen Akadiko was put into the regular class in the mornings, I told the teacher it was true that he couldn't see, but he had ears to hear. An intelligent boy, he learned well.

In the afternoons, he was taught how to weave a bed mat. Before class, his teacher went to the forest to cut the needed bamboo and raffia (from leafstalks of a palm tree). A Braille alphabet metal sheet gave him the opportunity to read and write. In training Akadiko, we said to the people of Congo: don't kill children who are deaf or blind; they are valuable; they too can earn a living. (Akadiko eventually became a village evangelist.)

Two o'clock in the afternoon was work time for all school children. We assigned projects according to the mission needs of the day. Workers obtained firewood from the nearby forest.

When building a new mud-and-stick dorm for the boys, older workers cut the large trees that termites wouldn't eat. Younger boys cut the smaller sticks to place between poles. They used raffia to tie the poles and sticks together. Girls carried red dirt (for plastering) in baskets on their heads. The roof was elephant grass, cut just before the dry season.

Thanks to these measures, dorm buildings cost the mission only the small amount pupils received for their work. They usually spent their hard-earned wages to supplement their protein of grass hoppers, flying ants and caterpillars. The boys would walk long distances on weekends to get food from their mothers' gardens.

In back of the school dorm, paths led to the girl's "bathtub," which was a river. They had their water hole for bathing and drawing water on one end of the mission property, while the boys had theirs on the other end. Surrounding this was thick foliage where they found kindling (to cook their meals), building materials and greens growing wild (for their supper).

About a year later, a Belgian school inspector came to our mission station. He insisted that if we wanted subsidies, our older students must leave. After complying with this order, we soon received money for our teachers' pay. This also meant that certificates handed out by us would be recognized by the Belgian Education Department of the Belgian Congo.

One day, Zola came from the girls' dorm to see me. She asked me if I would help her to get dressed for her wedding. Zola had come to the mission school at an age when she should have been finishing fifth grade instead of starting second grade.

Before the wedding day, the church elders asked the groom (one of our school teachers) what he had paid for his bride. He had given a goat, a piece of cloth and palm wine to the mother of the bride. His uncle on his mother's side, who arranged the marriage, had helped him get the money together for the last payment. Now he felt his marriage would be secure, by also asking the Lord's blessing.

On that particular Sunday afternoon, I walked over to where the bride was being dressed. In my hands was a rosecolored, streetlength dress Susie Brucks had made. Frieda Martens had utilized leftovers from her mosquito netting and made a short veil. Nellie Sidone combed her hair and put knee-length man's socks on her - a 15-minute process for each leg.

As Zola tried to fit into a pair of second-hand shoes with buckles, one buckle came off. After running home for a large needle and heavy-duty thread, I sewed it back on. Zola's friend tried to get the bride's shoe on, but was putting the left shoe on the right foot. When this was corrected, the bride stumbled around trying to learn to walk in unaccustomed shoes. In the early days at Kipungu, girls wore neither shoes nor socks.

A brown homemade suit, sewed with light-colored thread, looked good on the groom. Zola, besides her rose-colored dress and finger-tipped, mosquito-netting veil, had bright bougainvillea blossoms artfully set in her veil and carried a bouquet of the same colorful flowers.

Citizen Ngolo and Zola marched hand-in-hand up the walkway to missionary Theodor and Frieda Marten's home. A bed mat had been placed in front of the home, upon which two chairs awaited them. Had it not been for Ngolo's arm holding her up, Zola would have fallen; first, because of her unaccustomed shoes, and secondly, because she put her head down to display her shyness - an action that pleased both her and his relatives.

My Heavenly Father's strong arm held me up, or I would have stumbled in this overwhelming task of being an ambassador for Christ.

After being pronounced husband and wife, the happy couple went to the end of the walk-way to be greeted by the white powdered faces of their families and friends. Most of the women came to the ceremonies dressed in a two-yard piece of brightly printed, wrap-around, skirt-like cloth. They each carefully placed one over the other on the heads of the bride and groom. Some fifteen or so pieces of cloth gave a roof-like effect over the couple as they sang while they marched around the mission compound, that led to the prepared arbor of palm branches.

At an earlier wedding, I remember a 7-year-old boy who decided he too was going to celebrate. He had one problem: his pants just wouldn't do. He had two shirts, so he improvised. Placing two skinny, black legs through the sleeves of the extra shirt, he tied the shirt tail around his waist.

Trailing the marching crowd, he sang happily, oblivious to his appearance. I wonder if my frequent display of self-righteousness, replacing the Lord's righteousness, didn't look more ridiculous to Him than this innocent child.

Following the custom for new brides, Zola pulled up all the manioc plants she had cultivated for the school garden. Since she would no longer profit from the plants, she destroyed them so no one would profit. Mama Zola worked hard replanting the manioc field.

In the Congo, many newly wedded couples go to their ancestors' graves and pour blood on them as a witness to the fact that they have fully paid for their bride. The husband knew that later on he would again have to pay her family each time she would give birth.

Students like Sidone Nellie brought real joy. Sweet and submissive, she did exceptional work in school. Her father worked for a store; therefore, her background was different from the other girls. *Tata* Nsukami convinced her to leave school before she could finish. They married and moved to Leopoldville, where he later worked for Air-Zaire.

On a never-to-be-forgotten Saturday, excitement ran high at Kipungu Mission Station. Bill Goertzen and his Congolese masons and helpers had completed the stone church building. Next day, they would dedicate the building to the Lord. Many had carried rocks, sand, water and heavy bags of cement to the site to form this unique Kipungu church.

The middle large arch drew our eyes upward until they rested on its modest church bell tower. It pointed heavenward calling all to climb Kipungu's steep mountain to join us in our mountaintop mission worship service

With three arches above the front door, the middle larger one drew our eyes upward until they rested on its modest, neat, church bell tower. It pointed heavenward to God, calling everyone to come and climb Kipungu's steep mountain and join us in our mountaintop mission worship service.

Everyone tried to help in our Thanksgiving celebration and church dedication. School dorm girls went into the forest to pick flowers and native wild fruit. They gathered branches of palm trees and wove them artfully with flowers, forming an arch for the front door of the church. Five open windows along the sides served as shelves where the girls placed their flowers and wild fruit.

School boys went to the forest to cut down trees. After stripping them of branches, they carried them up the steep mountain and into the church for temporary benches. Though the carpenter shop kept busy making the benches, they were not quite ready for this important dedication.

When Sunday morning arrived at last, the first bell from the new bell tower brought the dorm girls dressed in their finest. The school boys, wearing their one allotted pair of pants, stood in line with their teachers.

Village women wore their oiled, unwashed loin clothes, matching their red mud curls and unwashed bodies. They climbed up the steep Kipungu hill with babies on their backs and carried an offering of dried corn on their heads. They, too, had an offering for this day of Thanksgiving.

Five hundred people stood outside the church, in three lines. They joined in as the dedicatory prayer was offered for God's house. It was theirs. They had helped in carrying stones and sand on their heads as part of their gift to God.

Sefu, one of our teachers, happily rang the bell again as Elsie Brucks played on the small pump organ: "What can wash away my sins? Nothing but the blood of Jesus." All 500 piled into the church. Some squeezed onto an already filled log bench. A log cracked, so displaced worshippers found another crowded log.

Henry Brucks conducted the service, while a Congolese man led the singing. Most of the villagers didn't know the songs, but the school children made up for them. They sang their joyful praises to the Lord in four-part harmony.

Tata Elie, a Congolese village pastor, spoke on I Corinthians 15:58, "Be ye steadfast." Teachers from both the mission and village schools sang special numbers. Bible school students home for this occasion also sang.

Morning and afternoon meetings led to a great climax as our guest speaker, a missionary from a neighboring mission, Brother Chambers, (father of twins Nancy and Gordon, students of mine at Ecole Belle Vue in 1952-53) spoke on the theme, "Thanks be to God for His unspeakable gift." Many villagers listened intently and responded as they glimpsed the reality of God's wonderful gift of salvation.

What good news it was when I learned that Martha Willems, an education missionary, would be moving to Kipungu. She would take charge of the sixth grade, which had been moved to Djongo Sanga with Henry Derksen in charge. Since this station was being given over to another mission, the Brethren decided to move it here, and at the same time add grade seven.

Since missionaries studying French in Belgium would not come until after the opening of the school year, it was decided to have Martha's sister, Kathryn Willems, the Kituba language expert, to come fill in until the missionaries from Belgium would arrive. Forty pupils entered that school, hoping to prepare themselves to enter college.

Martha had spent a year in Belgium learning French. The Congolese could not believe that she could learn a language in that short a time, without a talisman. She testified that the Lord helped her.

An Indian firm, seeking to defraud the Congolese, told them if they bought a magic talisman, they would not have to study. Some tried this, having to learn the hard way. Many of the Congolese still worshipped idols and wanted a tangible mediator to reach God. They still wore fetishes around their necks, waists and arms to ward off evil spirits. Thus, the Congolese student was easy prey to this kind of fraud.

School girls on our mission station were protected by a large fence around their living quarters. Because of this protective barrier, the girls here were called fence girls. Their kitchen included in the protected area - the place where they pounded their manioc and entertained. Actually, the kitchen was only a number of poles, with no walls, holding up a grass roof that protected them from tropical storms (to some degree, at least).

Kipungu had two-room mud-and-stick buildings for sleeping quarters. From 10 to 15 beds filled each room. On Saturdays, all the beds were taken out and washed to help ward off bed bugs and ticks.

In their spare time, the girls often kept busy knitting sweaters to sell for food. One evening, some of them came over to tell me of an urgent need. Their kitchen was falling down. The roof had become thinner and thinner. When the girls made a fire, they would use some of the grass from the overhanging roof. It was now leaking badly. They were begging for a new kitchen.

"Why are you tearing down the roof over your heads?" I asked. "It's your fault that it's leaking. Maybe next year we will be able to build another one for you."

Not many nights later, I heard the howling wind as a tropical downpour beat against our house, built of cement bricks. It swirled in a way I have never experienced before or since. As I lay in bed, I began to pray. "Lord, we'll understand if You take the girl's kitchen, for they have already stripped it, handful by handful. But please save the rest of the mission buildings."

Just then, the wind drove the rain between the walls and the overhanging roof. It came through the ceiling, dumping an avalanche of water right above me as I lay in bed. Since I had my bed covered with plastic, nothing was ruined. I found my two friends, Martha and Kathryn, already in the front room pushing the furniture around to the driest spot. Then they mopped up the flooded cement floor.

As I walked about with my camera the next day, I took pictures of the damaged grass roofs, toppled trees and the blown-down kitchen that the girls had ruined beforehand. So that the school might continue, we divided the newly built church into makeshift classes until the damaged roof could be repaired. The partitions were taken down for Sunday services.

Temporarily, the girls had to learn their lesson by cooking outside, rain or shine. They had to stack their food and pots into already overcrowded bedrooms.

Meanwhile, Ernie and Lyddia Dyck now served at Matendi, Ernie as principal of our monitor's school. To help our mission primary school to raise its standards, we held a seminar at his school. Because it was the dry season, all of the students were on vacation. We challenged our teachers to accept a week of training.

The only way to get to Matendi on these one-way trails was by carryall or truck. Arriving at Kafumba from Kipungu, Margaret Dyck and I profited by going with Irvin Friesen, the Bible school teacher at Kafumba. On the back of the pickup, we had the company of 14 school teachers. They joyfully bumped along with us, singing harmoniously in praise to their Creator. Even the mountains, hills and valleys echoed the message to small villages and jungles along the way.

School soon began, with Irvin Friesen teaching the Bible lessons and leading devotions for 32 teachers. Mrs. Buschman, an educator; Martha Willems, now directing school at Lusemvu; Ernie Dyck, from Matendi; Margaret Dyck and I taught them, specializing in pedagogy. Nettie Berg, a nurse, shared ways in which they could apply practical health habits

At the end of the school year, Mr. Martens and I talked to each prospective fifth-grade graduate. We tried to learn their interests and goals.

Meanwhile, Kipungu primary school needed teachers for classes added because of increased enrollment. We encouraged the most promising students to take advantage of the sixth and seventh grades now offered at Kipungu. Those interested in becoming pastors were directed towards Kafumba for Bible training. Prospective teachers went to Matendi for the monitor's school. A few went right to teaching, so great was the need.

At Kipungu, we heard many voices calling us. One was the voice of the sick. Susie Brucks, Henry's sister, looked after those who were ill but needed better buildings and more help.

Another voice, the mission church, included all who were on the mission station. Villagers all around us pleaded, "Please tell us the story of Jesus. We want to hear, but you never come." The field was too vast for one couple to handle. Village pastors and teachers needed guidance. How could one couple hope to answer so many voices?

When John and Ruth Kliewer opened this mission station, and later left for furlough, the Theodor Martens took their place. Henry and Elsie Brucks also came and helped when needed. Clearly more teachers were needed. We had to help the Congolese in their tribal errors. To them, telling on someone who committed a sin was as bad as doing it. Hidden sin wasn't sin until it was found out.

In spite of this, many found their way to the Savior. Village pastors and medical workers all worked together with mission schools at Panzi, Kajiji, Kafumba, Lusemvu and Kipungu to build the body of Christ. Daily Bible lessons taught them to turn from dead idols to the living God.

One evening, when we missionaries had met together, a group of girls came and began coughing outside the door. We called six in, and they confessed they had done wrong by not obeying.

After a while, we noticed they still had not gone. We called them back in, only to hear them confess another sin. We thought that was all, but still they didn't leave. Finally, Elsie went out to give all the girls time to talk. They confessed several other things the Lord had shown them. We praised the Lord that He was convicting hearts of wrong doings in spite of their heathen teachings.

CHAPTER 7

PANZI

Four years after coming to the Belgian Congo I found myself moving to Panzi Mission Station. Begun in 1930, it was turned over to Mennonite Brethren Missions/Services in 1953.

Driving up the last slippery, red-mud, one-way, unpaved road, we turned the corner. On the right, we saw piles of stones and a foundation laid for a large, permanent church. I saw the usual temporary buildings, - the boys' dorm, the church, the fenced-in girls' dorm and kitchen, and the homes of teachers and workers.

We greeted a missionary couple, John and Agnes Esau, and their children, who had charge of this primitive mission station. Then we drove to the dried mud-brick home Elsie Guenther and I were to share. It had a thatched roof over an adequate verandah.

As we entered the house, we walked on uneven bamboowoven floors which were laid in the front room, living room and kitchen. Elsie had thoughtfully insisted on laying a good cement floor in my bedroom just before I arrived.

Looking into Elsie's room, I noticed that her furniture consisted mostly of covered wooden boxes. How grateful I became for the furniture Theodore Martens, together with Congolese carpenters, had made for me at Kipungu, and for the gifts that came from home to help pay for it.

Panzi kept us missionaries busy, with up to 500 students attending grades one through five. Elsie, as principal, showed me around. She indicated which classrooms would be mine to supervise. I was given the first-grade class and four second-grades classes.

These classrooms and their equipment proved to be even more primitive than Kipungu's mission school. One classroom didn't even have the split logs as desks to write on. They even lacked the minimum required school books. How would we raise the school up to standard in a year's time, so that the Belgians would pay its teachers? Most of the teachers had no more than a fourth-grade education.

Elsie and I realized these weaknesses and did all we could to encourage better teaching methods. That included checking lesson plans and class journals. We found ourselves rising at 5:00 a. m. and eating breakfast together at 6:00, just as the sun always peeked its head over the horizon.

Singing God's praises together with the students and workmen, then listening to the morning challenge in chapel, proved to be a wonderful way to set our hearts right for the work day ahead. We enjoyed our morning break while the students ate at 8:30. Then, we placed our chairs outside classrooms or walked around to listen to the different teachers. Often I took out students for personal coaching until noon.

Belgian colonizers insisted on teaching more handwork, so we divided the students into four different groups. One group came to me for a week at a time to learn some kind of trade. Other students kept busy getting poles from the forest for a new dorm house, cutting grass around the school buildings, or gathering sticks and mud for the building program.

At 6:00 o'clock, while the sun was setting, they ate their second meal of the day. Each village group cooked for themselves over an open fire. The stove consisted of four stones to hold up the kettle. Every other weekend, as at Kipungu, they made the long walk to their villages in search of food from mother's garden.

Most of the students excelled in language learning; however, acquiring other knowledge was a different matter. How could we best teach our children so they would reason for themselves?

One Bible school graduate, a promising first-grade teacher, wanted to have a class of older children. Since the Word of God was taught in all classrooms, he wanted to profit by this. First-graders were just too young to grasp the deeper truths he wanted to teach. John Esau told him either he took this class or he was through.

While the teacher battled with the offer for several days, the class was without a teacher. One Monday morning, the children asked me about a teacher.

"Well," I said, "I guess Mahenzi Wilson will have to teach."

Being the brightest one in the class, Mahenzi stood up and actually taught. He showed flash cards to the students, and they responded. He wrote arithmetic problems on the board; they faithfully worked on them.

Later, he led singing - even beating out the time correctly. But he did have his troubles. Other students, finding out who was teaching, tried to push their way through the bamboo door. I managed to chase away the culprits. Though Wilson did a good job, the children wanted a "real" teacher the next day.

Later, in his adult life, Mahenzi Wilson continued to use the talents the Lord gave him. Among other responsibilities, he became a secondary school inspector for our mission's schools.

One day, I woke up to find that our whole house - except Elsie's and my bedrooms - had been invaded by drivers ants. These unique insects live in a hole and march in a row, the width depending upon the size of their colony. On the outside, soldier ants protect their marching workers and hold on to one another. Once, I picked up a whole string of the ants simply by just raising the stick I had placed underneath them.

When I went into the kitchen to ask why they hadn't awakened me to open the door for the cook, they said they were too busy fighting ants outside the house. When John Esau came for the morning service, he graciously invited us to eat with his family. It was impossible to prepare anything in a kitchen covered with drivers ants. Congolese found the nest and tried to burn them out.

Our bamboo-woven floors gave many a cockroach a hiding place, but eventually they became a feast for the ants. They worked as our insect terminator. In the afternoon, the ants returned. They climbed up the outside bathroom wall. With a blow torch in hand, John stooped to kill them from the bottom up. Suddenly, they all let loose and landed on John.

Jumping up in a hurry, a frenzied John shook them off then picked off the stragglers one by one. They bit like a wasp. Though

John worked for half a day, killing many of them with his blow torch, they still kept coming.

That evening, they appeared on my side of the house again. We put kerosene around the doors, and that discouraged them from crossing over. Elsie kept her parrot in her room that night, so that if the ants got in he wouldn't be eaten. Drivers ants have even killed and eaten people who were too drunk or too sick to move.

One night, the Esaus' two-year-old daughter suddenly awoke. "Ants are biting me! Ants are biting me!" she screamed.

Her parents searched her crib but found none. Going into the adjoining room, they found the floor covered with ants. God must have sent an angel to awaken the child and to let her parents know they were in the adjoining room. God loves and takes care of the missionaries' children; otherwise, she could have been eaten alive.

Meanwhile, village teachers came to me on special days for further class work. Many had only a second-grade education. It seemed an insurmountable task to get them to teach even the basics in their primitive village schools. Had I been able to supervise them properly every day, that would have certainly helped. But I had my hands full with other tasks.

About a month before Christmas, we began practicing a Christmas play. How they loved to be the soldiers who insisted that all come to be registered for taxation; or shepherds who saw the angels and heard them sing.

At Kajiji, when Mrs. Shannon directed the Christmas pageant, villagers would walk days to attend. After the play, many would flock to the altar. They found this true story the answer to their personal desire to know the loving Saviour.

Before our students went home for Christmas, we bought 145 kilos of their staple food, manioc, which the girls prepared for us. Students and teachers with borrowed dishes, found their way into the grass-roofed church, where servers dished up luku, buffalo meat, sweet mango sauce and orange juice. What a treat for them - and us - to have such a variety of things within their culture. We all said grace together. I doubt if many of them had prayed before eating a meal, truly a learning experience.

After the school children left for their Christmas vacation, hun-

Missionary Willie Baerg making contact with a village chief.

Many women came with the typical basket piled high with a bed mat, food, cooking pot and firewood.

dreds of followers (*balandi*) streamed from their villages to the mission station for a week of instruction. Women dressed in oily loin cloths carried long baskets strapped to their backs. The typical basket included a bed mat, food from the garden, a cooking pot and firewood. Baby strapped in front completed the usual picture.

Some Congolese walked days to get to Panzi. Village teachers encouraged them to come. Their school children who returned for food had aroused their curiosity with tales of the white man. Missionary Willie Baerg had made many contacts in the small villages, giving people courage and a desire to hear more of God's Word. He had organized this great gathering, and was supervising the building of this permanent stone church.

These visiting villagers took up residence in the school buildings, boys' dorm, and even built mud-and-stick huts where they stayed during the week. Early morning meant chapel, where challenging messages touched the hearts of many. Bible lessons were taught in the simplest language possible, for many of the dear Congolese were illiterate. Many believed that baptism would save them. We had to show them from the Word of God that salvation involved a change of heart.

In the afternoons, faithful and willing workers served by carrying rocks or sand for the large permanent church being built. Walls were going up on the foundation I had seen on arrival at Panzi.

Another conference took place during the school children's Easter vacation. All the students could go home, but a number decided to stay. They wanted to get right with God. When the invitation was given, many Christians came to confess sins. Others trusted Christ for the first time. Some came to pray for their home villagers.

Many became candidates for baptism. The missionaries and mission pastor led by William Baerg spent days listening to hundreds who wanted to be baptized, to make sure they understood what it was all about. Some lacked evidence of spiritual life; others needed more instruction. Many were accepted. That year, at Panzi alone, some 200 baptisms evidenced vital signs of a new life in Christ.

Sunday mornings, Elsie and I ate breakfast together at 7:00 o'clock so that we could review the Sunday school lesson we would soon teach. A good teacher, Elsie had taught this lesson to the Congolese teachers the night before. Now they prepared to meet with their pupils.

As the drums beat, Sunday school pupils followed different paths to their open-air classrooms. Some sat on a verandah, others on someone's lawn. My third-grade boys and I took our places on a fallen log in the Brucks' back yard under a big tree.

Even before I arose from siesta, the missionaries' children had already appeared at my door for their Sunday School lesson. I found these dear children a joy to teach. On this Sunday, the story centered around the prodigal son. Two-year-old Katherine saw that the prodigal son had bare feet in the picture shown.

"He will get chiggers," she said. These tiny, pinhead -sized creatures loved to crawl under the toenail and breed. She remembered when her mother had to dig them out of her toes with a sewing needle.

After Sunday school, we gathered in the church for the morning worship service. Somehow, Panzi's singing just didn't compare with Kipungu. Mrs. Agnes Esau and her three children came over for dinner. After this, we all took a siesta.

Mr. and Mrs. Willie Bearg had returned to America for health reasons. Henry and Elsie Brucks and family took their place. When Henry and John Esau toured the villages, they found the Spirit of the Lord working among the Congolese. Men cried in repentance over their sins, an unusual occurrence in Congo.

Later, John and Henry went back to hold regional conferences with them, walking or riding a bicycle for days to reach some of the remote villages. Earlier, one of our teachers talked about the tree that grew from the smallest seed. "All the birds of the field found a nesting place there," he said. "Somehow, we at the mission station were like the birds in that tree. We sing nice songs and relax, but become complacent. Jesus wants us to go out and sow the seed of the Word of God in the villages, he reminded us."

One weekend, we decided we should indeed get into the villages that were far from Panzi. We knew that those teachers needed our help and encouragement. We left Panzi at 10:30 in the morning, skirting Angola, traveling west. At about noon, we arrived at the mammoth falls, Chute Guillaume, now called Tembo Falls.

We walked across the corn fields which towered above our heads and entered a miniature rain forest. Mist from the waterfalls covered us continually. Spellbound, I gazed at the great sight - the historic water falls that separate the Belgian Congo from Angola. My eyes followed the flow of swift, tumbling, turbulent waters into the deep ravine it had cut into mother earth.

Somehow, I wanted to stick my feet into its cleansing waters. I remembered Peter saying to Jesus when He wanted to wash his feet, "Lord, doest thou wash my feet?" Jesus answered, "If I wash thee not thou hast no part with me." Our Creator's marvelous display drew me closer to Him and gave me peace in His presence.

Soon we found the path leading to the shore below. Looking at the upper part of the falls, we saw that this breathtaking phenomenon - almost an eighth of mile wide - had made many paths, leaving strips in between where shrubs, trees and rocks struggled to survive.

Congolese told of people who had hid underneath the falling waters when the Angolans and Congolese were at war. Awestruck by the magnificent display, we sat there eating our picnic lunch. Inwardly, we praised our great, majestic, all-powerful Creator.

We soon made ourselves break away from this awesome specta-

Th higher the door and the more colorful the picture above the door, the more important the residents were to their village clan.

The children pushed the sand aside. With sticks for a pencil they wrote upon the ground. Poor, yes, but they were determined to use what they had.

cle, as we had traveled only halfway to our destination. Finally, after hours through grass-lands, forests and jungles, crossing many log-covered bridges, we came to our destination, the tribal village of Kibenga. A bare-breasted lady, wearing only a loin cloth, gleefully ran longside as she tried to keep up with the carryall - her way of welcoming us to her village.

Though it was almost dark, hundreds joined in singing a welcome song that included John Esau's name. Most of the men had only a string around their waist, a piece of cloth draped between their legs. Just a few years earlier, the entire tribe wore only animals' skin for dress.

Little girls, with beads around their necks and waists, wore only a piece of cloth that hung in front the waist down.

Boholo village homes looked like a huge beehive, with elephant grass woven in - not only on the roof, but all the way down the sides as well. They looked like huge, rounded baskets turned upside down and covered with elephant grass. Doorways differed according to the importance of the dweller. The higher the bamboo door, and the more colorful the picture above it, the more important were the residents to their village clan.

While in Kibenga, we held morning worship services before all the women left for their fields. All classes had school in the mornings. On that first morning, I walked around to see the school in session. I couldn't believe my eyes. In one class, meeting outside, the children had pushed the sand aside and with a stick as a pencil, wrote on the ground. Though poor, they determined to utilize whatever they could to learn.

Since this village had their teachers occupied in the mornings, we decided to reach some nearby villages during that time. Mr. Buck, a missionary residing in this region; John, a Congolese pastor, and I started out on the car trail, as far as it went. Then, we followed the footpath to the target village. Many people came out to meet us and carried our lunch and flannelgraph on their heads.

When we arrived, we decided not to eat breakfast first, lest village women would leave for their fields. A good-sized crowd gathered to listen to us. After my flannelgraph Bible story, John gave the morning message. How much of the trade language they comprehended, we didn't know, but we trusted the Lord to speak to some.

While I was eating breakfast in the teacher's hut, the the pastor called me to see a sick child. He led me to a girl about 11 years of age, sitting on the ground in the heat of the tropical sun. She said she was thirsty and hungry. Her reddish hair indicated poor nutrition. With her pale face, she looked like a living skeleton. I asked about her.

"Oh, Mademoiselle, you know our ways," the village pastor said. "When a person has been sick for a while, we don't give them much food. We starve them." That kind of mercy killing sounds familiar today, as if some in America might be promoting it.

Though her mother had left for the fields, I asked that someone give the girl food. The spiritual leader of the village offered her leftover luku, while I handed her some meat. Then I told her of our living hope, Christ Jesus, and how He loved her. The pastor translated where he thought necessary.

By early afternoon, the rain had driven the villagers back from their fields. After another worship service with them, we started back for Kibenga. Despite the rain, we stopped at another village.

Many people came to greet us in the downpour. Their oiled loin cloths shielded their bodies from the rain. Asked if there was a place to hold a service, the villagers said *no*. The only available house was filled with *mingolos* they had gathered to sell. Could we stand under a roof or a verandah of a house for a service? No verandah or overhanging roof was large enough, they said.

"We will go and look," the Congolese pastor said. "Maybe Satan is deceiving us with lies."

As we walked out into the rain, the women cheered us and made us feel welcome. We ended up having a service with the men standing on the verandah while we women stood outside in the rain. I opened my umbrella. As many women as possible cuddled up close for shelter. John held an umbrella over the Congolese pastor while he gave a short message.

These people, refugees from Angola, had very little housing for so many people. We wondered if they must have been sleeping like pencils in a pencil box.

The women's hair, in French braids and matted down with red mud, would have looked nice indeed if it had been clean. When village people come to Christ, God cleans up the inside with His precious blood and they start to clean up on the outside as well.

Early next morning, we went out to another village. This time John's wife, Agnes, and their three children accompanied us. Three white children MKs (missionary kids) proved to be a main attraction: Mary Lois, 3 1/2; Kathy, 2 and baby John Irwin, 8 months old.

Mrs. Esau sat outside the church with her babies, so that all eyes - and ears - could concentrate on the message. A church overflowing with listeners gave village mothers an excuse to sit beside Agnes, and her unusual pale-faced little ones.

Though the minister's words could be plainly heard from where they sat, they may not have heard much of what he said. But the missionary family had a message for them. They learned from the

Panzi mission school children saluting their flag.

John Esau and a Congolese teacher counting villages without schools or a Christian witness.

loving, Christ-like parents' concern for each other, and their way of disciplining their children in love.

Upon talking to one of the teachers in the village, we learned he had only a first-grade education. He taught 140 pupils. We wondered how someone with only first-grade education could do justice to 140 pupils. But they made the most of what they had.

After my flannelgraph lesson and John's stirring message, we went to the carryall - the whole village walking with us. They wanted to sell a large stock of bananas, floor mats and native beans.

Even though we hadn't eaten breakfast, we didn't dare do so. Too many children had whooping cough. Leprosy also was prevalent there. At other times, when we did eat in the open, we felt like a monkey in a cage. The village children watched every bite we took. After we had left, the children searched for crumbs. They wanted to taste our odd food, which was usually sandwiches.

Now we drove the bumpy, one-way trail to the river to wash our hands before we ate breakfast. After eating and while we were resting, John and the Congolese went hunting. They did get a monkey or two. You can guess what we had for supper that night. As my Mother would say in German when we as children were slow in eating something we didn't like, I ate "with long teeth."

In the afternoon, I again resumed my work of trying in three days to instruct the teachers in how to reach the school children more effectively. Often, village teachers were persecuted, laughed at and cursed at, tempting them to use heathen methods of witchcraft and ancestral worship. They had to lean heavily on God.

One man told a missionary how he turned to the Lord from heathen practices.

"I was fishing. My wife was far from there. I was thinking of all that was going on in my village of Kibenga. I had helped to decide who should drink the last poison cup. Individuals who had drunk them had died. I believe that soon the villagers will find out that I was the one. They will ask me to drink it. This will mean certain death.

"Now my wife was watching me fish. She met me as she was coming from her fields of manioc. She carried her roots of kasava to soak in the stream below. She had heard rumors that more poison had been made from the dead who were buried and dug up.

"She had a real concern, wondering who would be the next one to die in our village. A missionary led me to the Lord Jesus Christ who forgave me my awful sins. I am praying that the Lord's will might be done."

Since this story was told, others from this village have died, but we haven't heard whether this man has or not. Even today, poisoning has not been stamped out. We continue to pray that the Christians stand firm in their new-found faith.

At Kibenga, on the last day, after we had our teachers' session, I asked the pastor to accompany me on a tour of this unique village. The rounded, miniature replicas of their houses in the backyards fascinated me. I was determined to look into them. Before I had permission to look into one, I glanced in. Because it was so dark, however, I couldn't see anything.

In response to my questions, they explained that they had some bracelets from their ancestors in there. They were supposed to bring them good luck. Bracelets in Congo often were made from muscles of someone who had been killed.

As I walked and talked with the pastor, he assured me this village was free from any idols. He also said I could look into one of the little huts. After a long discussion in their tribal tongue, he persuaded the owner to open the mat door to the food storage hut. To the pastor's surprise, it had an idol with some food in front of it. Food was being dedicated to the idol.

The second one had the back partitioned off with a bed mat. It hid whatever was precious to them. He took out a home-made bamboo box and showed me the bracelets worn on the ankles by his ancestors.

When I said that I still believed there were idols in back of that mat, he brought forth a long stick with a face carved on it. Congolese believed that their one God was so far removed from them that they needed idols as a mediator between them and God. They worship the spirit that possessed the idol. Trusting idols is like a vine climbing a dead tree. Both must soon perish!

The pastor laughed to cover up his embarrassment. I told the owner of the idol that I hadn't come here to laugh at them, but only to point them to Christ our Mediator. We didn't have to use idols to get to God, for Christ Jesus does that for us. Our Saviour gave me joy and peace, and I wanted them to know Him as I did.

As in America, some of the adults in the village appeared hardhearted, disinterested in Christ. But many others came, including children. Many wanted to be baptized. When I told John and Agnes about the idols, they decided not to baptize any others until the village received further teaching from God's Word.

Just before leaving Kibenga, John and a Congolese busily marked something in the sand. Looking over their shoulders, I listen as I watched. They counted the villages in this region for which we were responsible. Their final count came to 48 villages - and only ten teachers for all these villages. That meant 38 villages still had no Christian witness and no school. Truly, the Lord of the harvest needs more workers to reach these untouched villages.

After we returned to Panzi Mission Station to finish out the school year, final exams for all grades had to be given and corrected. Three exams given during the year, together with daily grades, would decide which children should be promoted.

Fifth-grade graduates now had a larger choice of schools that they could choose from for further education. Their choices increased annually. Not only could they choose between the sixth and seventh grades at Kipungu, but also Bible school at Kafumba, the monitor's school at Matendi, and Kajiji now offered a medical school as well.

Entrance exams were given by placing each student a yard apart on church benches. They were placed in rows directly one in front of the other. We sat watching them, for they were clever at cheating.

In the middle of the school year, the girls' work had been given over to me. Other missionary wives had helped the girls in the primary school by teaching them to sew. After sewing underpants for some time, the girls vowed never to wear them. This was all new to them.

Now, after sewing handkerchiefs and bras, they were asking me to make - of all things - underpants again. As they began to see the need of such garments, their sewing was well done. The Congolese girls weren't unintelligent, they simply lacked opportunity.

Girls in the surrounding villages of Panzi usually stayed in their villages, caring for their younger siblings so that mother could do her demanding field work. She not only took care of her younger brothers and sisters but her cousins as well. She considered them her brothers and sisters, too.

Many a 3-year-old already had a baby strapped to her back. This was her task until she entered puberty. When her uncle on her mother's side decided it was time to go to the mission school, she was sent. In that way her family could obtain a better bride price. Because of the work demanded of her, many girls in the lower grades should have already graduated from fifth grade.

The woman of Congo was a slave. If it wasn't for her, the Congolese would starve. Beast of burden and childbearer, she also cooked all the meals. The man supplied protein by hunting and fishing. He also built the house.

As an educator, I sought to educate the families to send us their girls while they were young enough and interested in learning to read and write. They must realize that the girl was smart, but had much to learn to become better wives and mothers. We needed to do something special for the girls to elevate our church families in the Congo.

Chapter 8

My First Furlough

In 1957, while en route to America, I stopped in Bangui, French Equatorial Africa, bordering the Congo. While riding to my friend's mission station, I spied a girl with a grass skirt running as if to hide.

Margerie Benedict, a missionary nurse, whose friendship I had made while attending Simpson Bible Institute, explained that soon after puberty, Africans circumcise their girls. Thus, when they are married, they would be faithful to their husbands. Wearing a grass skirt signified that this had just been accomplished. Margerie had eased my curiosity.

What a joy it was to see my friend and her work! Permanent small huts had greeted our gaze as we traveled from the airport to the mission station. Government officials had set a date when no more mud-and-stick or grass huts would be allowed. They destroyed all the remaining huts built with temporary materials.

This act forced the inhabitants of the country to obey the requirement by building with bricks. I rejoiced as I reflect on the firm foundation God had provided for my life in the person of His Son, the Lord Jesus Christ.

Margerie not only nursed at the dispensary and maternity ward, way out in the bush, but she also had to provide ambulance service in emergencies, using her own vehicle. She drove the critical patient to the nearest hospital to consult with the resident doctor. During camp season, Margerie still found time to teach hungry youths the Word of God.

After a week's stay, I had to travel on.

When we arrived in Paris, the customs officer told me to follow a certain lady into a small room.

"Do you speak French?" she asked.

"A little," I said.

"Undress!" she ordered.

I was intimidated. Why would she suspect me of smuggling something? Since she was a lady, I obeyed. Finally pointing to my watch, pinned on to my dress, I said in French, *"C'est cassée!"* (It is broken.)

"Oh!" she said, "I guess that is what they saw."

She then let me go. Though mortified by the experience, I knew that diamond-rich African countries had many smugglers. I wondered if other passengers noticed my ordeal - an apparent suspect of smuggling diamonds. Except for the grace of God, I realized, I might have been one of those guilty as jewel thieves.

When we reached Brussels, Belgium, I met up with other missionaries traveling home, including Henry and Helen Derksen and their sons. We soon boarded the plane and headed for the Atlantic Ocean. Being the curious type, I always begged for a window seat.

Suddenly, I saw the wheels of our plane go down. Looking below, I searched for a possible landing field. A short time later, not having noticed that our wheels had been retracted, I saw them come down again. When this happened a third time, I wondered what was going on.

At Shannon, Ireland, the pilot informed us that we had time to look around the curio shops in the air terminal. After we had looked around for some time, an announcement came over the loud speaker: "Your plane was struck by lightning. It has been repaired. We will be loading in 15 minutes."

The Lord had been gracious in protecting us. That night, as we flew over the Atlantic, the wind literally howled. Finally, the pilot explained that we had hit the tail end of Hurricane Audrey. Although delayed by the storm, we made it safely. Again, the Lord was with us. "Underneath are His everlasting arms" (Deuteronomy 33:27).

On landing in New York, we soon learned that we had missed our connecting flights home.

The next morning after taking leave of my missionary friends, I boarded a direct flight to Los Angeles. My mind raced ahead, wondering who would be at the airport to greet me. I could hardly believe I had been gone for five years. I longed to see my mother, my brothers, my sisters again.

As we approached the landing strip, suddenly the plane jerked upward. Steadily gaining altitude, we found ourselves circling the airfield.

"I believe the pilot missed the runway," I said to my seat companion.

"That never happens," he said - and he was a pilot himself.

Just then a voice came over the loudspeaker. "Another plane was on the runway. I saw it just in time. We will be landing in three minutes."

Again, the Lord's protective hand had saved our lives. He must still have work for me to do.

Coming home was quite traumatic. Everyone I met had changed. My oldest nephew Ron Newfield, 10 years old when I left, was now taller than I was. Before, when he and his sisters came over, we often enjoyed the record about Rip Van Winkle, asleep in the Catskill Mountains. Now it almost seemed as if I, after five years of sleeping, had wakened to my dear ones in America.

Further education was required of me if I wanted to continue the work of a missionary teacher. After a year and a summer of hard work, I received my B.A. in education and two California teacher's certificates.

Because I was worn out, to pack up and go directly to Belgium for an arduous year of French studies was out of the question. A physician ordered a good amoebic dysentery cure, after which I felt like a new person.

That reminded me of the first time I contracted this hard-to-get-rid-of amoeba. It had happened back at Kipungu, and it forced me to spend a whole month under our mission doctor's care at Kajiji. Oh, how I learned to appreciate our mission doctors who took care of us as well as the Congolese. I recall Dr. Luke also served many in the name of Christ.

Meanwhile, I spent a year commuting between Fresno State College, studying French, and our Mennonite Brethren Biblical Seminary, where I was enriched spiritually by studying the Word of God.

By this time, I was more than ready to return to Congo, the land to which the Lord had called me. After arriving in New York, I found myself boarding the *S.S. Rhyndam* on July 1, 1959, on my way to Belgium. We had a pleasant though sometimes bumpy trip.

In Brussels, many single missionaries lived together at a Christian pension (boarding house). Most of us attended the Colonial school to learn French, a must for all educators entering the Congo who wanted to be recognized and paid by the Belgian education system. On the first day, a French dictation determined which class we would enter. Our French tutors had prepared us well, so most Mennonite Brethren missionaries made the strong class.

Studying in my room, with a hot water bottle at my feet, and a blanket to keep warm, I had earphones to listen to my tutor's voice. That enabled my lovely roommate, Louise Moore, to study without distraction.

No matter how hard I studied, my teacher really frightened me. I flunked his oral exam. The board graciously allowed me to stay in Belgium a month longer to enroll in Alliance Francaise de Belgique, where I received my coveted French certificate.

One day, an 18-year-old neighbor girl stumbled upon our boarding house. In Belgium taking care of children in order to learn French, she had one English parent and one German. She knew both languages well. We became good friends, and I introduced her to my best friend, Jesus. A little later, she responded to His claim on her life.

In 1958, a few selected Congolese had been allowed to visit the Brussels World's Fair. When these men returned home, they started agitating. A number of political parties sprang up. Now, when we arrived in 1959, Belgians and Congolese met constantly to try to iron out their differences.

Almost daily, our teacher at the Colonial school reported to us what progress had been made. The Congolese wanted their independence. The Belgians needed this colony to give their people work outside of their small, efficiently run country.

Laws were so worded that the Congolese never should have received their independence. King Baudouin did not want war. The Belgians knew, however, that only 14 Congolese were university graduates; only 12 had risen to administrative positions in the Colonial government. How could the Congolese successfully run their own country?

On June 30, 1960, the Congolese received their independence. Wearing the maroon sash of the order of the crown, Belgium's highest decoration, which he had received the previous night, Patric Lumumba, prime minister of the Democratic Republic of the Congo, addressed the assembly of diplomats and guests, including Belgium's King Baudouin.

They listened in stunned silence as Lumumba recounted the sufferings of the people of the Congo and all Africa at the hands of the Europeans. He stated that only independence could end the humiliation and slavery which had been imposed on them by force.

On Independence Day, all Congo was reported to be calm. Soon all women and children of expatriates were evacuated. We missionaries from the Mennonite Brethren Board of Missions went to the airport to see our missionary men leave for Congo. It was heart-rending to see them say goodbye to their wives and children.

In 1960, new reports came saying that we had a membership of 5,399 in our Congolese churches. The new Christians needed our support in these difficult days. Rev. John Toews, secretary of our Mission Board, came to Belgium on a visit.

In subsequent conversations, I mentioned my concern for the girls and women of Congo. After all, it was the woman who raised the child. The Congolese man needed someone equal in education to stand by him. He needed someone who knew the Lord and could lead their children to the Saviour.

"If we start a girl's work," Rev. Toews said, "the Congolese themselves will have to pay for it. We can't afford to do that type of work."

Though discouraged, I was not crushed. Somehow or another, I knew that God would some day allow me to help the Congolese women.

In July 1960, Moise Tshombe, together with some Congolese, headed the secession of the richest part of the Congo, Katanga. Without these mines of copper, tin, gold and silver, manganese, cobalt and zinc concentrate, this new independent African country could hardly survive.

It soon became evident that, with the evacuation of all missionary women and children from the troubled Congo, we in Belgium would be going home instead. Some evacuees suffered pitifully.

Congolese villagers stopped them and searched their four-wheel-drive panel, making them unload, then reload their things. The driver asked what they were searching for.

"Independence!" they answered. Some hadn't a clue what that meant.

From Belgium, we went to Holland, then on September 13 sailed on the Statendam to New York, arriving there on the 21st.

By December 12, I found myself at Balch Camp, a Pacific Gas and Electric project settlement in the mountains near Fresno, California. In this isolated community, I taught third, fourth, and fifth grades.

My brother and sister-in-law, Rev. Ed and Margaret Kopper, took my things up the mountains for me. Mother traveled with me. Delayed from following them immediately, we met them on their way back. They assured me two gentlemen already had offered to help me move into my home. Because it was getting late, they suggested that mother go back with them.

"But, Dorothy," mother said, "will you be all right?"

"Mother," Ed reminded her, "she has just gone to Africa and back by herself. I think she is able to handle this one."

True to their word, two men met me. They asked me which apartment was mine. The gentleman who lived there was only half moved out.

"Look and see which room has his bed in it," I suggested. "I'll take the other one."

"Yes," they teased. "You just enter this man's apartment, push his clothes aside and make yourself at home."

I have no choice, I thought to myself, *they told me this apartment would be ready on this date.*

One of the fellows, a divorcee, asked me to join them for a party that night given by Pacific Gas and Electric. When I declined, saying I had to get settled, they kept teasing me.

"You can put a broom from the door to that wall so no one can get in," they suggested. Still a little uneasy, I actually did that.

That night, I slept fitfully. Bells clanged periodically through the night. Was I losing my mind, or were these men so angry at me that they were ringing bells?

Not many days later, I asked someone about the bells. Deer had been tagged in the region to study their wanderings, they explained.

At Christmas time, I joined a gathering at which I again saw the two men who had teased me. "Hello, Miss Kopper!" one said. Then he poked the other and said, "Introduce me to her; I met her under adverse circumstances."

Meanwhile, my main attraction to Balch camp was their need of a Sunday school teacher. When I asked about it, they said, "I believe you are the answer to our prayers."

Though I enjoyed the rare beauty of the place, its people and my school teaching, I enjoyed the Sunday school even more. What a thrill to share the Word of God with others.

In the Congo, meanwhile, things had been changing fast. History was being enacted. On February 12, 1961, assassins brutally killed Lumumba. He was quickly replaced by Antoine Gizenga of Stanleyville.

Back home, a Christian couple moved to Balch Camp and took over the little Sunday school. During the next school year, Hanford, California, beckoned me to teach third and fourth grades. This church town had almost every denomination represented except ours.

After seeing my African film, a woman said to me.

"I know why you are here. It is because this church prayed for you." Truly the Lord directs His servants.

Among my combination class of third-and fourth-graders, I had 16 problem children. Some had brain damage. Others had experienced trauma in their young lives that had hindered their educational progress. They all needed individual attention.

A young, inexperienced teacher had been lined up for the class. The mother feared that if the young woman would teach the class, she might think her child was completely off, for he had been brain damaged at birth. Since I was a little older, more experienced and a child of the King, she had more confidence in me.

At this time, single missionaries from Congo received word from the Board of Foreign Missions. We should never expect to go back there again. After all, the Congolese now had received their independence. They felt no need of any more help. We should adjust into American society again and forget Congo.

When the news came, I cried bitter tears. My word from the Lord was still 2 Peter 1:12. "Wherefore, I will not be negligent to put you always in remembrance of these things, though you know them, and be established in the present truth." God would show me the way.

Soon application forms came from the Peace Corps and other mission organizations. One interdenominational organization worked in the Congo. Congo Poly-Technic Institute needed farmers, educators, and especially some to help them train Congolese girls and women for their new role. Mary Toews, from our mission, already worked with them. She encouraged me to join the organization.

A supervisor of the Hanford grade school encouraged me to apply. *Doesn't she know that the Board of Foreign Missions/Services told me to forget Congo,* I thought. *Why is she always asking me about these opportunities in the Congo? Could it be that the Lord is working through her?*

I continued to pray, asking the Lord of the harvest for direction. I did so much want to help the needy other half of the Congolese family, the woman. Would this open door lead to that very thing?

When Poly-Technic Institute accepted my application to work in Congo, this meant first going to the East Coast for orientation. After spending some time at Drew University, we soon found ourselves in Washington D.C., taking refresher courses in Home Economics at Howard University. In the afternoon, we studied French together with Peace Corps personnel.

In between classes, we still found time to visit our famous capital. I learned anew that the Lord has richly blessed our country. May we live out our thanks to our fore-fathers who brought us here, and to our heavenly Father who permitted us to be born in this country.

Connie Russel and I flew out of of New York on September 11, boarding a jet for Europe and then another to the Democratic Republic of the Congo.

Now I appreciated the privilege of being a missionary even more. How thrilling to return to my adopted country and the Congolese people!

PART TWO
MEETING THE CHALLENGE
OF THE HOUR
1962–1971

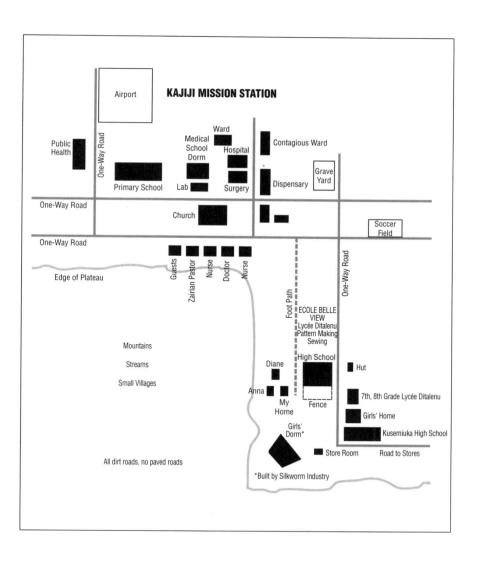

Margerie didn't only nurse at the dispensary and maternity which was located way in the bush, but she had to provide ambulance service when she ran into a complicated case.

CHAPTER 9

LIKE SWALLOWING AN OCEAN

Coming back to Congo with Institute Polytechnic Congaise, an interdenominational organization, I was now in Leopoldville, a large city and the capital of the Republic of Congo. Looking around, I noticed that all statues - including those of Stanley and Leopold 11, which the Belgians had erected to depict the history of their former colony - had been torn down. The main avenue in this city was now called Thirtieth of June, the date of their independence.

When I arrived, on September 14, 1962, I was taken to four apartments made into a secondary school dorm. Its condition was typical of all Belgian-built homes left empty between 1960 and 1962. Not a door handle, lock or key could be found. If per chance the lock was welded into the medal door, its key was gone.

Light fixtures had been torn out. Not a bookcase, cupboard or detachable clothes closet had been left in this shell of a building. My job was to make a list of all items missing in this dorm. My chauffeur and I were to comb Leopoldville for all these things.

A date had been set for the girls to enter the dorm, at which time a new girl's secondary school would begin.

It took two weeks to fix the electric wiring and water pipes before the electric power could be turned on. Other major items, such as keys to the main entrance, had been obtained.

The twenty-six girls came from various homes and backgrounds. Some of their parents suddenly found themselves trying to make the adjustment from living in a mud-and-stick hut to beautiful, abandoned, Belgian-built homes. Many of the wives of Congo didn't know how to cook in their modern kitchens.

Often, when the man of the house came home with his business friends, he was embarrassed to find his wife outside cooking over an open fire just as her people had done for generations. Mary Toews and others taught the wives to bridge the gap.

Many of our students came from village-type homes surrounding Leopoldville. Mostly small, mud-and-stick huts with thatched roofs, they had bamboo shutters instead of windows. Dirt floors had been watered down to settle the dust and to discourage insects. Eating and entertaining friends and family took place in the courtyard.

Villagers who had moved to the big city, now crowded together, had settled in the area where their tribe was located. Sanitation was worse here than the bush villages from which they came. A few faucets in the backyard supplied running water; otherwise, they found a stream of water where they bathed and fetched water for drinking and cooking.

Although the affluent part of Leopoldville had electricity, except when it was in need of repair, no electricity could be found here, for their meager wages wouldn't allow such luxury.

At the dorm, even the most mundane things had to be taught. For instance, the girls learned to line up next to the outside shower instead of going to a stream of water. Constance Russell worked hard to teach these precious girls these things. She lived upstairs with the girls, while I lived downstairs.

Each girl had her own bed, a desk, a drawer, and a corner in a clothes closet where she learned to hang her clothes on hangers. This was all new to them. Her daily task had to be done before breakfast. Congolese girls were admitted to this secondary school based on their scholastic standard and good reputation. At about 7 a.m., Connie led them the five blocks to the school grounds.

Even though I taught part-time in this French-speaking secondary school, my main job was to draw plans for the kitchen cupboards and furniture needed for the dining room and front room. I spent months combing Leopoldville for the best bargains.

Traveling down the Leopoldville streets, we saw that cement brick walls surrounded the homes. On top of the fences, either broken glass or arrows of metal had been cemented in. That discouraged would-be thieves. Larger homes had sentinels and fierce, barking dogs to guard their places. Behind this city of walls, lush green lawns blossomed with tropical flowers and bushes.

Bars guarded the lower floor of our dorm, while a low but meaningful fence surrounded the building. These pliable girls adapted to this new way of life and proudly entertained guests who came for our open house. People of different shades of skin came dressed in their best. While signing our guest book, visitors heard the students carry on a good conversation in French. Girls liked to describe their dorm life, meal time, work, study and devotions.

One girl explained that they all attended the interdenominational church on the same grounds as the Union Mission Guest house. The more educated people in Kinshasa mostly attended these French services.

Besides having Bible study in their classroom, they had daily devotions before going to bed. Learning memory verses had the promise of a gift at the end to all who completed the program. When all girls gained the prize, I rejoiced with them. "My Word will not return unto me void," God promised.

To celebrate Christ's birthday, the girls took an active part in the church's Christmas program. Then they went home for the holidays.

In January 1963, Moise Tshombe and the Katangese government again united with the Republic Democratic of Congo. Now the secession had ended and all of Congo could again profit from the riches of their mines found in the Katanga.

On the last day of school, we invited guests to join us. Parents came with joy to hear their girls recite. Fathers came with their tailored, Congolese cut suits, followed by their wives in long, colorful wrap-around skirts with matching blouses. Colorful head scarves artfully chosen, matched their outfits.

Somber faces of the students surprised me as they stumbled through what had been a well-practiced program. Something hindered their usual jovial spirit. Not until later did I learn what it was.

The girls had heard rumors that most of them had failed in their studies, so they refused to put any real effort into the program. Later, when they received their report cards, however, they learned that the rumors had not been true. Joyful surprise replaced their somber spirit. At Christmas time, Mary Toews and I visited friends in Kikwit, then on to Polytechnic Institute farming school. A huge river lined with tropical foliage separated the farm school and the beautiful new Home economics building from the Baptist mission station Vanga.

Looking down the river, we could see Hippo Island. Hippos actually did live there, and they had been known to attack in earlier years. (Just before I retired, they again attacked and killed an internist learning tropical diseases at the Vanga hospital.)

On Saturday, we went to Kipungu mission station, where I had been principal of the grade school last term. Fighting red mud, slippery roads, we finally succeeded in climbing up the steep mountain. I met some former students who had gone on for further education and were now busy teaching, nursing or preaching the Word of God. That thrilled me, for God had given the increase.

Some teachers asked many questions: "Whom shall we marry? Can you tell us someone from your school whom we can marry? Can we come down and see the school? What are the qualifications for entry? When are you going to come back here to help our girls?"

Truly realizing the vast need for girls' schools would be like swallowing an ocean. This school in Leopoldville was only one of many that should be opened all over Congo. If we fail the Congolese woman and girl, cultists will move in and take over.

CHAPTER 10

SECESSION WAS OVER

A s cousins of the crickets (makalele) and many other small creatures sing their lullabies, the sun sinks and leaves only a trace of light outlining the palm and mango trees. We pause for a visit at a Methodist mission station, Mwajinga Sandoa.

Institute Polytechnic had long promised that when the Katanga again became safe for women missionaries, a teacher would come to train the wives of secondary school and farm students. Now that the Katanga again belonged to the Republic of Congo, the promise became a reality.

Some 200 tribes in the Congo have different tongues, customs and manners, with more than four major trade languages and a number of others related to these. Moving to the Katanga meant switching from the Kituba trade language to Swahili. Most village women didn't know this trade language, either, so we learned it together.

In the afternoon of Tuesday, October 22, 1963, I arrived at Mwajinga Sandoa in the Katanga, on the border of Congo's southern tip. My new apartment wasn't completed yet, so Mr. and Mrs. Lou Hammond, teachers at the agricultural school, kindly let me live with them.

At this Methodist mission station, as well as Vanga, close to our Kipungu station, and Gemena in the north, Institute Polytechnic set up schools to teach Congolese men wholesale farming. Up to this point, farming had been strictly a woman's job.

A new home economics school for their wives accompanied each farm school. It taught practical housekeeping, conversational French, and the Word of God. Dean Freudenburger served as principal of Mwajinga Sandoa's farm school. Monday, October 28, began like any other day. After breakfast, we went to teach our classes; Lou to his agricultural class, Betty Hammond to her English class, and I to teach French to secondary school and agricultural wives.

At 7:00 o'clock, the house help came in and told us that we were surrounded by soldiers of the Congolese National Army, called ANC. We looked out and saw the builder, Mr. Pattrikious. He had been stopped in front of our house by two soldiers. He left his car there, and after a while walked off.

Word came to us that we were to stay in our houses. About an hour later, we were told to go and teach as if nothing had happened. Mrs. Hammond and I started out in their car. Soldiers in front of our house stopped us and asked where we were going, and if we spoke English.

Evading the last question, I told them I spoke French and Kituba. Then they gave us permission to drive to class. Two more soldiers stopped us along the way, asking us the same questions. I told them the other soldiers had given us permission to drive because it might rain. Actually, we felt safer in the car than to have to walk by these soldiers.

By 10 a.m., the soldiers ordered us back to our houses. They followed us into our homes and even followed me into my bedroom. They asked for my papers. I explained that since I had just moved from Leopoldville, I had not been able to get registered here. They took knapsacks, camp cots and other possible army equipment from the homes. They accused us of espionage.

The Allens, Methodist missionaries, monitored the two-way short-wave transmitter - the only way this mission kept in contact with the outside world. Each station responded twice a day as they were called. All planes reported their flight plans, weather conditions and hours of arrival by this method.

Soldiers took the Allens' receiver and their tape recorder. They tore down the antenna and left it in ruins. Then they went off with two barrels of aviation gas. Other soldiers took the keys for the one-motored aircraft that Ken Enright, village evangelist and pilot, had purchased about two weeks before. They wanted Ken Enright to dismantle the airplane, then put it on the truck to burn at Sandoa.

When Ken refused, the soldiers left thinking they had taken the only key for the plane. They called the airfield a military landing strip. One soldier charged that Ken was the personal pilot of Moise Tshombe.

On Tuesday, October 29, 1963, all the men went to Sandoa, about 30 miles from the mission station of Mwajinga Sandoa, to get their legal papers straightened out. Some still had Katanga identification cards, linking them to this part of the Congo that had seceded with Moise Tshombe.

On Wednesday, October 23, the Congolese Army soldiers would have killed Ken, had not United Nations Army bigwigs warded them off.

On Thursday, Ken Enright and the others again went into town to clear up the matter. The Congolese National Army arrested Ken, insisting he must go to Delolo for trial, charged with treason. The United Nations took Ken in for protection. His wife and daughter went with them to Sandoa to spend the night with Ken.

Meanwhile, the Allens came to sleep in the room next to me. They feared that the soldiers had their eyes on Ken, and if they came after him and didn't find him, they would nab the Allens because they were the radio operators.

We were told that if we heard a lot of commotion in the night, just to head for the bushes, follow the road down the hill, and then follow the path to the springs.

Dean Fraudenburger, in charge of Sandoa's farm school project, called a meeting of the workers. He told us that since the United Nations was guarding the Congo soldiers, we would be safe. They had contact with Sandoa every half hour, and they would alert us right away if the Congolese National Army started anything. We were told that the safest place was right in our homes. We felt better and went to sleep.

On Friday, the men went back to Sandoa. They said the United Nations Army and the Congolese National Army opposed one another. They had to go back to stand trial.

Five days after Belgian Congo received their independence, discontented Congolese soldiers in the lower part of the Congo had revolted against these Belgian officers. Disaster struck the country.

As attacks on Belgian nationals increased, the Belgian government flew troops into the country to restore law and order.

At the same time, in the mineral-rich Katanga Province, Moise Tshombe, backed by local Europeans, declared the province an independent state. With the new country disintegrating around them, Kasavubu and Lumumba accused Belgium of aggression and appealed to the United Nations Security Council for assistance. The United Nations responded by sending in a peace force.

Initially, the United Nations operation was effective. United Nations policy, under Dag Hammarskjold, supported the unity of the country, without putting down the secessionist governments of Katanga and Kasai.

Since UN officials and Lumumba disagreed over what action to take in regard to Katanga, Lumumba turned to the Communist nations for help. He was not disappointed. They sent in guns, airplanes and trucks.

Negotiations between Adula and Tshombe began, but the secession was not finally crushed until forces moved decisively in January, 1963. Perhaps that review of history will help us better understand why the Congolese soldiers were suspicious of missionaries, and why they and the UN soldiers were so at odds.

With UN permission, Ken flew into Elizabethville that afternoon. During the week before, he had spent hours making the second set of keys for his plane. Jonathan Dean of Elizabethville's American Consulate, Captain Bense NGA and Vo Luzolo Eugian Marie came to settle things.

On Saturday evening, we had a meeting at the Hammond house. The American Consulate, with Captain Bense and Vo Luzolo Eugian Marie, explained that when a group of Congolese soldiers came into a new area, they tried to scare the people so that they wouldn't have any trouble with them.

After they realized there wasn't anything going on, such as espionage, they pretty well left them alone. They suggested that we have some of these fellows over to show them the farm and school on a friendly basis.

An American Embassy official came to my rescue. Since I had a dual citizenship, my representative before God, His Son, was my real rescuer.

After I took pictures of our guests, our Embassy friends left by way of Sandoa to go to Joddotville, where the soldiers received reinforcements. This was also where ANC soldiers had taken many vehicles which had been stolen from the businessmen of Sandoa. This delegation from the consulate of Elizabethville expected to get them all back.

On November 19, just three weeks after my arrival and three days after I moved into my apartment, we women were told that we would be evacuated to Elizabethville. That would be our home until the United Nations Army was replaced by the Congolese National Army. Even though we faced no immediate danger, I could now empathize with others who have fled - and are fleeing - for their lives.

Meanwhile, Betty Hammond and I went shopping in the mornings for our women's school of 50 students. We studied Swahili in the afternoons. On November 22, 1963, while shopping in an open market in Elizabethville, the shocking news reached us of President Kennedy's assassination.

A few days later, all foreigners in town, including American missionaries, and foreign diplomats from the embassies, gathered together for a memorial service. On entering the Methodist church, we signed our names to declare our sympathies to the Kennedy family.

On December 14, we flew back to our mission station, Mwajinga Sandoa, located in the back bush country of Central Africa, called Katanga. Though rich in minerals — cobalt, copper and zinc — these riches did not filter down to the common villager. Chokwe and Lunda tribes remained poor. After school for several more days, we let the women go for Christmas vacation.

Both Protestant and Catholic missions geared their schools mainly to the needs of men. This meant that the women stayed 10 years behind the men in public education. They served as slaves who had to raise all the food for the family. The man was responsible only for the protein that fishing and hunting could provide, and to build the house.

Women carried wood and water on their heads. They arose

before dawn, babies tied on their backs, baskets on their heads. They cultivated three manioc fields. They had to prepare a large, new field before the cassava root manioc could be planted. This meant clearing the ground of underbrush, shrubs, clinging vines and trees. Their husbands might help with the very tallest and hardest-to-cut trees.

Corn, peanuts, sweet potatoes, pineapple and banana groves also must be cultivated. No wonder they had so little time for housework, since they also had to soak the root of the cassava plant to rid it of all toxic materials before further preparation could be made for daily meals. House cleaning usually meant just throwing water over her dirt floor after sweeping.

In the garden of Eden, you will remember, gardening was given over to Adam. Why, then, was the Congolese woman obliged to bear the child and also to do the garden work?

For the woman whose husband received training as a farmer, her world changed fast. Not she, but her husband, now attended agricultural school. He would try his hand at wholesale farming, instead of her having only the family plot. She must find a new identity.

She must learn to meet her husband's business associates. She might live in a more modern home. How could we best prepare her for this new role? That was why the interdenominational organization had built a three-room home economics school building and a two-room nursery at each agricultural center. Except for the farmers' wives, all over Congo the woman still has to raise the food for her family's table.

Oral conversational French was taught. Everyday lessons on house cleaning were given, for now she had only a simple village hut where spiders and their webs were good for catching the buzzing, malaria-carrying mosquito. Her low, homemade bamboo bed had a mat for a mattress. The "blanket" was a fire in the middle of the room.

Now she faced a new Congo with two cultures merging. For many a husband, getting a better education and being exposed to some of the ideas of a big city tempted him to leave his village and his untrained wife for someone who could mix with his newfound friends.

A Congolese girl preparing her supper in her outside kitchen

Our students ranged from having no education at all to having sixth-grade primary schooling. We had to start from zero with most to teach them the rudiments of housekeeping. They had to adjust from bamboo shutters to glass windows, from mud floors to linoleum, from wearing torn clothes until they wore out, to mending them, to sewing new things, from cooking outside over an open fire to cooking on a modern range, from pounding clothes on a rock to washing in a sanitary tub with a scrub board, from using the bush as an outhouse to using a modern flush toilet.

Typical students had to have a taste of all of it, for who knew which wife would some day live in a modern city and which had to continue to exist in the most primitive jungle home in this bush country?

Three holes were dug into the sides of the high rise ants apartment, one on top of the other. By placing fire in all holes, we burned out these termites. After homemade doors were made, fire was placed in the upper and lower holes. The oven was now ready to bake.

Given instructions, I set up ovens in the food laboratory. Since the oven was new to their culture, they ordered different kinds of baking facilities many of which they could duplicate in their isolated villages. No matter where the Congolese woman would find herself later on in life, whether in Leopoldville in a modern kitchen, or in the most backwards village, she could feel at home using an oven.

In one unit, the girls learned to place a layer of sand in a large kettle, put the kettle over an open flame, then lay the bread - which was in a pan - atop the sand, with live coals on the lid. It baked well.

Another unit had a kerosene hot plate with a tin, box- like oven that fit over the burner. In this food lab, still another unit had a wood-burning stove that each group had to learn to use. Another unit, a modern butane stove.

The last unit proved the most practical of all. In the Katanga, the sun often seemed obscure even with no clouds. Looking around to see why, we noticed millions of flying ants that came out of the tall, red, termite hills. Some of the hills towered above the houses.

Congolese took banana leaves, forming them into a cup, then placed them over the top of the hills. In this way, they caught the protein-filled insects as they flew out for their mating flight. Popping them into their mouths, after throwing away their wings, they ate them. Missionaries' children said these flying ants tasted like bacon bits.

Three holes were dug into the sides of the high-rise, ants apartments, one on top of the other. Placing fire in all the holes, we burned out the ants. After making a homemade door for the middle holes and placing fire in the upper and lower holes, we considered the oven ready to be used. Smoke came out of the natural chimney the ants had built into their condominiums. Banana bread baked in these ovens was delicious.

Last but not least, I was in the Katanga to help the whole person. These precious women were already here, where I could teach them the Word of Life. Since I was still learning Swahili, I bought some flannelgraph lessons written in that language.

While placing the figures on the board, I read the lessons in Swahili. One Congolese teacher translated this into either Chokwe or Lunda. On the fifth day, we sang hymns in Swahili.

One day, the Minister of Education came to visit us. He arrived at 11:30 a.m. instead of the scheduled 9:00 o'clock. Just the same, we admired him for not letting overflowing banks of water, running across the road, stop him.

About once a year, the River Lulua between the city Sandoa and the mission station Mwajinga Sandoa overflowed its banks. Fortunately, the Minister of Education did get through.

Two guards led the way as the Minister entered the church. Guards had been placed at all doorways. After the Congolese sang their National Anthem, a primary and secondary student both welcomed him with speeches in French. This was followed with two discourses from him, one in French and the other in an African tongue.

He left the church with his guards and made a tour of the primary, secondary, and agricultural schools. Even though temporary classes in the nursery continued until completion of our three-room school, he stopped to look at this building. Following him and his entourage, the mission teachers entered the washing and ironing rooms, the sewing room and the food lab.

At the nursery, our students served homemade cookies they had baked. How proud I was when I saw these raw village women, my students, rise up to meet this challenge.

While we had a period of calm, the northeastern part of Congo suffered great unrest. Some of our young Congolese were inspired by the Communists to oppose the government for having killed Lumumba. Pierre Mulele, the rebel leader, gathered youths ages 10 through 21 to carry out their deadly mission. They called themselves *Simbas* (lions).

Witch doctors pronounced a protective covering over them, effective only as long as they kept the rules. A *Simba* couldn't steal. If they stole, their immunity to bullets and other dangers no longer worked. Sometimes they would put a gun on the table or in the stomach of the victim and say, "I'd like that food, that radio and that pair of scissors." These things would be quickly handed over.

If they even touched a white man, they would lose their protection. Some white men didn't know this. Trying to be friendly in touching them, they were shot. If they touched a woman, the same thing would happen. They would come into a village and demand so many chickens, eggs, stalks of bananas and women. Then they were free to handle these women at will. Since they drank a lot and smoked hemp daily, this led to terrible cruelties.

In January 1964, the *Simbas* attacked companies and educated Congolese who wouldn't join them in killing foreign diplomats and missionaries. They did not exempt Congolese church members and pastors.

The *Simbas* believed that if they destroyed even what the missionaries had helped them build up, their ancestors would come with big trucks and bring to them everything the *mundele* (white ghost) had held back from them. The Congolese army was humiliated by the defeat this opposing rebel group inflicted upon them. This dealt a fatal blow to the Adoula Government.

Startling as it seems, in July 1964, Moise Tshombe, the very one who had headed the Katanga secession, was made Prime Minister of the Republic of Congo. "The most high God is ruler over the realm of mankind and bestows it on whomever He wishes" (Daniel 4:25b).

Seeing the dilemma of his own army, Tshombe hired several hundred white mercenaries to reinforce the Congolese army in order to save Congo from Communism. He also obtained military aid from Belgium and the United States.

As a young child, Pastor Jimbo at Kafumba had attended the mission primary school. As a slave, his captors let him attend this strange new school even though the ruling tribe didn't let their own children go. Jimbo trusted Christ as his Saviour and Lord. Later, he became a leader as pastor of the Mennonite Brethren Church at Kafumba.

Simbas didn't bypass Kafumba but came there to continue their deadly deeds. Many Christians, including missionaries, had to flee for their lives. Missionaries could evacuate, but what about the people of this land? After Pastor Kasai was buried up to his neck in sand, fellow Christians dug him up at night and saved his life. Pastor Jimbo fled to the forest, where he and his wife lived with many others for more than a year. Kafumba was destroyed.

In September, the mercenaries began to push the rebels back. Hostages held Stanleyville and, on November 24 at Kilometer Eight, Belgian paratroopers rescued them. They had been dropped from United States Air Force planes on Stanleyville. *Simbas* killed many that day - at least a hundred paratroopers, Congolese and missionaries.

On that same day, a mercenary-led army column reached the rebel capital and consolidated government control. In the weeks that followed, the eastern rebellion fell apart. Katanga had no part in this struggle. We in the southern part of Congo, by the grace of God, carried on our mission work uninterrupted.

After two years, my contract with Institute Polytechnic expired.

This meant I could go home for a few months, but I did not feel ready to do this. I asked if they would pay my way to the Holy Land instead. When a positive answer came, I finalized my plans.

On the plane crossing over Africa, I prayed, "Lord, I'm going to see Jerusalem. If You take me to the heavenly Jerusalem or the earthly Jerusalem, either one is all right with me."

After stopping at Addis Ababa to visit Valdene Neuman, a distant cousin and a missionary nurse, I flew on to Egypt. I took a train up the Nile River, where Moses had been hid in the reeds.

On arrival at Luxor. I saw the temples and tombs of the kings. In Cairo, I found the pyramids and museums very interesting. After leaving Egypt, I went to Jerusalem. My greatest thrill came when I walked where Jesus had walked. We saw the triumphal entry gate which has been sealed since the 16th century. We saw where Jesus cried over Jerusalem, and where He was arrested.

We followed the worn cobblestones of the way of the cross. We saw where Simon carried Christ's cross, and the place of the skull where Christ was crucified. We saw the borrowed tomb. It was empty! Christ Jesus our Lord is alive today! Because He lives, we also shall live - with Him, forever and ever.

After tucking away the passport I used on the Arab side of Jerusalem, I walked across the Mandelbaum passageway, to reach the Jewish side. Soon I looked at a bar of soap with a number on it. It had once been a Jew, who had been reduced to this by Hitler's regime. We saw whole Arab villages still intact, where they lived in peace and safety.

On the other side of the border, large camps of Arab refugees cried to the world that they wanted their homes back. I had no answer for all this. Both the Arabs and Jews are sons of Abraham. The sin of Abraham and Sarah seemed evident in this continual struggle. I was deeply impressed to have witnessed a modern miracle, the reality of the rebirth of the nation of Israel.

In 1987, I again visited Jerusalem - this time with Margaret (Dyck) Krahn. When we reached the wailing wall, we saw our Jewish friends slip notes into the small holes in this wall. As I stood there with them, my tears mingled with theirs. I prayed for enlightenment of the Jewish nation to their Messiah, Jesus Christ.

Now, on my way back to Mwajinga Sandoa, as I passed through Elizabethville, rumors circulated that the newly elected Prime Minister, Moise Tshombe, would make his appearance there. This first appearance since the secession fascinated me. I went to the main square to wait his arrival, even though I should have stayed at the guest house to wait for the Methodist plane ride back to Mwajinga Sandoa.

When Tshombe appeared, crowds of people awaited him. Everyone gave a loving, low sign of love, like an "OHHhhhooo," crescendo at first, then lower and lower. Their voices became like an echo and ended in a whisper. What adoration they showed in this emotional moment in history! After he spoke, Tshombe walked from the middle of town down the main avenue that was lined with orchid-blooming, jacaranda trees. He held his arms up all the way while crowds followed him in loving adoration.

Coming back to Mwajinga Sandoa for another year, my two Congolese teachers, other missionaries and I again immersed our-

Coming back to Mwajinga Sandoa for another year, I, together with the Congolese teachers, and missionaries such as Mrs. Hammond, immersed ourselves in teaching these precious Congolese women.

selves in teaching these precious Congolese wives and mothers. David Tshombe, brother of Moise, often would come from Sandoa where his father had a sawmill and owned many stores. He came to encourage us in the work we did for his people. He said that now the women of the Katanga had their chance of a lifetime to advance and to learn something useful.

At Christmas, we gave a learning experience program. Our students sang "Silent Night" while acting it out. The first scene portrayed the manger scene, with Mary and Joseph kneeling down to worship the baby Jesus, our Saviour.

As the second verse began, shepherds came to worship the baby. The third scene portrayed the wise men. While the last verse was sung, all the wives fell down in front of the baby, worshipping Jesus our Lord. The pastor of our church closed with prayer. Many of these precious wives trusted Jesus Christ as their Lord and Saviour.

Twenty of the wives wore blouses they had sewn by hand-turned sewing machines. They presented a fashion show. In addition, they displayed women's dresses, men's shirts, children's clothes and baby clothes.

Soon, precious little children sang "Away in the Manger," and one of the women read the Christmas story! Given a chance, these village women took real pride in what they accomplished.

On November 17, 1965, E. Stanley Jones, well-known Methodist evangelist, came to this out-of-the-way station. He held two days of meetings with our high school, agricultural school and women's home economics school. Among other things, he stressed that we should always leave a place cleaner than we found it.

Even though he held meetings all day, giving forth the Word of Life, he found time to send the students out to clean up the campus. Then he challenge them all to clean up their personal lives. Many responded.

When this man of God reached the airstrip, ready to fly home, he pulled out a picture to show to us - one I will never forget. It was the Gospel of John, hand-written on a large piece of paper, the delicate shadings of the words clearly portraying a picture of Jesus Christ.

"And the Word became flesh and dwelt among us and we beheld His glory, glory as of the only begotten from the Father, full of grace

Mar. 17, 65 E. Stanley Jones. 116 Glen Rd., Wellesley Hills, 81, Mass

At the airport, E. Stnley Jones showed us a picture I will never for-get. It was the Gospel according to John printed by hand on a large piece of paper. The shadings on these letters were so delicately print-ed that the words portrayed the picture of the Lord Jesus Christ. "And the Word became Flesh and dwelt among us." Missionary pilot Amstutz, E. Stanley Jones, Missionary Crowder.

and truth." (John 1:14) How real this passage of Scripture became to all of us after seeing this picture!

Later, the directors of the various schools on the mission station were called to the city of Sandoa to meet his highness, Prime Min-ister Moise Tshombe. After we waited for about a half hour. he walked into the room and shook hands with all of us - an unforget-table moment. He sat down and chatted with us for quite a while.

A Methodist who spoke freely to us that day, Tshombe seemed to display common sense. When he saw our Congolese director of the secondary school sporting a beard, he simply said, "When people see beards like yours, they think of Russia." I am sure our Con-golese director took this to heart, for Tshombe had just been fight-

Man 20, 65 Tshombe Moïse J. Léopoldville

A little later the directors of the various schools on the mission station were called to the city of Sandoa to meet his highness, Premier Minister Moise Tshombe. On the way out he signed my guest book.

ing the Communists with the help of mercenaries.

Tshombe continued, "Other countries come in here and smuggle out diamonds. At first no one knew what I was trying to do. They called it the 'little America.' Now there are some people who understand what I'm trying to do."

When he talked to government workers about misunderstandings, he simply said, "Yes, you think that way, but at Sandoa they think differently." He knew well that the 200 tribes in the Congo held different opinions.

On the way out, he signed my guest book, after which he yielded to picture-taking.

Though I recognize that a sovereign God permitted this to happen, it was a sad day for the Congo when on November 24, 1965, Mobutu Se-Se-Seko took the office of Prime Minister by force. Moise Tshombe's plane was hijacked, then his enemies flew him to

Algeria where he later died.

Earlier, in March, Institute Polytechnic faced a crisis. Many of their workers had become dissatisfied. The Methodist Board of Foreign Missions came for a visit to see what should be done. My new contract came, but I felt no liberty to sign it.

I prayed earnestly that the Lord would show me just how and where I could continue to help the Congolese women.

Meanwhile, our stations at Kwilu and Kwango offered me the opportunity to serve again with Mennonite Brethren Missions/Services.

"Dear Dorothy," Irvin Friesen wrote me, "at our recent administrative committee meeting we again mourned over the fact that we have nothing appropriate to offer our girls in the way of an educational program adapted for girls. At that time we decided to propose to the board again that a school for girls be opened.

"It was also decided that I write you to find out if you would be at all interested to return to our field for work....Bob and Wanda have given me your letter of May 1. Perhaps your hesitation to sign the contract is of the Lord so that you will be able to return to our work and to open a school for us. Please let me know as soon as possible what your reaction to such a proposal is so that I may inform our board of it.

"We hope that you will be able to come. How long have you been on the field and when will your furlough actually be due? If you could come to us, when would you be able to come? May the Lord guide you in this."

After further correspondence, asking them just what they had in mind, I packed my bags to join the missionaries of the Mennonite Brethren Church again. My destination: the very mission station where I first served, Ecole Belle Vue, Kajiji.

In the dry season of 1965, as I neared the station, I remembered the earlier cries of our Zairian brothers and sisters, "When are you coming back to help our girls?"

Now, with the Lord's help, perhaps I could reach some of these precious young girls. I could teach them how to tell their children about our wonderful Saviour. I could help them set up family devotions so that they might grow in their spiritual lives. The Lord was leading; He had heard and answered my prayers.

Jolice explained the colorful dresses they had made for the girls.

Parting after living together for three-and-a-half months was difficult, but we knew that some day we would be together again forever.

CHAPTER 11

A DREAM PARTLY THWARTED

A short-wave message came from Leopoldville. Citizeness Sidone Nellie wanted to join us at Kajiji. Should she come, even though she was more advanced in housekeeping than my other students would be?

"Yes!" I responded. "I am delighted to have her come."

She had been a star pupil at Kipungu primary school until her husband made her drop out to marry him. They now resided in Leopoldville where her husband worked for an airline.

Since Belgian Congo's independence, the children of missionaries had gone to school in Leopoldville. Medical students now lived in the dorm they had formerly occupied. Because the Congolese elders decided that the men students should no longer be housed in the same building as the women, one half of the building was vacated for the woman's school and dorm.

It became necessary for me to hire a mason to repair the wall that was crumbling. The former laundry room had been remodeled into a much-needed food laboratory. We invited two women from each of our Mennonite Brethren Mission Stations to join us.

In 1963, before the Simba rebellion, the Congolese had reported a total church membership of 8,870. In 1965 it decreased slightly to 8,689, due to the persecution during those terrible years. Malnutrition and exposure killed many of our Christians. Others had been threatened by death at some time or another. Now we saw the opportunity to build up the Mennonite Brethren home again starting with the women.

Women from Panzi, Kajiji, Lusemvu, Kafumba, Kipungu, Matendi and large centers such as Leopoldville and Kikwit came to our school. Each woman had the option of bringing one child with her. I would be living with them in a dorm, teaching them needed practical lessons, including semi-modern housekeeping, for three-and-a-half months.

When citizeness Sidone came, we embraced warmly. She appeared as dedicated as I was to learn new ways of keeping house and to study the Word of God.

Eva, another former student from Kipungu, also joined us. She had been married to Sammie Mboloko, a pastor, currently serving at a palm nut village. They worked hard together. She took a real interest in the women of that church. Even though schooling wasn't her cup of tea, she faithfully plugged along. God's love shone through her. She learned to teach children's Sunday school classes and how to be a better pastor's wife.

After three-and-a-half months of living, learning and having devotions together, graduation time came. The women were ready to return to their villages to join their husbands and families, to put into practice what they had learned. We joined them at their closing dinner and looked at their displays.

Rolls and cookies had been baked the day before in various types of ovens. They served Spanish rice, squash with bananas, and salad. Mint tea had been made from plants growing in our school garden.

"Now we will hear from two ladies who were at the head of their class," I told the group.

Citizeness Sidone, mother of several children, petite and neatly dressed, drew us with her expressive, dark eyes and graceful gestures as she described our sewing classes.

"We first made large, sack-like mattresses and stuffed them with dried grass," she said. "Next we sewed sheets for our beds, then sheets for our infants."

As she spoke, our minds went over the display we had just seen before entering the banquet hall. The first display featured six different items every mother had made for a new-born infant. A large, black doll had been dressed to substitute for the real thing.

We saw many sunsuits and tailored shirts, and an exhibit of colorful dresses. On a counter was a display of kitchen items, including hotpot holders and aprons already in use in the food lab.

On the mantelpiece were serving trays made of bamboo. The bulletin board was covered with colorful mottoes of "GOD IS LOVE" done with yarn in petit point.

Citizeness Sidone then reported on other classes: mothering and child care, oral French, washing and ironing, and mending classes. She concluded by explaining that the woman's school should be continued in order to teach others how to keep house, how to be better wives and how to better raise their children.

After attending these classes, she said, the mothers and wives felt better qualified to do their part in elevating their country, the Republic of Congo.

Citizeness Jolice, a tall stately woman from Kajiji, told of the 33 Bible stories they had studied. She related how the story of Joseph deeply touched her. Even though his brothers had sold him, Joseph returned good for evil.

She concluded by asking the women questions about the plan of salvation. They responded by quoting appropriate Bible verses. The students then recited the 23rd Psalm and prayed the Lord's Prayer together. All joined in a meaningful song, praising Jesus for His great promises and for the hope of our future with Him forever.

Parting, after living together for three-and-a-half months, was difficult, but we knew that they were going to be more useful to their husbands and families and to other wives in their congregations. Some day we would be together again forever, nevermore to part.

I now taught all students in the secondary classes, and taught girls home economics in the afternoons. The program's future remained uncertain. I gathered materials and waited for the missionary brethren, together with the Africans, to help me decide on the future of the girls' and women's work.

One day, the girls were to bring clothes to mend. We had obtained sewing kits from the Congo Protestant Relief Association, mainly supplied by the Mennonite Central Committee. That gave us the needed scissors, needles, pins and measuring tapes. We also received a bale of cloth.

While attending the mixed high school, 20 secondary school girls joined the five from last semester in the practical housekeeping dorm. Until they had completed their mattresses and sheets, they slept on bamboo mats rolled up in a blanket. Then they learned how to sleep between sheets, something new to them.

Dorm girls made their own clothes bags, and then learned to put their dirty laundry in them. They swept cobwebs from their walls before they washed the floors.

In 1956-57, a famine hit Kajiji and its surrounding villages. The cassava or manioc plant, their staple food, had rotted in the ground, or had tubers full of bugs. At Kajiji, the Mennonite Central Committee set up a warehouse from which they distributed food for the hungry, plus sticks of sweet manioc to plant. A different strain, it resisted disease.

The Congolese didn't like to continue to cultivate sweet manioc because that meant it took very little preparation and people passing by would steal it. They ate it right out of their fields. The other type could never be eaten out of the fields, but had to soak for three days to get rid of the natural toxic. After a while, the Zairian women replanted the regular type they liked. The disease went away on its own.

During the rebellion of 1964-66, they didn't plant their fields. This led to a great shortage of food. East of us, the same disease which broke out in 1956-57 repeated itself in 1966-67. Peanut fields also suffered. Sadly, the sweet manioc sticks that the Congolese planted to combat this very dilemma were now almost nonexistent. Planting must be constant for three consecutive years before a balance of steady food can be assured any given family.

This made it hard for us to buy manioc to feed the dorm girls. Had it not been for Congo Relief Association, supplied mainly by the Mennonite Central Committee, relief food would have been scarce. We praise the Lord for Christians at home who gave to make supplies possible.

Instead of eating out of one pot, the girls would set the table and eat family style. They learned how to wash dishes with hot, soapy water, rather than wash out in the open or at a stream of water. Instead of wearing torn clothes, they learned to mend them. They learned hand-stitching first, then advanced to machine-stitching.

Every girl had her task to do each day. They were changed each week. No one worked long hours, for they had to study many hours in preparation for their secondary school exams. School began at 6:45 a.m. and continued until 12:20 p.m. From 2:00 to 4:00 p.m., every afternoon except Wednesdays and Saturdays, they attended classes or study hall. School continued six days a week.

On one occasion, when the girls had a holiday, I sent them down to the stream to wash their clothes. The German-made water system (called a ram) wasn't shooting up water. It had been brought in by the silkworm industry.

When I arrived in 1952, it was working well. It ran without any motor, fuel or electricity. By the force of the river, a piston was set into motion, shooting the water up into the pipes, forcing it to run uphill where it filled a large storage tank. Citizen Kamanda, a faithful Congolese, learned how to keep the waterway running by clearing out the constant sand that collected in its pipes.

Living in a dorm with five different tribes was like training a lot of children, starting when they were teenagers. Some really wanted to obey. Others had to submit to punishment. Several confessed their sins and asked the Lord to help them, for which we gave thanks. A number of them responded to the altar call.

Mathilda, a Christian girl, came to me and said that François always took too much food. When she had said something to her about it, François had cursed her and asked, "Why do you torture me little by little? Why don't you get out your fetishes and heathen medicine and kill me all at once?"

Mathilda said if she told her parents what François had said, it would start an argument among their different tribes. They would also ask whether she had told me. I called for François and talked to her. She agreed it wasn't the right thing to say.

I told her I was glad that some time ago she had asked us to pray for her. I had also asked her to pray for me. Now, I wanted to know how I could pray for her. She expressed a desire to change her ways.

"You have tried again and again, haven't you?" I asked.

"Yes," she said.

We read 1 Corinthians 10:13, "There hath no temptation taken you, but such as is common to man; but God is faithful, who will not suffer you to be tempted above that ye are able; but will with the temptation also make a way to escape, that ye may be able to bear it."

She then read verses on salvation, asking God to forgive her and became a born-again child of God.

After reading 1 John 1:9, she decided she should confess everything. "If we confess our sins, He is faithful and just to forgive us our sins, and to cleanse us from all unrighteousness."

When I suggested that she ask Mathilda's forgiveness, she agreed. François gave Mathilda a clear testimony about confessing her sins to Christ. Then, she asked Mathilda to forgive her. Mathilda's beautiful smile radiated throughout the room as she forgave her friend. It was the breakthrough we had been praying for.

With the new school year came changes. Given a full teaching schedule of 20 hours a week, I continued living in the dorm. Each day after study hall, the dorm girls and I had our evening devotions together. It was a joy to have them take an active part with me.

One day, in late afternoon, I decided to join the students outside in their recreation time. Some played volleyball; others played rugby football. Some sat on a grass mat and embroidered. Two lonely children shot basketballs. Other students prepared the evening meal, consisting of luku, and caterpillars (*mingolos*).

Mothers came by on the trail, walking home from their gardens. On the back of one was strapped her baby. How content their little ones were, being so close to their mother. It gave them a wonderful feeling of security.

Older children, at home, with knife in hand, carved their latest toy from bamboo. It was an airplane, like the one they had seen flying out missionaries to conference. Another boy made a truck, complete with a clicking sound made by placing spikes of the bamboo outer bark to hit against a wheel. A long stick, connected to the drive shaft, with a steering wheel at the end, guided this toy with precision.

Under the citrus trees, some of the boys - lacking a ball - had picked several green oranges and played catch with them. They little realized, of course, that if they left them to ripen, the oranges might save the lives of some youngsters in need of the vitamins.

Another mother came by with a basket on her head, a smaller one on the head of her 3-year-old. The child had taken her clothes and learned how to wash them by pounding the dirty clothes on the rocks in a stream of water. From now on, she must keep her own clothes washed. One girl was holding a chicken, another fed a monkey a mango.

A grade school teacher, who taught me the Kituba trade language, walked up holding something in his hands. Moving closer, I could see it was the a skin of a large snake. The cobra had killed his dog so he killed the snake. I bought the large snake skin.

Meanwhile, it was almost time for a furlough. *United States, here I come!* I worked feverishly to get ready for my trip home. On Monday, the mission plane would bring forms and letters. Short-wave reported that it was coming in the afternoon. The next report added that if they came late, they would spend the night there at Kajiji. Missionary Aviation Fellowship isn't equipped to fly after dark.

Before I received another report, the plane had landed. My neighbor, Katy Penner, a nurse and teacher at the hospital, knocked at my door. "The plane is leaving right away," she said. "Since I had to come for my letters, I can take your letters as well." The airport, behind the hospital, was two miles from Ecole Belle Vue, where Katy and I lived.

"Thanks," I responded, "but I must meet the plane myself. I need to fill out forms for a new passport and visa while the plane is being fueled and loaded with passengers."

I ran to school to get Gladys from chapel. We drove on the one-way path to the airstrip. This trail skirts the edge of the mission station. When we rounded the corner, Africans - mostly medical students - tried to stop us. We proceeded slowly, then we saw a motorbike lying on the road.

"An accident happened to this motorbike," they said. "When a car came around the corner, Mademoiselle Penner was on her motorbike coming in the opposite direction. The narrow path did not allow for two cars to pass each other. Both vehicles and wind made much noise. Tall elephant grass hid the two vehicles from each other. They collided."

The Congolese did not want us to go by, but finally they pulled the motorbike out of the way and permitted us to pass. My passport and visa forms did not come that day.

Later on in the day, I drove the car involved in the accident to the hospital. I wanted to check on medical tests being done for my dorm girls. Several medical students came out waving their arms angrily.

One carried a butcher knife, ready to slash the tires of the car. (In an animistic culture, the spirit in the object is as guilty as the driver of the car, hence the attack on the car.)

Another more level-headed man and Elsie Fisher, a missionary nurse, warded him off. "We need this car," they said. "It's the only car on this mission station to take Mlle. Katy home."

Some of the medical students shouted at me, "Never come to the hospital with this car again."

When the students refused to let me enter the front door of the hospital, I walked in the back way. Some more mature workers took time to help me find the laboratory results for the tests done on my dorm girls.

After parking the car at Helen Toew's home, I walked to the other residences to talk to my friends. At the guest house, someone handed me a note. "Please come with the car so you can take Katy home," it read.

I persuaded one of the missionary men to ride with me for protection. The crowd did not say a word as medics wheeled Katy out beside the car. The doctor lifted Katy into the car. She was conscious and talking. Her bandaged nose evidenced where the doctor had spent hours sewing her up. She had no broken bones. The students gasped as they realized that Katy Penner agreed to get into the very car that had almost killed her.

Later, one of my students approached me, "What do you have against the medical students?" he asked.

"Nothing, why?" I responded.

"They plan to beat you up."

A couple of hours later, I met some of them. "What have you against me?" I asked them.

"Nothing," they replied, "just against the car."

Oh! I thought, Animism! Hadn't Kamanda, the worker who kept the water pump running, said earlier, "That tree tried to kill me while I was walking in the forest"?

We know that God is everywhere, but He doesn't live in objects. How can our adopted people grasp these truths overnight? Again I realized how much teaching they needed from the Word of God.

Nice dorm rooms, civilized ways and modern methods didn't change the hearts of Congolese students. Their heathen religion of animism, witchcraft and evil spirits was very real to them. We taught them that lying and adultery were wrong. From devotions in the dorm, Bible classes and chapel, they learned that the Lord Jesus Christ alone could change their lives.

"I would like to explain how I took Jesus Christ into my heart," one student said. "Pastor Simon, a Congolese, taught us that Jesus will come to take His children who have trusted Him. Those who haven't received Him when the Son of Man comes, will experience much pain.

"One day, I dreamed I saw the Son of Man come. In this dream, I saw the children of God go up to heaven with His angels. Then I saw fire that scorched the whole earth, and people were running, but the fire followed them everywhere.

"Where the people of God were, there wasn't any fire. The fire didn't go there. I marveled greatly. Then I awoke and called my brothers and sisters and parents. I told them what I had seen that night. They said I must make my heart ready, because on that day the Son of God will come like that.

"Today, I know that my heart is ready even when I die. I am sure I will go to heaven to our Father of all blessings, all grace, all kindness and all love. I will go to be with all His children. The verse that spoke to me was Philippians 1:21, 'For to me to live is Christ and to die is gain.'"

Meanwhile, five more years had passed since I had put foot on American soil. It was furlough time. Betty Funk, studying in Belgium, would take my place in the practical teaching dorm for secondary school students, and teach home economics. The school wasn't the all-girls' school we wanted, hence my efforts were partly thwarted. However, the girls learned practical lessons in sewing, nutrition and semi-modern housekeeping.

For Betty, it would be her first taste of this culture. I would stay and work together with her for a month. Something detained her in Belgium longer than expected. I met her only briefly in passing through Leopoldville on my way out for furlough.

Margaret Dyck, a missionary who worked with Bible correspondence students, and I said good-bye to Congo on September 15, 1967, a day earlier than planned. Unrest in the country brought this about and made it impossible for me to get my things packed at Kajiji. Packing my things in a barrel became someone else's responsibility.

In Leopoldville, as we made our way to the ferry to cross the Congo river to Brazzaville, we became aware of the All-African Conference taking place there. The Africans had laid a leopard carpet, about two blocks long, in the middle of the street. This led right into the special ferry for the ruler of Brazzaville to walk upon. He would be royally received back into his country, the Congo.

At the Brazzaville airport, a group of Africans sung harmoniously - farewell songs for the parting missionaries. Since they no longer could have long services, the leader of the church called for more choir rehearsals and incorporated short Bible studies with them. Didn't the Word of God say we were to be as wise as serpents and as harmless as doves?

Margaret and I decided, since we had to change planes in Europe, one of our orientation stops would be Rome. We visited the coliseums where many Christians had been eaten alive by lions. Then we entered the catacombs, where others - because of their faith - hid out in times of great persecution.

We also saw the Sistine Chapel, where Michelangelo's Last Judgment is magnificently portrayed. What awesome testimonies great men of faith have left for us!

After arriving in Venice, Margaret and I made reservations at a hotel - just a ferry trip across a wide waterway. We were asked whether we wanted a guide.

"No," we said, for that would be extra, unnecessary expense. We could certainly cross by ferry and find the hotel by ourselves.

Margaret bought two tickets and handed them to me. She held

on to the address of our room reservations. I walked ahead with my suitcase and boarded on the ferry. Unexpectedly, it took off, with no Margaret in sight. What should I do? Which hotel was it? I seemed to remember that we should get off at the first stop.

Before I knew it, we had crossed the large canal. The ferry stopped, but to my dismay it quickly started again before I had time to get oriented. At the next stop, I jumped off in a hurry. What should I do now? No address, no Margaret.

Just as I thought about returning to the ferry and retracing my steps, another ferry came. Who should step off but Margaret.

"Margaret, what happened?" I asked. "Why didn't you get on to the same ferry with me?"

"They charge a separate ticket for each suitcase," she explained. "I didn't known that, so I had to buy more tickets."

"How come you got off here instead of the first stop?" I asked.

"The ferry made that first stop in such a hurry I didn't have time to get off."

We laughed, marveling how God brought us together by having both of us make the same mistake.

On September 27, Margaret and I boarded a plane and flew across the great Atlantic Ocean, finally landing in Montreal. Rev. Shannon, a former missionary at Kajiji, met us and took us straight to the Sermon from Science Pavilion at World's Fair. Here his wife and many other French-speaking missionaries shared their faith.

While at the pavilion of the Republic of Congo, I recognized one of my former students. She had lived with us in the dorm in Leopoldville in 1963. When we saw one another, we ran into each other's arms as startled fairgoers stared in bewilderment. A week later, I flew to Baltimore, then took a bus to Washington D. C. I wanted to get in touch with Clara Nickel, who had been in orientation before leaving for Kimpala with the United States Agency for International Development. We spent a lovely evening together, marveling at how the Lord had led us both to Africa.

For the last leg of the journey, I chose to stop in San Francisco instead of Los Angeles, to change planes for my hometown, Bakersfield. Before I realized it, we flew over Bakersfield, stopping in

Los Angeles to get to San Francisco!

A couple of days later, when I wanted to catch a direct plane to Bakersfield, they told me it was booked solid. Then they sent me via Los Angeles to transfer over. Again I flew over Bakersfield for the third time in trying to reach it.

Fog filled the airport. No planes could now fly out of Los Angeles. The airline ended up sending me to Bakersfield by Greyhound Bus. I arrived on Thursday, October 12, 1967, at 2:30 in the morning.

Sometimes in life, we may be led in roundabout ways, but when the Lord is leading, not even detours are a mistake.

CHAPTER 12

GIRLS, GIRLS, GIRLS

I had been home a year for my needed furlough. In that time, I got reacquainted with my family, furthered my French studies at Fresno State College, and spliced the 35 mm. movie films I had taken in the Belgian Congo. Now I showed them in the churches.

On my way back to the Congo, I was asked to visit some dear friends I had never met. They had taken a great interest in the girls' work, deciding to supply us with needed things to equip our food lab and our girls' department office.

After meeting me at the Buffalo airport, Mrs. Wichert and her lovely family thoughtfully took me to the pride of that whole region, one of the wonders of God's creation.

How fabulous to see the lights on Niagara Falls glistening as if lit by flames of sparkling firecrackers. They reflected from every visible drop of water as the river plunged over the great precipice and rushed on its turbulent way.

That evening, 80 women entered an ample basement to get an idea where their hard-earned money had been and would be spent. My home movie presented the girls' work. Over cookies and tea, they asked many intelligent questions which I attempted to answer. They greatly encouraged me to continue teaching the girls and women of the Congo.

On Sunday morning, before the whole church, I spoke a greeting in my mother tongue, German, as requested. Then I added greetings in French, the education language, and in Kituba, the trade language of our area in the Congo. This gave the audience a broader picture of what languages Mennonite Brethren churches now used. They worship or minister in about 50 languages worldwide.

On my way back to the Congo, I enjoyed a stopover in Belgium, using the time for purchasing a few things for the school. While visiting with missionaries studying French there before they too returned to the Congo, we listened by shortwave to news from Africa.

Brazzaville, we heard, was quite upset over the Republic of Congo. The new government had offered safe return to all Congolese who wanted to come back to their country. But they had not kept their word; they had assassinated Pierre Mulele, the main Communist-inspired leader in the rebellion of 1964-65.

I arrived in Leopoldville, the capital of Congo, in October 1968. Flying over Kikwit, I observed that the city was built upon rocky hills, its two sides surrounded by the Kwilu river. On the hilly outskirts of this hot, sandy city stood small, authentic, village-type Congolese huts. A fence circled each modest hut.

Skimming lower, we saw that the main stores were built at the lowest part of the saucer-like basin. They stood close to the picturesque, crocodile-infested Kwilu River. A ferry and dugout canoes constantly carried people back and forth, uniting the two sides.

Gliding toward the airport, we noticed great rifts in the landscape. The main road, leading from the shopping area to the government buildings, open market and Congolese homes, faced erosion threats.

A few years later, a great washout almost divided the city by nearly cutting into this road. Some Congolese believed that an enormous cobra bored its way down the caved-in hillsides. To appease the cobra, some threw in great quantities of rock salt, while others offered money.

At last, the government called in an engineer who figured out just how to build retention walls and a proper run-off to rectify the situation. The cave-in was halted just half a block away from the main connecting road. Our new babes in Christ had much to learn to rid themselves of their old superstitions.

After I walked into the small air terminal, I presented my passport and visa. Picking up my luggage in the sweltering heat, I explained to the baggage inspector that I would be living in Kikwit

To stop the erosion, some threw in great quantities of rock salt, while others decided that they must appease this cobra with money, to stop it from further boring into the earth.

to teach their high school students.

The missionary who had come to pick me up handed out tracts to out-stretched hands.

Arriving at the apartments, two blocks from the Kwilu river, I noticed Nettie Berg waving a welcome from our combination Bible school correspondence office and Christian Book Store which she managed. In the back of this bookroom was the apartment for the couple who manned the two-way radio. Going upstairs, I was welcomed by Martha Willems, with whom I was to live.

When I was home on furlough, the Mission Board, the brethren on the field and I had tried to reach an agreement on how to tackle the huge task of educating women and girls in the Congo.

"Since Betty Funk has worked her way into this work (at Kajiji), we feel that she should stay with the work," J. H. Epp wrote me. "We, however, are seriously considering the erection of a girls' dormitory at Kikwit. These girls will also need home economics training..."

I wrote back to him: "It is good to hear of the advancement and good job Betty Funk has been doing. It gives me joy to hear that Betty enjoys and plans to stay in the field of the formation of our girls. It is only normal that she be left in charge of a work that she is capable of doing so well.

"We have only scratched the surface of this project. We do need more missionaries who are willing to do the same. I am willing to be placed wherever the Zairians need me. If it is to start a new work in Kikwit, this is fine."

Now I found myself at Kikwit, attached to the secondary school with both boy and girl students. At 7:00 o'clock every morning, six days a week, we teachers caught a ride with fellow missionaries. If, along the way, we saw the Congolese raising their flag, we had to stop the car on the road until they had finished singing their National Anthem and put the flag in place.

Soon we pulled up between the high school, called Mbandu, and the apartments that had been built for the expatriate teachers. We could use them as long as we needed them. Later, the Mennonite Brethren Church of Congo would take full ownership of them.

Arriving at the Athenee, a government school, we left Martha off to teach her religion classes that Ivan Elric had turned over to her. On other days, she went to the Bible Institute to supervise the practice teaching of our students. She also had charge of the library as well as the high school.

With Henry Derksen at the wheel, I accompanied him up the main road leading toward the airport. On a side road, a small rift could be seen between the main road and the lesser one. This dirt road led to the largest Mennonite Brethren church in Kikwit.

Dodging bicycles and pedestrians, we hoped to make the jump over this ditch-like rift without harming ourselves or the car. As we traveled, then and later, the Lord provided His guardian angels in every time of need.

As we pulled in between the church and the modest, 4-room Bible School building, Rev. Derksen greeted his students and joined the men for his day of teaching. I took the wheel and drove further up the unpredictable paths, dodging sand pits and road washouts. I always breathed a sigh of relief on arrival.

At the high school, which was Baptist, I greeted my eager students who wanted to learn English. Even teaching them for two long hours at a time proved to be a real joy. They wanted to learn the language that Congo considered the world's trade language.

We worked together with other missions in larger cities, exchanging teachers when we could be helpful in a single effort to show Christian love. When I drove back to the Bible school, where Henry Derksen taught, I often stayed in the middle of the path with one wheel on the far side of the unpaved road's shoulder so that the other wheels drove on the high middle part. In that way, my gas tank wouldn't be punctured.

I joined my students for a class in personal evangelism. After the men in Bible school learned a number of Bible verses, I tried to make it practical. Each student took a turn acting as an unbeliever. Another student had to persuade him of his need of a loving God. He was to attempt to lead him to a saving knowledge of Jesus Christ.

Earlier, I had mentioned to the students that it was possible to sit in classes for three years and still not know the Lord Jesus Christ

"When I pray," one of the students said to me, "I don't feel God hears me. What can I do to get through to God?"

After I showed him the promises of God and prayed with him, he came through to an assurance of his own salvation.

The more advanced Bible school men students did practice teaching in various Sunday schools. Martha and I graded them on this, and some did very well.

In our apartment, we had no refrigeration to cool us off. Our neighbors and Martha had electric fans which they used when they had electricity. After lunch, we rested until two o'clock. Except for Wednesday and Saturday afternoons, the carryall again picked us up for our classes at Mbandu, our mission's High School for both boys and girls.

Taking the girls aside, I taught them sewing, food lab, or had study hall, for their benefit. This became necessary when five girls flunked and we had to expel them.

On arriving at home, we looked around to see if the electric refrigerator was running. If it was not running, we had to fix whatever would spoil if left. We checked to see if the city water was running. If it was, we filled up our two barrels with water, one in the kitchen and the other in the bathroom.

Depending upon modern conveniences and not having them was worse than setting up our own system of lights and barrels for rain water to supply our needs.

For Christmas vacation, the four-wheel drive carryall jerked over the last bumps of the one-way road leading to Kafumba, where Bob and Wanda Kroeker were stationed before the rebellion. It had plowed through a real downpour when we left Kikwit, but near Kafumba mission station the roads seemed just a little damp; therefore, the red-mud roads weren't slippery.

Rev. Bob and Wanda Kroeker, and children, were now missionaries in Leopoldville, now called Kinshasa. Agnes and Jake Kroeker, Bob's parents, who were my cousins, were visiting their son and family. We stopped to take pictures of ground orchids. Below this flower was an edible bulb that tasted much like citrus. Another type of orchid was found on a tall stem supporting from three to five blooms each.

The forested area on this humid, hot trip was enriched by different shades of green and orange. Blooming trees, shrubs, climbing vines and tropical ferns all fought for space. They thrived while closer together on the banks of the rushing river.

When we stopped, some small gnats surrounded us, protesting our actions. The trip took three hours instead of two. That was all right because we wanted to enjoy it this time. What else was a vacation for?

As we turned the corner at Kafumba mission station, we could see the ruins of the missionary dwellings, print shop, maternity ward, schools and church buildings. The *Jeunesse* (youth) *Simbas* (lions) had really done their devastating job in the rebellion of 1964. After that event, we left the Congolese in charge of this mission station.

We saw Pastor Timothy Jimbo coming up to greet us, one among many who had hid in the forest for years. We paused long enough to hear his story.

Ahead of us on the path, a group of Congolese became excited over a cow they had killed. They planned to have a feast, for tomorrow was New Year's Day.

A group of my secondary student girls sat on a mat around a manual, portable sewing machine. Citizeness Jimbo turned the handle on the side of the wheel while holding the garment being sewn with the other hand. She was intent upon what she was making.

"What are you sewing?" I asked.

"We are sewing a dress for grandmother (Pastor Timothy's wife)," they answered.

I asked the girls to call the children together and tell them the Christmas story. I was proud to see them putting into practice some of the things they had been taught in school.

Two weeks before, on a Monday afternoon, expectation filled the air as the third-year (first year high) secondary school girls rode home with me. They gathered in my kitchen, because the school's food lab was incomplete.

They were divided into four groups. Each group was to bake a batch of peanut butter cookies, something they had never done before. First, they roasted their home-grown peanuts to perfection. Someone had brought along a hollowed-out log with two poles.

Two girls from each group were chosen. They stood facing each other, with the homemade mortar between them. One girl lifted the pole way above her head, coming down with great force, striking the peanuts a fierce blow. When her pole came up over her head, the other girl pounded downward with her pole. Pounding in rhythm was their way of making this task fun, and it enabled two to work in one hollowed-out tree trunk.

For extra fun, on the third beat one of the girls would hit the outside rim of the log for special sound effects. Soon they scraped out the smooth peanut butter. Then, the second group of girls were ready to pound theirs.

Using the recipe, each group added the ingredients necessary.

Fifth and sixth grade girls showed the two-pieced dresses they had sewn. During the year, they learned the added technique of sewing sleeves and collars.

To follow a recipe was also new to them. After rereading it to make sure nothing was missing, they placed the dough by spoonfuls on the cookie sheet, marking them with a fork. They called this marking "fantasy."

On Tuesday afternoon, the fourth-grade girls came to my home to bake sugar and pineapple cookies. Wild forest pineapple had been bought at the door, ready for the girls to peel, cut into small pieces and cook before adding them to their cookie dough. When the last cookies were placed into the butane oven, the counters washed and dishes cleared away, each girl was allowed to sample her cookies. They rejoiced at the outcome.

Saturday came at last. After two hours of school, recreation time ensued. All teachers, both expatriates and Congolese, came for Christmas tea. One fifth-grade girl welcomed our guests and ushered them in, making them feel at home. Soon all sipped their tea, some eating a cookie for the first time in their lives.

By decree of the Congolese Education Department, all Congolese children had to wear uniforms. Our girls were taught how to sew the simple skirt. Yellow, sleeveless blouses became part of the school uniform.

Fifth-and sixth-graders exhibited their two-piece dresses. This year, they had learned to sew sleeves and collar. The girls wore the matching, wrap-around skirt, with the opening in the back, to distinguish them from the married women, who wore it open in the front.

Recreation time brought all 49 school girls together to enjoy tea and cookies. It was a learning experience, for many of them had never attended a tea. They learned it was not a time to fully satisfy their appetite, for it wasn't a meal. They should walk around to get acquainted, carrying their glass of tea and cookie while conversing with people.

The hostess presented a greeting card, signed by all the girls, to the principal of the secondary school, Ben Klassen. He had worked long hours to make the nice cupboards for the food lab and the sewing materials.

Some of the girls stayed for a singspiration. How these girls could sing! Singing in harmony came naturally to them. Earlier, ten of the girls had come to me asking the way of salvation. What a thrill to talk with each one, showing them from the Word of God how they could be forgiven and be adopted into the family of God.

At the singspiration, Martha and I talked about what they could do to help their families during vacation time. Not only could they help with their daily tasks, but they could also spread the good news of salvation. Many of the Kafumba girls put into practice what they had been taught, bringing great joy to their teacher.

Easter was just around the corner. A couple of weeks earlier, I had finally received the things we had packed while at home on furlough. Many of the items came from the Friendship Circle and Mission Sewing Circle of the Mennonite Brethren Church in Bakersfield, now called Heritage Bible Church. It seemed like Christmas as I did the unpacking.

During Easter vacation, the Congolese gave a lovely program about the resurrection of Christ Jesus. Some of our third-year secondary school girls sang. One girl had been quite a problem as a student at Kajiji. Now, in Kikwit, she told the girls in our sewing class about her earlier problems.

"Yes, Citizeness Mpasi, "I said to her, "we had our difficulties, didn't we?" She agreed.

"I hope you have learned something from that," I said.

"Yes," she said. "When I was a child, I spoke as a child, I understood as a child, I thought as a child, but when I became a man, I put away childish things"(quoting 1 Corinthians 12:11).

To start out the school year, we had very few girls but many boys. Already eight had dropped out with low grades or illness. Most of the ailments had been caused by living in sin. Many girls came from neighboring villages.

They knew that at Kajiji I lived with the dorm girls, while teaching full time at Kusemuka's secondary school. The Mission Board was considering building one in Kikwit, to teach them the rudiments of housekeeping, but were low on funds.

Walking long distances to and from their homes led them into temptation. They begged for a dorm to help them resist temptation, and to have time to study.

"You don't want to keep us in a dorm," they said to me, "because you now get more money for teaching." It was hard to convince them otherwise. Their culture just didn't lend itself to mixed schools.

A summons came for me to go to Pai for closing exercises and to inventory the school books. Another school year neared the end. The mission had just purchased a new pickup. Two sons of the Derksens accompanied me on the two-hour trip.

Starting out at about 5:00 o'clock in the afternoon, we enjoyed talking about their school experiences at the American School in Leopoldville. We took the muddy roads in stride, hitting bump after bump, enjoying the rich foliage of the tropical forest.

Looking to our left, we could see white birch bark shining in the fading afternoon sun. Fern-like umbrella trees shaded the roadside most of the way. Soon, however, we noticed a red warning light on the dashboard. Darkness was falling. What should we do?

We encountered few passersby and they knew nothing about engines. I recalled that if I turned left on a road a couple of blocks away and crossed a ferry, it would lead me to a palm nut oil factory run by the Portuguese. It was too dark to cross the ferry. We decided to sleep in the pickup and consult mechanics at the oil factory in the morning.

After waking at dawn, we drove up to the ferry. We signed the book and paid a small sum for crossing. Then I gingerly followed the signals of the ferry man who guided me up the slippery boards and onto the rickety vessel.

At the palm nut factory, mechanics checked the engine and found it was giving false signals. We could go on without worrying. Thanking them for their kindness, we soon went on our way.

After another hour's drive, we curved around and up the Pai mountain, viewing the hospital, dispensary, maternity ward, doctor's house and the nurses' dwelling places at the large center.

My mind went back to an earlier visit I had made there. We had gone to the dispensary for a visit when I spied Eva, one of my pupils who got married at Kipungu. She also had been my student at Kajiji.

"I knew you were coming," she said, embracing me. "I dreamt about you last night." It encouraged me to know that Eva apparently walked with the Lord.

A day later, I had to take inventory of the books used in the school. Each pupil handed in his books as they were called for, and a deposit was given back. We worked hard from early morning till 10:00 a.m., when suddenly the principal interrupted and asked me to take part in the closing exercises scheduled at 4:00 o'clock that afternoon. I would rely on the Lord to speak through me.

After a hurried lunch, I excused myself to prepare my talk. Then, at 2:00 o'clock I went back to school counting books. We worked feverishly until time for the program to begin.

My duffel bag with my overnight things and a change of clothes had not made it to the pick-up. How could I look presentable wearing rumpled, slept-in clothes?

Returning to my room to type out my speech, I saw that my girlfriend, Tilly Wall, had laid out her skirt and blouse for me to wear for the occasion.

When I used the borrowed clothes as an illustration during my talk, the children took new interest in what I had to say. Why were they in school learning to read and write? I asked them. Why was the mission establishing schools in their area? Wasn't it because we knew they were intelligent and we wanted them to be able to read the Word of God for themselves? As I had put on someone else's clothes, we were asked to put on Christ.

Back at Kikwit, on a Sunday, several of us missionaries decided to attend a new three-week-old church. We walked to the Kwilu river, crossed by ferry, then climbed the steep mountainside. Soon we came to a clearing in the thick foliage and saw a small group of homes. Under the trees, they had placed several makeshift seats. God became more real as we listened to the message from God's Word in their trade language.

Dr. Donald McGavran, noted missiologist, once said a church should be within walking distance of everyone in the world. Some of our Congolese had a vision of opening up churches in strategic places in Kikwit to reach those who lacked transportation to the larger churches. By this time, 9,205 Congolese had joined Mennonite Brethren churches in the Congo. Truly, God had given the increase.

On another Sunday, after leaving the church, we saw a strange-looking man dressed in a skull cap, a rough, woven, wrap-around skirt, with bracelets and gobs of stuff hanging from them. I asked my house help who he was.

"A medicine man," came the reply.

Dispensaries and hospitals in Congo kept busy. When ill, most Congolese immediately wondered who could have caused the illness. If they didn't recover quickly, they consulted the uncle on the mother's side.

As the disease worsened, the heathen would consult a medicine man. He would mix potions of medicine found in the forest. Sometimes they had medicinal value, but most often their dosages were not right.

The medicine man sold fetishes, to be worn around their waists, necks, ankles and wrists. They would ward off diseases caused by curses.

The oldest son of the family now consulted the dead to find out which dead ancestor or idol the sick one had offended. We had taught them that our God was stronger than these evil forces, but if they had offended someone, they should make restitution. They should also get right with their Creator.

One night, I was awakened by a loud voice. Sitting up in bed with a start, I heard someone preaching against the evils taking place in Kikwit. I ran to the window and saw a Congolese man dressed in a long flowing robe, with a huge horn from an animal as his loud-speaker. I suddenly realized he was the town crier I had heard about.

He announced loudly that all commercial buildings in Kikwit had to be repainted. The Prime Minister of Congo, Mobutu Se-Se-Seko, was expected soon and every part of town had to be repainted and cleaned up for him.

This time he kept his word by coming. All school children had to line up on the one paved road in Kikwit, leading from the airport to the main stores. We were all scattered to make the welcome as widespread as possible. I had charge of all the girls from our secondary school. We too had our place on the side of the road.

Suddenly, I noticed that our girls had all taken off their shoes. I asked about this but received no answer. I could see they were apprehensive. Finally, official motorcycles came, followed by a procession of cars. They cleared the way for the great leader of Congo.

When his car came closer, everybody around us started to run on the side of the vehicle. It soon became a great stampede. Now I knew why my girls had become apprehensive. Getting them out of this crowd alive proved challenging. The crowds could have easily trampled many people underfoot. I vowed never to take the girls to a reception like that again.

On another occasion, a group of us decided to go to the Kwilu church dedication, about an hour and a half from Kikwit. As we came nearer to the Kwengi river, we rocked back and forth and sideways on the treacherous road. We thought we would have to leave the vehicle beside the river, because we had heard that the ferry was out.

To our surprise, we soon learned that this was the first day the ferry again took vehicles across. As we walked up the ferry planks, hundreds of butterflies covered the path leading down to the water. They flew in our direction, and many landed on us. They looked like colorful, flying flowers, fluttering around the undergrowth and covering even the beaches.

After driving off the ferry, we again climbed into the carryall to travel the rest of the way. Between scattered villages of simple huts, healthy groves of palm trees had their huge clusters of orange and black palm nuts.

Some nut cutters, high up in the foliage of palm trees, had been strapped down to the tree trunk by vines made into ropes. They cut down big bundles of rich, thorny fruit. Further on, we saw piles of these orange and black palm nut clusters ready for the truck to pick up and haul to the palm oil press.

Upon arriving, we saw two buildings that looked almost identical. Both structures showed the work of masons' patient, meticulous skill. The walls of both the church and the school would weather the test of many a tropical downpour. These dear people responded to the Mission Board's promise. If they built the walls of permanent materials, the mission would furnish the roof. Crowds of people, waiting at the doorway, hoped to get into the small church building. Old village chiefs with their beaded hats, medicine men with skull caps and loin cloths, men with homemade Congolese cut suits - all attended.

Congolese women waited for entrance. Their babies were tied to their backs with the same printed cloth as their nice new dresses. Matching colorful scarves, artfully folded and pleated, hung around their heads. Others, with hair woven into many different designs, had spent hours in having their hair done.

Looking around, I saw Pastor Sammy Mboloko and his wife, Eva. We ran into each other's arms. She had dreamt I would be at Pai. We lived together at Kajiji for three and a half months. She had sewn her boy a shirt and shorts and had learned how to bake bread.

In student days, while baking a loaf of bread, she had said, "When my husband serves communion, I will bake the bread!"

Now she was again at her husband's side, able to entertain. She also taught Bible to the women from her congregation, as well as some sewing. Her class sang. Then later, they showed me some of the blouses they had made.

This little church, built brick by brick through many years, spoke of encouragement given by different missionaries such as

Looking around I saw Pastor Sammy Mboloko and his wife Eva. We fell into each other's arms. She had dreamt that I would be at Pai. We had lived together at Kajiji for three-and-a-half months.

John Kliewer, Ted Martens, and the Ortmans. Now, however, the group of masons and carpenters who had finished the task of laying the bricks sang a song.

When the first verse finished, they sang the second, then the third. Verse upon verse, they kept on singing. I had never before heard such a long, long song. Later, I asked them why they sang for such a long time. "Why shouldn't we sing a long, long song?" they said. "Didn't it taken a long time of many years of hard work to complete this church?"

When we see Jesus, surely we will sing long, long songs of praise throughout eternity.

A meaningful prayer asked God the Father, Son and Holy Spirit to bless His house and fill it with His presence. After the service, we enjoyed a banquet under a shelter of palm branches erected for the occasion. Congolese women had prepared large bowls of luku from manioc. They proudly carried their colorful serving dishes on their heads and placed them on long makeshift tables.

When registration time came for the new school year, girls, girls, girls, hundreds of them competed for the fewer than 20 places we had reserved for them. Tears of frustration streamed down my face as I had to turn so many girls away. Why, oh why, couldn't we start an all girls' school? The need overwhelmed me.

Secondary schools, added to our mission schools in the various districts, drew at least 100 girls.

In my spare time, I sewed samples, labeling them in French for the centers of education. Hope ran high that someone in each center would be found to teach the precious girls. As future wives and mothers, they at least needed to learn to mend their torn clothes.

My second year in Kikwit proved much like the first. Meanwhile, our mission board office at home went through financial hardship. In principle, they had agreed to build a girls' practical dorm - to teach housekeeping - close to the mixed secondary school. But they had no money. The mission had gone into debt to keep us on the field. They asked me to either get myself recognized by the Education Office in Kinshasa, and thus get paid for my teaching, or come home.

When Brother Wiebe came from the Foreign Board of Missions Office for a visit, he confirmed that I must earn money by teaching. Until now, the Congolese government had paid the mission for my teaching by the hour, on the same scale as the Zairians.

This didn't suffice. I must get the amount earned by all foreigners whose teaching credentials were in order and recognized by the Congolese Education Department. I understand the World Bank supplied the money for this.

I spent days in Leopoldville gathering all my necessary papers. I brought my college degrees to Mr. Brott, who spoke French perfectly and did the translation work on all the certificates: B.A. in Missionary Anthropology, B.A. in Education, two California teacher's certificates, a French certificate, and a copy of an inspector's report on my teaching.

I took copies of all these papers, with their translations into French, to the American Embassy for the official stamp confirming that these were exact translations.

What a relief later to hear that I had been accepted and would

Traditional dress for the Zairian man.

thus be paid for my teaching. The money went directly to our Mission Board, which in turn paid me a regular salary.

Suddenly, word came that Betty Funk could no longer stay at Kajiji. She had become susceptible to certain strain of malaria. The doctor said she had to change climates within the country or go home for good. So we were to exchange places. One serious catch arose.

In order to receive subsidies for my teaching, I had to teach high school. Kajiji, thus far, had only junior high. Not long after this, however, the Education Committee of our mission in Kikwit decided to add a third year of secondary school to Kajiji's junior high. This meant that now all obstacles to my teaching at Kajiji had been removed.

School started at Kajiji on the first Monday in September of 1970. On Tuesday, at about 6:30 a.m., all my belongings including my dog "Viringo," had been loaded into a truck, with several passengers and myself, headed for Ecole Belle Vue, Kajiji.

We bumped along on an unpaved road, over many sand pits and

red-mud holes, averaging about 25 miles an hour. Suddenly, the chauffeur stopped the truck. The brakes were on all the time, and he couldn't release them. The tires smoked badly. When they cooled off, we would proceed.

Finally, it was safe to go the five miles to a palm oil factory, where a Portuguese there kindly let his Congolese mechanic fix our brakes. About noon we drove on. Halfway to Kajiji, the motor made an awful noise. Stopping again, the chauffeur said, "We can't go on or we will ruin the motor."

In the middle of nowhere, the grasslands of Congo had just started to grow after they had been burnt in the dry season. Not far from where we were parked, we came upon a home. A kind Congolese woman informed us that her husband was out in the villages working for the Congo government. She took me in for the three nights that we camped on the road.

By day, I sat in the truck to discourage looters. My dog "Viringo," a Godsend, made the passing villagers afraid to come too close, unless they wanted to talk. I had packed fresh water in a plastic jug. We didn't dare drink unboiled water. This lasted for the entire time we stayed there.

Fresh meat, in an ice chest, didn't spoil. We had also brought canned goods along, which had been stored in the back of the truck. I had a Scrabble game with me and played it with a Congolese English student traveling with me.

In the evenings, when the chauffeur took up the surveillance of the truck and slept in it, I went to my hostess' home, where we ate luku for the evening meal. Then she would take her youngest child, place him in her lap and cradle him until he was asleep.

After this, she got out the only school book she had, which happened to be on geography. She explained this simple book over and over again, her way of making conversation.

She gave me a room with just a metal bed. Fortunately, I had my sleeping bag, air mattress and mosquito netting with me. Crawling into the bag with the netting over me, I was soon fast asleep.

Two days later, at about 9 p.m., we heard the sound of a truck. Word had finally reached our missionaries in Kikwit. They had sent another truck so that I could continue my journey to Ecole

Belle Vue. That evening, the men reloaded everything. At about 3:00 o'clock the next morning, we resumed our journey. We left the mechanic to repair the truck we had to abandon.

Arriving at Ecole Belle Vue at about 11 a.m., I could hardly believe I was actually back at the first mission station I had ever worked at in the Congo. Again, I stood on the verandah to behold the wonders of God's creation. Again, I was welcomed to my favorite mission station, Ecole Belle Vue. Truly, the Lord is good!

CHAPTER 13

TRAVELING WITHOUT THE MAIN DRIVE SHAFT

Girls from five different tribes in the Democratic Republic of Congo greeted me with their typical handshake. I had just moved from Kikwit back to Kajiji and would again live with them as a dorm mother while teaching full time in the mixed secondary school.

These dorm girls soon made coat hangers, mattresses and fitted sheets in their spare time. When the grass was a little longer, they cut it with their short-handled hoes, let it dry and stuffed their sack-like mattresses with it.

One afternoon, as I checked on the school skirts and blouses they tried on, I noticed an interesting underslip. It was made of row upon row of sewn together strips. Further observation confirmed my suspicion.

"Bandages from old sheets you got from the dispensary and sewed together were not sent for this purpose," I said.

"Yes, I realize that," the student admitted. "They wear out too soon."

Most torn sheets rolled into bandages are used as such in different dispensaries and hospitals in the Congo and are desperately needed.

My neighbor, Helen Toews, also became a dorm mother, but for medical students. She nursed and taught full time. Our dorms, on opposite ends of a V-shaped building, had been built originally by the silk worm company.

As our dorm girls got ready for school, Helen and I had breakfast together. No bakery shops or grocery stores could be found around this bush station, so all breads, buns and sweet rolls had to be baked in our own kitchens.

One day, I counted 25 bundles of bananas in my banana grove. The Congolese had stolen more than that, until I marked each bunch with red paint. Just as we stopped banana thieves by markings, so Satan has lost his hold on us because we have been marked by Christ's precious blood.

Pineapple, guava, passion fruit, paipai, mango and citric fruits all grew in my garden. What a variety we had for our breakfasts.

No buses, trains or cars traveled out to this isolated spot. Our mission truck came occasionally with supplies for the hospital, schools and mission workers. The Klassens in Leopoldville kindly bought the necessary supplies and loaded the truck. Their great service allowed us to stay at our tasks.

After a day's travel, the driver would stop in Kikwit for the night. Finally, the truck arrived with our needed supplies. Too, many of our students sat on top of these barrels and cartons - the only means of transportation inland to our isolated mission station and schools. Many came to enter our scientific section taught at the high school.

After a day of rest, the truck driver returned with a load of empty kerosene and gas barrels, and propane containers, to be filled for us. Students wanting to enter Kikwit's Mennonite Brethren high school profited by this ride. Many others had to walk days from the surrounding villages to attend our schools.

After breakfast, I checked the rooms to see if the girls had done their tasks before going to school. At the same time, I looked around to see if any of the students stayed home because of illness.

At 7:00 a.m., I locked my front door, satchel in hand, cut across the empty basketball court and followed the grassy path to the school office. On my way, I heard the usual slogans being repeated by our junior high and high school students.

Standing in a circle in their school uniforms, they shouted: "Above all, discipline! We must serve! Serve who? Serve ourselves? No: *Serve others!*"

When I entered the classroom, my pupils stood at attention until I told them to sit down. Crude desks filled this room, often with two pupils at each desk.

When the flag was being raised and they sang their National Anthem, everyone came to attention until the flag was in position and the second bell rang.

After greeting the principal, two secretaries and seven other teachers, I signed in, picked up my chalk for the day and entered my assigned class for that hour.

When I entered a classroom, the pupils stood at attention until told to sit down. Crude desks filled the room, often with two pupils at each desk. Some desks needing repair had been abandoned in one corner until money for nails could be found.

Before new desks were needed, the village sawyer was notified weeks in advance. When we heard that our truck had to go in their direction, we asked the driver to stop for our precious boards.

Arriving at their work site, the sawyers busily cut a fallen log. The sawyer on top of the log pushed on a handle attached to a long blade, cutting the large trunk. In a trench that had been dug under the fallen log, the other sawyer pulled on the handle attached to the other end of the cutting tool.

My sister Alice and Art Newfield had given me some tithe money, which paid for hand-sawn planks bought from the sawyers in the forest. When the boards were somewhat dry, our carpenter, working in the shade of a large tree, made window frames and doors for the classroom.

Back and forth they sawed, taxing their strength. Finally, they came toward us, wiping their foreheads with their left hand. After shaking our right hand, they pointed to a small stack of crudely cut planks - only a part of what we had ordered. They insisted that they couldn't keep up with the demands placed upon them.

When we drove back to the mission, the carpenter spied us. He left his hand plane, clamps, hand saw and square on his crudely made carpenter's table under a tree while he inspected the boards needed for the finishing of school desks. He tried to pick out the driest board, but shook his head knowing that any of the boards would shrink and later crack while drying. The boards were placed in our attic to dry.

The inside and outside of the classrooms were whitewashed, with a mixture of slaked lime and water. For commercial use, the company adds whiting, glue and sometimes salt. Village women found deposits of a beige type in their fields. They carried up baskets full of it, formed into balls of a clay-like substance, on their heads.

Looking around at my pupils, I couldn't help but notice that they all wore uniforms. Others had been refused entrance until they too wore the uniform that had been chosen. The boys had opted for a white shirt and black pants.

One fellow, who was at the head of the class, was voted in to help each teacher with discipline problems. He must take down the names of all who were unruly. One morning, he told the class how they were to behave, then before I could say a word he leaped out the glassless window and fled.

Later, this same fellow trusted Christ and decided to serve the Lord. He became a mechanic for Missionary Aviation Fellowship.

All three classes, totaling about 100 pupils, were my responsibility for two hours of Bible study each week. Just before the morning recess, chapel was held three days a week. Each teacher took a turn giving forth the Word of God.

As a follow-up to chapel, students brought their questions or problems to me from 4:00 to 6:00 p.m. on certain afternoons. Many a third-grade student asked the way of salvation. Through the Four Spiritual Laws, in French, each found saving faith in Jesus Christ.

"Dorothy," a surgeon said to me one day, "we can't go on with surgery if you keep on moving your little toe."

In the operating room at Kajiji hospital, I had received a local anesthetic before removing one of my little toes. For years, it had laid over the second toe and became as sore as a boil. Ill-fitting shoes as a youngster had caused this.

Now, after surgery, I stayed over night with my friends, Sarah Peters and Arlene Gerdes, missionary nurses. Several Congolese teachers visited me. I had asked the doctor to place my severed toe in a bottle to preserve it. This bottle was at my bedside. When my friends came to see me, I showed them the toe.

"Are you going to take it home to your parents?" they asked me, over and over again.

"No!" I answered, not catching on right away. As others came over, I quit talking about my little toe. I finally realized that a Congolese hunter would give almost anything to make heathen medicine from a part of the human body.

In order to get rid of it, I later buried that tiny part of my body in my backyard at Ecole Belle Vue. A letter came from mother asking whether my painful toe had been taken care of.

"Yes, mother," I responded, "my toe is gone, buried. Now I will be able to walk without pain. I will enjoy my next trip home."

In 1971, the nationalism campaign resulted in the renaming of the Democratic Republic of Congo to the Democratic Republic of Zaire. Zaire is a 15th century Portuguese version of the local name for the Congo (now Zaire) river. Its citizens were now called Zairians. Its currency and even the great Congo river now bore the name Zaire. Many of its larger cities also received Zairian names. All Christian names would be dropped.

Learning to know some of their hidden beliefs, which included ancestral worship, I realized my responsibility for what I knew. I must show them the right and truthful way.

Chokwe tribesmen buried two types of people close to a stream of water, then later wondered why the tribespeople became ill when they drank the contaminated water.

First, powerful chiefs were thus buried at night, when no one save the family would know where they had been buried. They didn't want others digging up the body to make heathen medicines utilizing the power he had experienced in his lifetime. They placed watchers over his grave. If anyone came close, they would shoot.

Lepers also were buried there, but everyone knew where their graves were. No one wanted to become a leper.

Chiefs in the old culture were believed to be able to reincarnate themselves in the form of ferocious animals. Hunters often made medicine that would kill either humans or animals.

If someone had made medicine to kill an animal, one that had killed a person, and made heathen medicine out of the victim's heart, while hunting with this medicine, the hunter saw an animal with the chief's form hovering over it, but they didn't kill that animal, the hunter has to pay money, after which the thing is forgotten. Such was their weird superstition.

If, however, the hunter shot in spite of seeing the form of a human being above the animal, and the big chief was suddenly struck with pain right where they had shot and killed the animal, he was responsible for the death of that chief. After a Zairian pastor told me this, I went home more puzzled than ever.

The fear of Ndoki's power in the hands of their enemies is a daily threat to all Zairians. They believe that if someone had a *ndoki* (evil spirit) to throw onto someone else, but it hadn't been covered with human blood, it could come back and kill the one who had it.

One day, while making a volleyball court in our backyard, we realized that our girls needed to play with other schools for good clean recreation and competition. One way to get the court completed faster was to make all rule-breaking girls fill the chuck holes by carrying baskets full of dirt on their heads and dumping it on the court.

Medical students who lived right next door eventually played on their finished court. We watched them play the boys one time when suddenly, a student fell and broke his hip. A fellow student began to weep. They tried to console her, but to no avail.

She finally muttered something about the accident being her fault. This seemed strange, for she was just watching the game and not directly involved at all. She finally explained that it was her fault because she had dreamt all about it the night before. Zairians believe that when they sleep, their spirits can go outside their body and do evil things.

Besides the six hours of graded Bible lessons in three different classes, I also taught seven hours of English as a foreign language. Home economics, including housekeeping, food lab and sewing, filled the afternoons. Study hall for the dorm girls after the evening meal greatly helped those not used to the discipline of study. Evening devotions followed, after which I saw that the girls retired on time and in their proper beds.

One class of girls had sewn a shirt-maker's-style blouse, including set-in sleeves and collars. Now it was exam time. How could I be sure they had learned how to cut another like it and sew it when needed? I came up with a very practical exam.

Zaire Protestant Relief Association, mainly fed by Mennonite Central Committee, had sent us thousands of straight pins. With lots of pattern paper in the school storeroom, why not cut out two patterns for each student who had made this blouse and make her pin it together as if she were sewing it?

We placed the students in different corners of two adjoining sewing rooms. Unused plyboards, propped up between them, prevented them from seeing the progress of their neighbors. About 100 straight pins were given to each pupil. Would they be able to pin the yoke to the back and get the front part as if it had buttons to open it? Sleeves had to be set in just right.

Two hours passed before they started handing me their pinned-together blouses. One had turned the sleeves upside down, but most of them had done very well. I knew now that since they had already cut out the things they had sewn in the classroom, they wouldn't be afraid to cut out and sew the blouse together properly.

Another school year came and went. Report cards were given out, and the girls had gone home for vacation. A week later, Dr. Bob Buhr, his wife Jan and children; Katy Penner; Helen Toews; some Zairians and I traveled to Kikwit for a missionary conference.

I carried my typewriter, tape recorder, radio and sewing machine. All these things had been damaged on the rough ride when I moved from Kikwit to Kajiji. After the conference, I planned to pay overweight on my flight to Kinshasa in order to get these things repaired. They were worthless otherwise.

On our way to the conference, we had to stop at two different places so the medical staff could give entrance exams to prospective students.

With Dr. Buhr driving, we traveled mile after mile when suddenly we saw our first traveler. He rode a bicycle. Seeing us so close, he lost his balance and fell off the bicycle. He landed on the side of the one-way trail. Unhurt, he soon stood up and waved us on.

Small villages consisting of red-mud, plastered huts became easier to spot. The tall elephant grass surrounding them had been burnt. Sometimes there were only three huts to a village. Others were considerably larger. Old village chiefs ruled each of these isolated villages. When deaths or disagreements came, they divided.

Kamiala, a Mennonite mission station, was the first stop where medical entrance exams were given. Mrs. Eidse graciously announced that all women missionaries were invited to enjoy an evening together at the nearby city of Kahemba. After the exams, we ladies drove the 20 miles to accept the welcome invitation. We passed the airstrip without any buildings.

A little later, we stopped at the door of a mission home. Catholic sisters greeted us, leading the way into their simple but adequate frontroom. Classical music, played on a phonograph, soon filled the room. We imagined ourselves sitting in a grand auditorium in Belgium as the orchestra so artfully entertained us.

Tasty sandwiches delighted us as we conversed in French about the happenings on our separate mission stations. After a dessert of Belgian pudding, we took to the road again, finally spending the night at Kamiala.

Why was this such a treat? All missionaries need a complete change from their daily routine to stay healthy, both physically and mentally. Classical music did this for me. "...the people were playing on flutes, and rejoicing with great joy, so that the earth shook at their noise" (1 Kings 1:40).

Around the breakfast table, Mr Eidse spoke of his progress as a translator of the Chokwe Bible. He mentioned as helpers two Zairians, Khege Mwata-Swana and Mutunda Funda, who faithfully edited his work to bring out a clearer meaning to the Bantu mind.

After saying goodbye with thanks to our nearest missionary neighbors, we again proceeded on our way to Kikwit. About half an hour from Kamiala, while traveling on a one-way deserted road, the car suddenly stopped. Dr. Buhr looked under the carryall and said the main drive shaft was broken. He took it off and put it into the back of the carryall.

We got back into the carryall, but the vehicle wouldn't start. He opened up the hood and found some wires that had jiggled loose. Dr. Buhr fixed them, then we drove further until we got stuck in deep sand. We dug ourselves out and drove on.

How did we drive when the main drive shaft was broken? Four-wheel drive. Practically all vehicles in this part of Zaire came with that feature. Sand in the dry season and red-mud roads in the rainy season made this a necessity. When the vehicle was in this mode, just the front wheels were in action.

We wondered just how far we could go on like this when two travelers came driving from the opposite direction. It was the first vehicle we had met since our breakdown. We found a wide spot in the narrow trail and parked to let them go by.

Then, we noticed that they were veterinarians from our mission in Kikwit, on their way to Kamiala. We told them about our difficulties. When they arrived at their destination, they contacted our Mennonite Brethren Mission in Kikwit by shortwave, explaining our predicament to them.

Finally, we reached a small town called Gungu to give more medical entrance exams. The tang of smoked, dried fish and rock salt greeted us as we passed open markets on our way to the pastor's home. We went by a few small government offices, then the usual simple Zairian homes with stick fences partitioning off each yard.

At the pastor's house, he introduced us to the prospective medical students. After giving exams and sharing our mutual joys and concerns in the work, we again went on our way to Kikwit.

When the hill became too steep, we got out and walked beside the slow-moving vehicle. When sand got too deep, we pushed with the four-wheel drive. At other times, the men got out their shovels and had to dig us out.

Just as darkness overtook us, we came to a ferry. Who should be on the other side of the river but our good friends from our mission in Kikwit? They had gotten the message by shortwave from Kamiala and had come to help us.

Slowly, we crossed the river by the hand-drawn ferry. Our friends unloaded the drive shaft they had taken out of another identical carryall. By the light of their pickup, they put it into place. Now able to drive the rest of the curvy mountainous roads, we had assurance that we would get there. Our Lord looked after every need.

CHAPTER 14

CROSSING A RUSHING RIVER ON ROLLING POLES

E very day for over a week Sarah Peters and I had been hiking down the steep mountain on which Ecole Belle Vue was built. It took us a good 20 minutes to get to the fields, and another 25 minutes to climb back up. We were getting into condition for our two-and-a-half to three-hour walk to a woman's convention. In this village, no cars had ever appeared; roads were nonexistent.

Friday came at last. I could hardly contain myself long enough to teach my two hours of classes before we could start. When at last we were ready to go, we had a lightning-and-thunder flash flood. It would be impossible to start until the pouring rain ceased.

Finally, at 2:30 o'clock, our bed rolls, flashlights, drinking water and some food were put into the pickup for our five-mile ride to the road's end. Our group included five medical students, the pastor's wife, Mama Makeka, Pakisa Tshimika's mother, Sarah Peters and myself. Traveling along a one-way trail, cutting into tall grass, curving around fallen trees, bumping and swaying from side to side over washouts in the road, we drove until we got to the dead end.

From there, we had to walk to our destination. Carriers sent from the villages waited for us. They picked up our things, put them on their heads, then blazed the trail before us.

After an hour of steady walking downhill, we came to a large, rushing river, the Lutshimi. The bridge was made of a number of

We from Kajiji included five medical students: Sarah Peters, the pastor's wife, mama Makeka, and myself. After an hour of steady walking downhill we came to the large rushing river, the Lutshimi.

large logs tied together, placed end to end. Cross sticks, tied down with vines on top of these logs, were being washed by the high waters. Many sticks had been swept away.

"Please," I said to one who was accustomed to passing that way, "may I hold on the back of your shoulders while you guide me step by step? Otherwise, I don't know how to get across such a rising river."

Looking down at my shoes, he must have wondered why I did not take them off. He had his shoes slung over his shoulders, while his bare, callused but sure-footed feet led the way. He walked slowly - for my sake.

As I gingerly stepped along, I don't know how I would have crossed if I hadn't used him for my guide and balance. I would have had to crawl on all fours. Halfway across, some of the sticks started rolling. We all arrived on the other side without any accidents, however.

As we climbed up a steep embankment, Sarah and I were glad we had taken our conditioning seriously. The last time we had made such a trip, it had been much harder because we were out of shape.

Growing close to this path, the wild fruit would quench our thirst. Student nurses pointed out various plants used for expectant mothers. Other types of medicinal herbs found growing here could be used for gastritis. Zairians have effective medications in their forests and in their heathen culture that can be used, but it would take a lot of research to properly identify each and to establish valid dosages.

Many with us on this hike had already put their faith in Jesus Christ; others hadn't yet made that decision. One of the hikers placed a branch at a fork in the path believing it would prevent any further rain that day. Their quick, trained eyes spied scampering snakes that slithered off the trail for cover.

Extra food in a Zairian household or an extra large field of whatever crop the wife was raising meant that relatives and friends felt freer to sponge off of them. To avoid the curse of someone saying, "Your field is so large!" and thus causing it to be quickly used up, villagers planted a certain plant that all recognized to protect it against this curse. Such superstitions still prevail among some of our friends.

After more than two hours of steady walking from the river, we saw a village where the lawns were being cut and fertilized automatically by cows, woolless sheep and goats. Small, traditional village homes were artfully placed along a well-swept path. We visited the village basket-maker.

Every household had one of his baskets to carry food, firewood and hoes to and from the homes to the fields. Another type of basket, the manioc flour sifter, was elongated and closely woven. It had a substantial rim at the top, where the powder was introduced. After filling the basket and gripping the rim with two hands, they sifted by keeping rhythm, twisting the basket back and forth from side to side.

A third type of basket, for fishing, had sharp, swirling spikes inside, pointing downward. When a fish got inside, it couldn't get back out. They had all the materials needed for these baskets, growing right in their backyard forest.

A blacksmith worked under a wall-less roof, with homemade bellows, his feet fanning the small flame. Arrows for hunting animals were his priority. He displayed homemade knives, hoping we would be a customer.

Under a large tree, we visited the village carver. He chipped away at a large log to hollow it out. He aimed to make it tall enough and deep enough that mortar wouldn't cause manioc flour to fly out while it was being pounded. This was their blender and food mill. I felt that God was so good in providing all these materials and the know-how to hand fashion them.

Surprisingly, the village women and their children coming from

22 surrounding villages were better dressed than most isolated Zairian villages. We asked how they did it. We were told it was because of rocks.

"Rocks?" I asked. " What do you mean?"

"They pick up diamonds out of the stream close by and exchange clothes for them," they replied.

During instruction, Sarah, Mama Makeka and I each taught them a different subject. Mine covered *Kindokism* (witchcraft or witch hunting), something they dealt with every day. When someone became ill, they thought of their enemies.

"Who have I offended?" they would ask. "Why do they wish me evil or death?"

In their eyes, they were being cursed. In the old culture, there were no natural deaths. All came from curses. Some students asked me at different times where Cain was. Since God placed a mark on him to protect him, he should still be alive today.

We explained that we as Christians had no right to indulge in this. If we had injured or wronged someone, we must go and make it right. We who are truly born again are in the hands of God. His blood covers us. No evil power can touch us without His permission. No one can take us out of God's hands.

In the second half of the service, we divided into three groups. Mama Makeka took the women who knew only the tribal language. Sarah took the other older women, while I took the younger ones.

Many women confessed they were either involved in or in fear of kindokism. Some confessed that since they had no children, they felt they had to prove they weren't the cause; therefore, they became unfaithful. Some said their husbands wanted to leave them. Others claimed they had already left.

The heathen believed in reincarnation into their direct descendant. That made them feel they had to have children. Many of the dear village women requested that we pray for them. They wanted to live victorious Christian lives.

Zairian pastors know they must preach from the Word of God so that their flocks may be fed and taught Bible truths about these erroneous beliefs. Then, they will grow in the faith and find perfect peace in the Lord.

CHAPTER 15

WATER BARRELS AND KEROSENE-RUN REFRIGERATORS

After only six weeks of furlough, I was on my way back to Zaire again for the new school year, so as not to lose the government pay for my teaching position and the return ticket from the United States. The mission board received my wages as a foreign teacher, then paid my regular salary.

Arriving in New York on our way back to Zaire, a missionary friend and I went through the metal detector at the airport. Unexpectedly, the machine went off when my companion went through the gate.

"Well, friend," I said, "take off your metal badge." Even though she did, it still sounded.

"You missionary," I teased, "what are you hiding?"

Later, she realized she had hid metal hair curlers on top of her head to make hairs stand up instead of ratting them. The machine knew all about it, just as our Heavenly Father knows everything about us - even though it may be hidden from our eyes.

After landing in Kinshasa on September 2, 1972, the Larry Priebs, Helen and I flew to Kajiji on a Missionary Aviation Fellowship plane. We could take only a few things along with us on this flight. Even some of the fresh foods we had bought in Kinshasa had to stay for the next flight or the truck to bring it to us.

I knew that when we arrived, even though we would be low on food, our neighbors would help us out until our things got there.

Each year, we saw changes in Zaire. Our goal was to turn over our jobs to the Zairians as soon as they were able to do them. Then, the role of girls' secondary school dorm mother would be transferred to one of them. The elders and a Zairian pastor would choose her. I would still oversee her at the dorm, but I had my 28 hours per week of teaching to prepare for.

Thus in 1972-73, we made good progress toward indigenizing God's work on this isolated mission station.

My home was only a stone's throw away from the renovated high school dorm. Built for our missionary high schoolers, it had served us well. Now, it became three much-needed apartments. Since independence, missionary children attended the American schools in Kinshasa.

One day, when I went to enter my front door, a snake had the same idea. I called Larry Prieb, a teacher at Kusemuka's Mennonite Brethren high school. He, together with some Zairian friends, killed it.

Ecole Belle Vue, purchased for the missionary children's school before Kajiji became our station, was about a mile and a half from the mission. Here could be found the medical school and Kusemuka's high school girls' dorm, the Mennonite Brethren high school, three apartments for expatriate teachers, and Zairian teachers' homes.

Walking the mile and a half to the mission from Ecole Belle Vue took time. Helen Toews and Arlene Gerdes, missionary nurses, decided to make a short-cut path just for themselves. They cut a path through tall elephant grass, starting from Arlene's front door, and heading north.

After about three-fourths of a mile, the path met the main one-way dirt road leading to the mission. Soon many of her medical students and friends found this supposedly hidden path and followed it daily.

Larry, a teacher at Kusemuka, and Grace Prieb and family lived next door. My dog let us know each time anyone came close to my door. This meant that he constantly awakened my neighbor's baby. Could I change the path to go outside my immediate yard?

Eventually, two trenches were dug around my yard, one on the east side and the other on the south. These deep ditches were

Our running water came from water caught in rain barrels set upon poles cut from the forest or stone platforms. Citizen Lubambu, mason and gardener.

filled with compost from dirt found under forest trees and table scraps from the kitchen compost hole.

Not long afterwards, cuttings from lantana bushes and bougainvillea and trumpet flowers were planted there. Outside of this was planted a row of thistles found in an abandoned yard at the mission. A convenient path then formed right outside of the hedge leading to the other path.

What a relief when my dog just let me know someone was coming to see me, instead of barking at everyone who passed! Now, cattle wandering around the mission were kept out of my yard. It was true that snakes could hide easier when the hedge got thicker, but it was worth the privacy.

When company came, my dog would lie down at my feet. When people said goodbye, he too had something to say. As they left, he too got up - on all fours - and demanded attention. When I corrected papers in the evening, he would often push my hand making it impossible to continue until I found out what he wanted.

After guests left one day, I suddenly remembered that I hadn't locked the home economics building. When I walked to the building a block away, he was at my heels to protect me all the way. At night, he slept outside near the night watchman.

As I walked into my home one day, I noticed water running down the hall. This hallway ran all the way from the front door to the door leading to the verandah connecting the two other apartments.

I followed the stream of water and soon discovered that it came from a precariously tilted rain barrel outside my bathroom wall. The forest poles on which the rain barrels stood needed replacing.

My house help soon got some of his friends to cut new poles, wood that white ants wouldn't eat. After placing the barrels on the new termite-repellent poles and after the hoses leading from these water barrels were connected leading into the bathroom, I prayed for rain so that I would again have running cold water in my bathroom. For without electricity we had no noises of a hot water tank.

I now eyed my kerosene-run refrigerator. It worked like an Aladdin lamp. Tonight it seemed to be doing all right. Just yesterday, I had worked hours on it, trying to regulate the wick. After I thought it was working well, I came back to see the wall and ceiling showing signs of smoke rising from the temperamental cooling apparatus.

My refrigerator would freeze the things on top, but the things in the refrigerator itself stayed warm..

A new refrigerator was ordered. Again, I was given a wick kerosene type, although I told them that I preferred a butane one. It ended up keeping the things cold on the bottom but wouldn't freeze anything on the top. It took two to keep my food from spoiling.

Finally, after using three barrels of kerosene and starting on the fourth, I found out that both refrigerators started to work properly. Dirty kerosene had hindered both from functioning as they should. I prayed that God would continually cleanse me so that a dirty heart wouldn't hinder me from functioning properly for Him.

No televisions, no concerts, no restaurants, no hotels for night lodging graced the area. No movie houses had ever been heard of on this bush station. Eating around a friend's table provided great enjoyment.

One evening, Jan and Bob Buhr invited all of us to join them for a fondue supper. As often happened, we hardly started eating before the doctor received an emergency call. He no sooner got back when we heard someone clearing his throat at the door.

Jan went to see who it was. She came back and asked her husband whether they should buy a piece of hippopotamus meat. After dickering price with the hunter and coming to an agreed amount, she hurriedly cut up small pieces of the "delicacy" to add to an already complete fondue.

A young intern, now learning all he could about tropical medicines, planned to stay for about two months. As he enjoyed the feast with us, his fork had a piece of meat on it. His appetite had already been satisfied, so he forgot about the added treat on the end of his fork. All of a sudden, he said, "Oh, my hippo!"

From then on, when something went wrong, we said, "Oh, my hippo!"

In mid-November, my thoughts turned to Christmas. Here in the bush, could I really successfully bake a fruitcake? This became a challenge. In my back yard was a tree we called Jerusalem cherry. What about those pineapples growing nearby, and the citric peelings from our few oranges?

Could I candy all these and add a variety to the batter? Raisins from California had been bought in Kinshasa. Dates shipped in from Egypt stayed in my barrel to keep them bug free.

In one offday I candied the fruit and cut it up. The next day, I sifted flour from the barrel with a silk stocking to remove the worms and bugs. I converted white sugar to brown by adding maple flavoring.

Eggs, brought to the door by a villager, received the usual test. Those that laid flat in the water always proved fresh. I had just enough for my fruitcake. What fun it would be to serve this treat!

One evening shortly before Christmas, I felt an urge to go down to the mission, after the light plant came on, to make divinity fudge. Carrying my electric beater in one hand and shining a flashlight in the other, I took the path to be sure not to step into a horde of drivers ants. (If I were a Zairian girl, this walking alone at night would be out of the question. Since I was an outsider, it was safe.)

When almost finished with candy-making, we noticed the lights flickering - warning that the electric plant was about to be turned off for the night. We brought out kerosene wick lamps to finish our task.

Now my spare time was spent baking Christmas cookies, for company was coming our way. Hopefully, the hunter would soon come around with meat to sell. It seemed that everyone from our mission in Kinshasa and Kikwit just had to get out of those cities at times to visit the scenic, cooler mission station at Kajiji, about ten miles from the Angolan border.

Kajiji had mail service every two weeks. If for some reason, when guests arrived by plane, the pilot had forgotten to pick up the mail bag, sad faces greeted the guests. This rarely happened. Mission aviation pilots knew the importance of mail. They did their job of mail carrier well.

At Kajiji, the last vehicle on the station had given up its ghost several months ago. Another one had been ordered, but hadn't come yet. Our guests that didn't come in carryalls had to beg rides from those who did, or walk.

On December 27, the plane brought Bob and Wanda Kroeker and their three children, Cherie, Gordon and Cindy. Some of the children had been born at Kajiji. Their parents knew that the mission doctor and Helen Toews, a midwife, would give them top medical care.

Now, the children looked over the mission station, climbed down the mountainside and waded in nearby rivers to get a feel of the place where some of them had been born. After dinner at my home, we played games.

That same day, the Ben Klassen family and friends - a party of seven - drove up. Not long afterwards, a group of six teachers came, and soon we had 17 guests in all. "Be not forgetful to entertain strangers: for thereby some have entertained angels unawares" (Hebrews 13:2).

We missionaries always enjoyed every minute of guest visits. In this way, we learned what was going on in the outside world.

On Sunday, Bob Kroeker and I walked down the steep mountainside together with the congregation for a baptismal service. It was held in a dammed-up stream, just below the water-wheel Jake

Nickel had built. It would have worked well if the Zairians hadn't continually stolen the pipes leading to the hospital and homes to make homemade guns out of them.

Camera in hand, I took pictures of five of my girls being baptized. Singing and praising the Lord, in between the candidates' coming and going into the water, proved very meaningful.

The road on the west side of the mountain leading up to a former leper village and tuberculosis camp, looked so inviting, because it wasn't as steep. I decided to go back that way.

Church started at 9:30 and always featured many songs. Helen counted 13 in one service. I recalled a former student of mine from Panzi. He now worked as a chauffeur helper on a truck that traveled between Kikwit and Kajiji. One day while at Kajiji, he patted his brief case.

"This is full of new songs," he said.

Last year, when he was in school, we had a group from Panzi mission station singing for church services. They sang some lovely hymns, Zairian fashion - swaying rhythmically. He asked whether different groups still sang for us. When I said *yes*, he said, "I am ready to teach them some new songs."

I finally learned that he was the author of most of the songs that Zairians now sang.

After the song service, a pastoral prayer preceded Bob Kroeker's fine message in the trade language, Kituba. He helped the new candidates for church membership as they learned to grow in the Lord.

Communion was served just after the new baptized members were received into the church by laying on of hands and prayer over each one of them.

My mind at times strayed to the kitchen, wondering about Sunday dinner. When they announced a business meeting, Wanda and I walked out, knowing we had hungry children - among others - to feed. Our Zairian friends looked upon time so differently.

In between entertaining our guests, we wrote letters to go off on the plane when our guests left. When all 17 had taken to the road, either by plane or vehicle, we could relax. Two missionary nurses, Sarah Peters and Arlene Gerdes, invited us over for borsht and games - a most enjoyable time for the whole missionary staff.

When New Year's day came, I still had many cookies and part of my fruit-cake left. I went to the mission for a coffee break. Someone had made the traditional fritters, called *porzelchen*. I even exchanged some of my Christmas bakings for Jan Buhr's fresh New Year's cookies!

One pygmie played a home made stringed instrument.

CHAPTER 16

HELEN AND I, GORILLAS AND PYGMIES

Both missionaries on a bush mission station close to the Angolan border, Helen and I had a limited amount we could spend on a vacation. Since the Mission Board paid for our trip to Kinshasa for a missionary conference, we decided to benefit from already being in the capital city and go from there to begin our vacation.

I had to get away from the six-day-a-week school. Helen needed to escape for a while from the constant day-and-night knocking at her door for medical help. We were not tired *of* the work, but tired *in* the work. We decided to go east, to see gorillas out of Bukavu and pygmies in the jungles outside of Beni, both close to the eastern border.

On July 16,1973, we drove through the congested traffic of Kinshasa, dodging overcrowded mini-buses with both well-dressed and ragged men hanging on to the back for lack of space inside. We had to stop suddenly when a driver in front of us stopped his car to talk to someone on the side of the road. We could hardly wait to get out of this kind of jam.

At the travel agency, they told us that our plane had changed its schedule. Instead of boarding for a 2:00 a.m. departure, it would leave at 12:30 p.m. On the way to the airport, we passed hundreds of half-built brick houses. Zairians could not get loans to build, so each time they had a little money they would buy several cement bricks. They literally built their houses brick by brick, taking years to complete.

After flying for some time, we came to our first destination. Helen and I wondered about the crowds as we landed in Kisangani. We soon learned they were waiting for the leader of all Zaire, Mobutu Se-Se-Seko.

In the crowd, we finally spotted a familiar, pale face. Martha Willems, my friend from Kipungu and Kikwit days, met us. On furlough, she had earned her degree in Library Science and was now living here, employed by the University of Kisangani.

The next morning, our plane was scheduled to leave at 8:30. a.m. We finally boarded it at 1:00 p.m. This was typical Zaire. We heard no reason for the delay. At Kindu, we transferred to another plane. Quite a commotion ensued. The airline had overbooked.

A Zairian nun, already on the plane, had to give up her seat. Determined not to be put off, she pretended to faint. In spite of this, they pushed her out the door. The pilot cut off the motor and came back to see what was going on. The nun appeared at the door again, then fainted into the plane. Finally, they gave her a seat, saying they had miscounted.

We arrived at Bukavu, our second stop on a long list of goals. Our hotel, on the shore of the colorful Lake Kivu, had a hall window from which we could see two sides of this body of calm, blue water. The road wound out onto a peninsula covered with tropical beaches, blooming trees, ferns and clinging vines.

We were warned not to drink the water, but it came in bottles so we took a chance. We also bought strawberries and enjoyed them immensely.

After searching for some time, we finally met my friend Louise Moore from Belgian days. I had not seen her since 1960, when we studied French together. She had left for Rwanda as a missionary, while my goal had been to get back to Congo. After spending one night in the hotel, we accepted her invitation to spend the next two nights as her guest.

That evening, a Mr. Lovely from the American Embassy came to see Louise. At his request, she shared some of her experiences as a missionary while still across the border in Rwanda. She said there was a civil war, one tribe against the other. Every time their school would hire a new teacher, he would disappear.

Louise hid a black mother and her small children in her home. The mother's husband and two other members of her family had already disappeared. The lady she was protecting was sure that her husband was dead.

When the Rwandans would ask for this mother and her children, Louise would have to lie and say they were not there. She was able to protect them because they were Belgian citizens. Finally, the Belgians smuggled the black mother and her two children to safety. Louise now served as a missionary in Zaire until her adopted country would be safe for her to return.

On Friday, our guide took us around the lake on the airport road and then on a bumpy side road to see the gorillas. After seeing guinea pigs and monkeys, we came upon the gorillas. One seemed to be six feet tall. All had glistening black, short-cut hair. They watched us intently with their deep, inlaid eyes. As they moved slightly, we saw plainly their huge leathery black noses and black beards. They moved back and forth, displaying muscular legs as they analyzed our every move.

They put us on the alert, for they seemed to be beckoning us for a peace treaty. "Leave *the gorilla* alone and he'll leave you alone," said the Zairians, who knew well this proud, muscular creature.

It is a miracle that any of these peaceful animals still exist. In 1846, missionaries spied on them and published their existence. That brought scientists out to hunt skeletons for every museum in the civilized world. They tried to prove that man came from them. To justify such massacre, these "heroes" invented atrocity stories of the rape of women and murder of men. They drew imaginary pictures of hideous creatures more than six feet tall, swinging clubs.

In 1925, Baron Cartier de Marchienne coined the slogan, "The world must be made safe for gorillas." King Albert of Belgium organized a gorilla sanctuary, which later became the nucleus of the Kivu National Park, in Zaire.

Any animal, even the gorilla when it is provoked, will rise to protect himself. This great creature rises to his full height, beats his chest and cheeks, then bellows to frighten off the intruders. His family prudently melts away into the forest for security.

On Saturday, Helen and I decided to leave for Goma. We packed our bags and a lunch for a boat trip across Lake Kivu.

On that five-hour, smooth, but crowded trip, smoke from dry season burnings caused a heavy haze. In Zaire, every inch of burnable land is set ablaze while they hunt at the same time. The fire is to clear brush and filth from this third world country. They had already cleared a yard of brush away from their gardens and homes they want to save.

The air does not clear until after at least a month of good, tropical downpours. Smoke from the distant volcano adds to this haze. At Goma, we visited the lava fields - acres of hard lava wasteland. Later, we inquired at the tourist office about a safari to Park Virunga. We learned that two cars had just left that morning. We settled for going by taxi.

On the way, we saw different kinds of houses. The Zairians made use of any materials that could be easily obtained in their tropical forests. They also built houses according to tribal patterns.

When we reached the animal reserve, after seeing animals close to the road, we rented a nice room and ate tasty meals, but dared not drink their water. We had been warned by others who had become ill.

Our safari took us over a one-way trail, traveling about 25 miles per hour in order not to scare away any animals. We saw lions three different times. In a group of four or five, lions kill about 80 or 90 animals annually. Thus, a single lion kills only about 19 animals a year. He does not hunt every day. When he is satisfied and dozes on a river bank, or in the shade, zebras and antelopes browse quietly nearby.

Hyenas, wart hogs and many kinds of deer and antelope greeted us along the way. When we drove close to the lake, we gazed at water buffaloes and hundreds of hippopotamuses.

Entering the lobby of our motel, we met Jean Pierre Hallet, the author of *Congo Kitabu*. He once set up a curio shop in Bakersfield and lived next to us, but I had never met him there.

Early the next morning, we had coffee, then went out to watch the sunrise. At the same time, we saw early risers among the ani-

We saw lions three different times.

mal kingdom. At 8:00 o'clock, we went back to the motel for breakfast. After breakfast, we wanted to see a tiny African village. Elephants wandered in and out among the small, grass-roofed huts. We took pictures of one roaming aimlessly on the grassless courtyards.

Baby elephants, born after a gestation period of 20 to 25 months, weigh 200 pounds, the heaviest newborn of all land animals. For the first few days of life, it rests between the column-like legs of its mother. The cow, in the safety of the herd, could live for about a hundred years.

Among the docks on the wharf, we saw big birds. Some waded in the water. Vultures came close to the huge pile of fish. The fish were to be either salted down to dry or shipped, fresh, off to market.

Who can fathom the handiwork of the Lord's creation? Who gave our great Creator the ability to fashion a great variety of shapes and sizes of animal, bird and fish which survive using the self-defense God gave them? How can anyone deny God's existence after seeing them? "The fool said in his heart, there is no God."

Early the following day, at Goma, we went to a private airline to ask if there was a flight to Beni. They had received no gas but said if it came in, there might be a chance to fly in. We were strongly advised not to go, however. When we were told that gas had come in, our curiosity got the best of us. We decided to go to see the pygmies.

Arriving at a very small landing strip on the outskirts of a thick jungle, we made reservations for our return flight back to Bukavu. Then, we went to the only restaurant, attached to the only hotel, in this small village. After waiting for some time, the waiter came to ask us what we wanted. "Waiter, we would like to order a meal," we said. "Sorry, I'm not sure," he responded. "We have many guests today. I will see if there is enough food."

Helen glanced at me, saying nothing, but we both wondered how all this would turn out. To our great relief, they finally brought us good American food. When the waiter passed again, I asked, "You are also in charge of this fine motel *n'est-ce-pas*?"

"*Oui*," he replied, "why do you ask?"

"Do you perchance have a room with two beds for us?"

"Sorry, we are all filled up. We have special guests from Belgium and America. We have no room for you."

Looking around, we saw that Jean Pierre Hallet had a rich American with him, obviously to see the pygmies. He wanted financial support for his pet project, the pygmies.

We slowly made our way outside. Finding a bench, we sat down and wearily leaned against the motel for support. Helen's forehead creased even more than usual. She gave me a hopeless look that said, "What now?"

Soon a big truck pulled up to the side of the cafe. The motel manager came out to say that the truck driver would take us to the Catholic mission.

That night, we slept on old-fashioned camp cots without mattresses. The next morning, the sisters kindly served us breakfast, charging us only for the meal. We then asked the great question we were wondering about. "Where and how do we go to see the pygmies?"

The nuns said they had no work among them. We should go out in the middle of the main road in this town and stick out our thumb. A taxi would come by and take us to Mbau to see the pygmies.

Helen Toews greeting the Pygmies who are considered to be the earliest inhabitants of the Congo Basin.

The sisters took us to the circle on the main road in this mini-town. We stuck out our thumbs and *voila*, a taxi came by and stopped. All seats were already taken, but the driver told us to squeeze into the back seat. After we did, he took an old inner tube and tied the door shut. At least, now we wouldn't fall out or be pushed out.

We coasted down the unpaved mountainous road. At the bottom of the perilous jungle path, the driver got out and disappeared in the thick tropical foliage. He soon came back carrying full cans with water to fill the radiator.

After about an hour of swaying sideways and bouncing up and down, he told us to get out. "Walk down that jungle path," he said, "and you will run into another Catholic Mission. They will show you someone to lead you into the jungles to see the pygmies."

Specializing mostly in hunting and fishing, the pygmies lived in the forest. Agriculture remained secondary or non-existent. They are considered to be the earliest inhabitants of the Congo Basin. The remaining pygmies inhabit Tanganyika, Lualaba, Tshuapa,

Sankuru, and Bangi rivers. They also inhabit the forest of Kibali and Ituri and the region of Lake Kivu.

When we arrived, first, they danced stooping low. They wore a G-string with a piece of cloth hung onto it to make bikini pants. Next, they sang with their reed instruments. One man played a stringed instrument. It had a rounded, basket-like base. Extended from it was a long stick-like piece of wood, from which six cross pieces held the strings.

A woman sat by the open fire, preparing bananas. In the back of her, a very low hovel of a home had too low an entrance for even her to enter without stooping. The roof looked like old leaves, twigs and grass thrown over an oversized, rounded basket. One woman had found enough cloth to tie her baby to her back.

After leaving them, we walked to the dwelling place of a Belgian Catholic father. He sold us bows and arrows and bark cloth made by the pygmies. When he offered to take us to the Protestant Mission station Oicha, we didn't refuse.

We were soon outside Oicha's mission hospital. Jean showed us around, including a tour of the leper village. She demonstrated the making of shoes adapted to each individual crippled foot. If she did not make the shoes, her government subsidies would all be cut off.

Their reasoning was that leprosy caused them to lose all feelings in the affected areas. When they ran into things and wounded themselves, they ignored it. Because of this, fingers and toes became infected and fell off before they realized it. When I was young, the Lord dealt with me concerning the leprosy of sin. He forgave me and covered me with the shoe of His righteousness.

In the course of the conversation, we were told that their missionary neighbors had taken in a pygmy orphan. They came to the conclusion that they were no different from other Zairians except for their small stature.

Since Jean's neighbors had some business with the pilot of the plane we had reservations with, and since they offered us a ride, we spent the night free of charge, sleeping on the front-room floor at Jean's home.

Arriving at the airport the next morning, we couldn't help but see that the only indication that it was such was that it had a cleared area on the outskirts of a small village wide enough and long enough for a small plane to land and take off. No office or waiting room greeted its passengers on this jungle airstrip.

The clouds were low. We could clearly see that it wasn't good flying weather for a one-motored plane. We again met Jean Pierre Hallet and his rich friend. His friend nervously paced up and down the dirt runway, looking anxiously in the air for the small plane, while Pierre spun tall tales to amuse us. The secretary of this single-engine, five-seater plane was also there.

Upon arrival of the plane, the pilot checked the passenger list. "You have done it again," he said. "How could you have taken in more reservations than we have seats for? Will you ever learn?"

We all insisted that our reservations should be honored. Helen told me later that the rich American suggested that we bump her so that the rest of us could fly out. Would we get back to Goma in time for our reserved flight back to Kinshasa?

"The only way we can all go," the pilot said, looking for a solution, "is if you (pointing to a young lad) sit on the floor. This, however, will cancel out my insurance." That is what we did.

Viewing the clouds in the sky, mingled among the many towering, rocky mountains, provided a tremendous sight that again revealed God's awesome creation.

After landing at Goma, the pilot turned to me. "There are rocks in them there clouds," he said.

"What do you mean?" I asked.

"There are rocks in them there clouds," he repeated, explaining that the Ruwenzori mountains were the rocks in the clouds. They towered so high and were covered with clouds or snow, or overshadowed by tropical downpours, that many a pilot has gone down hitting those rocks, thinking they were clouds.

In Goma, we were told that the special plane that was to take us to Bukavu had already left. Would we get back to Kinshasa in time to meet our deadline for the reservation to fly into Kajiji? Helen stayed at the ticket office, for they had taken our tickets, but had not given us boarding passes.

To our relief, Amiza arranged reservations for us on a plane coming from Bukavu which was flying directly to Kinshasa. On the evening of August 27, we landed in Kinshasa. Our reservation on the Missionary Aviation Fellowship flight for Kajiji was for the next day.

Upon arrival at the airport on the morning of the 28th, we learned that the pilot did not believe we could fly from Goma to Kinshasa in one day, so they had filled up the flight with Zairians. Helen, however, managed to get on, leaving her baggage at Kinshasa. My teeth needed attention and I should see a medical doctor before flying to Kajiji. That must be why I couldn't fly in as planned. "All things work together for good to those who love the Lord." Since our missionaries also serve in Kinshasa and we have a guest house there, it was a pleasure to lengthen my stay.

After I completed my business in Kinshasa, another missionary friend and I decided to take a commercial flight to one of our mission centers leading me closer to Kajiji.

On Wednesday morning, we had someone take us to the airport. When we arrived, we found the passengers of two canceled flights waiting to take this one. Airline officials told my friend she wasn't on the list. I finally laid our tickets on the top of the rest of them when they weren't looking. They did find our names and verified our reservations.

Soon after, we happily flew over Kikwit. From here, to get to Kajiji, I needed only to have someone take me to a truck stop and pay for a two-day ride by truck over rough, one-way trails, or wait for another Missionary Aviation Fellowship flight into Kajiji. I had traveled both ways many a time, so this was old stuff to me.

CHAPTER 17

NO MORE BIBLE IN THE CLASSROOM

I n 1974, I had to hire a new cook. I introduced him to my back kitchen - a porch with a wood-burning stove. I asked him to start a fire. A few minutes later, I peeked around the corner to see what was going on. The doorway seemed to be lit up.

To my utter amazement, he had built an open, wood-burning fire right on top of the burners instead of in the fire box. Neither stove nor oven belonged in his culture. Wasn't this how he always made bonfires to cook their meals?

I called to him. After opening the fire box, I took one piece of firewood by its end, and placed the burning piece into the fire box. He marveled at this idea of caging the flames into something instead of using all the heat directly on the kettle. It took some doing to get every piece safely into the fire box.

That episode reminded me of the time I tried to introduce a Zairian cook to American-style cooking. Expecting guests, I had put a can of bouillon soup on the counter, alongside a can of fruit cocktail. When I came back from dressing for the occasion, he had opened both cans and added the fruit cocktail to the soup. I wondered how many times I made mistakes worse than these when not asking for guidance from the Lord.

Anna Goertzen had arrived and lived with me until her apartment, being renovated from a boy's dorm into a livable home, was completed. To introduce raw village girls to some of the miracles of civilization proved interesting.

Anna and I had found a battery-run slide projector, which we borrowed for the evening. Our dorm girls saw themselves on the screen for the first time. Oh, how they marveled at this! Yes, they had seen pictures of themselves, but this was different.

After showing the pictures, we took one small group at a time into my kitchen to show them the kernels of corn, like they were used to seeing. They were amazed to see these kernels jump up and come down all white and fluffy. What magic had we used in heating plain corn? We explained that this was special popping corn, not their field corn.

On Friday evenings, after our meals together, Anna and I would play games of Scrabble. We had to get our minds off of Kajiji and just have fun for a change. Even when she moved into her own apartment, we continued to eat some of our meals together.

Our teaching loads were more than full. Principal Tshinyama Aaron had given Anna several math classes (which was her specialty), as well as first- and second-grade Bible classes. Larry Prieb taught fifth-year Bible.

Mama Kabeya, dorm mother, prayed a timely prayer for the girls. While holding her youngest in her lap, she prayed for courage for each girl to deny the men.

I now had 28 teaching hours a week to prepare for, including third-year Bible. "Never a Man Spake Like This Man," written by missionary Ivan Elric, was duplicated for third-year students. They learned that the greatest teacher who ever lived was Jesus Christ.

Forty precious girls, now enrolled in this mixed junior high and high school, came to me in the afternoons for Home Economics classes. They needed to select their uniforms. After distributing them, they sat down to mend them.

For class devotions, I explained Proverbs 20. One girl

asked if that chapter comprised the dorm rules for the year. Mama Kabeya, dorm mother, prayed a most timely prayer for the girls. As she held her youngest in her lap, she prayed for courage for each girl.

Before we knew it, the school year had ended. Larry and Grace Prieb and family moved. Carry Johnson now occupied the middle apartment. Anna, Carry and I were the only expatriates left at Ecole Belle Vue. Then, without warning, the Government announced it was taking charge of all schools in Zaire.

With funds from the World Bank, the government had been paying all teachers who met their standards. Almost all schools had been started by either Catholic or Protestant Missions on mission property. We wondered if missionaries would be sent to any school they chose or placed on another station far from our own mission.

My heart missed a beat when the Government Education Office announced that after Christmas vacation no more Bible classes could be held in the schools, or during school hours. Instead, we must teach Mobutuism. Shocked, we turned to the Lord in prayer.

Wasn't the strength of our leaders and members of church due substantially to the fact that, since the first grade, they had studied graded Bible lessons? Our mission grade schools, junior high and high schools had equipped Christians to read the Word of God for themselves, to examine the Scriptures, to see that we were teaching them the truth. This edict would destroy the system.

Just before we had to quit teaching the Word of God, one of our missionary men came over and suggested that we should now turn over all Bible teaching to the Zairians. His reasoning; when pupils thought about the Word of God and what they had learned in their school days, they wouldn't think of it as something foreign, but that a Zairian had taught it. We agreed to this plan.

It was now December. The state said the children had to attend classes on Christmas Day, so we had to obey. When I turned it over and over in my mind, I finally decided maybe it wouldn't be so bad. When was Christ actually born? Who knew the actual date? Even though we could not have that day off, it didn't mean we wouldn't celebrate His birth.

Furthermore, the students from the mixed high school had been diligent in practicing the Christmas pageant they would give in church on Christmas Eve. Wasn't it much better for them to stay and present this play, instead of running off to their isolated small villages where there was almost nothing to occupy them?

Christmas day arrived. We still had liberty to teach the Word of God until January. That morning all classes marched to the mission church for a combined chapel hour. By this time, the membership of all our Zairian Mennonite Brethren churches had reached 15,900. In many communities, believers celebrated God's gift through Jesus.

I was thankful that Christmas happened to fall on Wednesday, my lightest teaching day. Second period was fourth-year English (for second-year high). They started to complain that they weren't ready for the vocabulary test I had promised them. Hadn't they stayed up late taking part in the Christmas play?

They could now study for 20 minutes, I told them, after which they would take the test. I knew that regular teaching that day was out of the question. I would be asking for trouble.

When fifth-hour came, I knew that I must face the same fourth-year English class. I met my students at the door, handing each of them a piece of typing paper. On the rail of the blackboard, easy-to-draw Christmas cards had been placed. A Bible verse in English - from the Christmas story - had already been written on the blackboard. All classes were taught in French, but this was a class to learn English.

At first, only two students walked in. The principal, looking into the classroom, asked where the rest were. I said I didn't know. Meanwhile, after looking into the classroom window, student after student slipped into their places, glad to be able to do something unusual.

Whoever heard of being given a sheet of typing paper to make a coveted Christmas card? What could be nicer than having different colors of felt tip pens to decorate this greeting card?

(Art classes with construction paper, crayons, paints and glue are not part of this poor country's school system. However, since Zaire had no patterns for sale, art classes - including water colors - were given in the sewing pattern-making school so students could draw their own. If there were any art classes, pupils came with their own simple, unlined notebook.)

By the time the class period ended, three-fourths of the pupils had successfully finished their English card and thus - in a measure, at least - celebrated Christmas.

Almost every evening, some students and teachers came knocking at my door for a place with light to study. From 7:00 o'clock to 9:00 o'clock every evening, they could prepare their lessons around my dining room table. Teachers, badly underpaid, often had no money to buy kerosene for their lamps.

This study plan proved to be a blessing in disguise. I had periodicals written in French, Kituba and Lingala, mostly Christian magazines. At 9:00 o'clock, just before they left, we had evening devotions together. Many asked questions, feeling free to talk in a small group.

Later, we would teach them in individual homes, on Saturday evenings, in connection with the church, as they showed interest. In that way, we continued to share the Word, even though we could no longer teach Bible during school hours.

The summer of 1976 found me attending a retreat at Deer Creek, Colorado. I had again received a round-trip ticket paid by the Zairian government. At the retreat, a former missionary to Zaire asked me why I even considered going back since the Bible was forbidden in the classroom. My answer: the Lord hasn't told me to stay home yet. I still had many opportunities to do personal work.

As I went back to my home, I asked myself whether the Lord wanted me to stay and take care of my aged mother or return as planned. While visiting with mother in a rest home, she said to me, "I can't even pray any more."

I reminded her that even groanings can be prayers. "....the Spirit itself maketh intercession for us with groanings which cannot be uttered" (Romans 8:26). At times, she prayed beautiful prayers. Through her prayers my answer came. She said the only thing that really mattered in life was to win others to the Savior.

My two sisters, Frances (and J.C. Krause) and Alice (and Art Newfield) lived in Bakersfield, and Art and Margie Kopper just 20 miles away, all close enough to care for Mother. Since she prayed like that, God gave me the assurance that Mother wanted me to return.

Since 1974, Pakisa Tshimika, a former English student of mine, took courses at Fresno Pacific College. He had just been accepted by a medical school in France. This would be his last year in the United States. On July 29, 1976, on his way to a fellow student's wedding, he fell asleep at the wheel. He next remembered waking up in the hospital with a broken neck.

On the evening of August 30, I flew to Fresno to see Pakisa. He lay paralyzed from the neck down. I had called long distance from Bakersfield to Fresno to my brother-in-law and sister, Lee and Florence Siebert.

"Please meet me at the airport," I said. "Could we go directly to the hospital? You know Pakisa has just been transferred there. I have *manioc* flour for him, and I must see him before I fly back to Zaire."

When Lee and I walked into the private hospital room, many college and church friends surrounded Pakisa's bed. I walked up to him and kissed him on the forehead.

"Pakisa, do you want to talk by tape to your folks?" I asked. "I am on my way back to Zaire. If so, I will take a tape back to them."

"Yes," he said, "but would everyone else please leave the room while I talk?"

"But you will be talking in a foreign language, anyway. Please, can't we stay?" pleaded the students.

"I was just kidding," said good-natured Pax (as his friends called him). "Yes, you can stay."

In Zaire, meanwhile, at the very same time that the accident occurred, his mother, Mama Makeka, had a dream.

"I saw Pakisa," she said. "All was cut. His neck was broken, but he was looking. He was not crying. I finished up the whole morning telling friends and relatives. They marveled. 'You are always having dreams,' they said. 'This gives us much pain.'"

While sitting outside their home at the mission station, Mama Makeka saw Sarah Peters, a nurse, and the doctor's wife coming down the path towards them. "They are coming to show me my dream," she said. "I have no strength."

After Pastor Tshimika and his wife walked into their home, Sarah said, "Let's pray. Pakisa has had an accident. His neck is broken. I don't know whether he will live. If he lives, his arms will not work. Nothing will work."

Mama Makeka picked up her story. "I began to cry. For 12 days I drank nothing, I ate nothing. If he dies, I will eat again. Pakisa has life. He is not eating. He is not working.

"Another day I dreamed again. Kasambashi (an elder in the church and a mission worker) accidentally set fire to our house. I had put Mukweka, our youngest, in bed.

"I said, 'Let me take my child.' The fire was burning. I entered the house. The grass roof fell all around me. It didn't fall on me. I took the child from the bed. I went outside. The fire did not touch me or the child.

"When I awoke, I said, 'Pastor (speaking to her husband, Pakisa's father),' God showed me Pakisa will bear much pain, but he will live.' "

Meanwhile, in Fresno hundreds of friends and even strangers donated money for his medical bills. Doctors, therefore, could continue therapy working all Pakisa's muscles in his arms and legs. The question still remained, Would Pakisa's arms and legs always be useless?

On September 3, I boarded a plane for Zaire. Some days later, a Missionary Aviation Fellowship plane flew us into Kajiji.

On the following Sunday after the morning message, Mama Makeka invited interested women to stay and hear the tape of Pakisa I had brought along. Even though I couldn't understand it, to see the sympathy on these Zairian women's faces told the story.

"If he had been in Zaire," his mother said, "he wouldn't have lived."

Meanwhile, my own Mother passed away at the age of 85 on October 26. She was laid to rest on the 29th. I received the message the day after she was buried. Why couldn't I have stayed with mother those last two months of her life? When groups of students and our pastor, together with elders, came over to comfort me and mourn her death, I had my answer.

"Are you going home?" they asked,

"That isn't necessary," I responded.

"Have you purchased her some material?"

"No. Why do you ask?"

"To remember you by."

"Mother's soul is with Jesus Christ her Savior, because she has received salvation as a gift. She doesn't need anything more on this earth. I mourn but not without hope."

I showed them the church album with mother's picture as she sewed to gain some money for missions. "She prayed for you and for me every day."

Again, I had the answer. God wanted me in Zaire at this time in order to witness to my students and fellow teachers in my time of sorrow.

As I returned to the task at hand, dorm food within the Zairian culture became a real challenge. Before their independence on June 30, 1960, the Belgians had made it a law that we couldn't feed our Congolese any bread. They knew that wheat could not grow in their country. If the people got hooked on bread, flour would have to be imported from that moment on.

If we insisted on feeding them our foods, imported into their country, and they craved it from then on, they would have to steal in order to keep eating like we eat. It certainly wasn't our goal to make thieves out of our friends. We tried to improve the nutrition value of their foods, but to stay within their culture as much as possible.

After independence, the American Government shipped many thousand sacks of flour to them to curb their hunger. Soon it was cheaper to buy bread on the streets of their larger centers than to buy their staple food made from the cassava root, manioc.

Zaire Protestant Relief Association, mainly supplied by the Mennonite Central Committee, shipped in bulgur (cracked wheat). We used it for two meals a week instead of rice. Soya flour and corn meal, mixed with their manioc flour, enriched its contents. We had to pay customs and transportation costs, for which dorm students were charged.

With a kilo scale in one hand, Tshilenga, a Zairian, followed me to the manioc storeroom to get the dorm's supply for a week. Without this particular food, the girls would say they hadn't eaten. We filled barrels with rice bought in season mostly at the door. That usually was served at the evening meal.

Going to another storeroom, I reached for a carton of dried fish just under the galvanized hot roof to keep it dry. He received enough pieces to feed the girls for one meal. From another barrel came *Min-*

golos (caterpillars), measured and handed out for two meals.

A barrel of thick orange palm fat was laid on its side so some of its contents could be poured into a gallon container. We added this to all meat sauces and greens. Canned fish, such as pilchards and sardines, also were given.

One day I noticed that the supply of manioc was running low. The mission truck had come. I hurriedly asked the driver to buy me a load. A runner, sent to the villages, told them which morning we would come to buy.

The day arrived. Since it was my day off from teaching, I had to make the trip with the chauffeur. We came to a village early that morning. The women came running with their baskets of smelly manioc on their heads and babies on their backs. The scale was hooked in the crook of an overhanging tree. Village women, with their colorful, worn work dresses, formed a line.

Each basket of manioc was weighed separately by placing a vine around the basket and balancing it on the lower hook. A piece of paper stating the amount of kilos her manioc weighed was given to each. Some tried to sell us wet manioc, which we refused. Although they argued loudly, they were paid the government set price.

Each basket of manioc was weighed separately by placing a vine around the basket and balancing it on the lower hook of kilo scales.

Some brought other produce from their gardens: stalks of bananas, palm nuts, dried beans, peanuts or corn. The humidity was high. So far, we had bought just one-fourth of what we needed. We inched along over the one-way trail to another center where we again set up our kilo scale. We again called for the women. Some had already left for their fields.

As we left the last village, we saw that rain threatened. The

As we left the last village, we saw that rain was threatening.

Ecole Belle Vue

Wet manioc was unloaded and put on bamboo shelves. Mama Nlemvo built a smoldering fire under the manioc to dry. Suddenly I heard screams. The manioc store room was in full flame.

truck driver, stopping to throw a tarpaulin over the manioc, grumbled under his breath. Then he made a long tssssaaa hissing sound which meant surprised anger or displeasure.

"What's the matter?" I asked.

"I forgot to tell you that the tarpaulin has holes in it," he said. "The manioc will get wet if it rains."

Just then, the rain began to fall. We decided to continue on our way to the mission station, knowing that some of the manioc - if not dried right - would mildew and spoil.

After the rain stopped, the manioc was unloaded and put into the storeroom on bamboo shelves. But we soon realized it was piled too thick to dry out. Citizeness Nlemvo, the dorm mother, knew just what to do. She built a slow, smoldering fire under the manioc to dry it out. She thought that everything was under control. She left it just for a little while.

About 9:30 that morning, we heard the students let out a loud ahhhhhaaaa! (a scream). The manioc storeroom was in full flames. With no fire truck or fire extinguisher, we quickly assembled a bucket brigade - to no avail. The hot flames consumed the bamboo storehouse in a few minutes.

The girls' dorm of the secondary school had only manioc in their part of the storeroom. A wall separated our storeroom from the medicals' food. Theirs had a whole year's supply to feed their 40 dorm students. Canned meat, powdered milk, barrels of rice and *mingolos* were all burned up.

Poor Citizeness Nlemvo had meant only good with her actions. She felt so bad that she wanted nothing more than to throw herself into the flames and die.

"What is food in comparison to a life?" we told her. "No one has died in the fire. We love you even though this accident has happened."

About five kilometers away lived an official whose office was in this region. He called me to his office to tell him just what had happened. Not long afterwards, another truck came to the station. We engaged the driver, who again drove a mission vehicle to buy a load of manioc - double expense for the dorm, but a much-needed supply.

When the government took over the schools in the larger cities, the Zairian teachers figured that it would take away a good many school supplies from our Mennonite Brethren secondary schools. The high school in Kikwit was in danger. If this occurred, the government might claim they had to distribute all things from the better-equipped schools to equalize them.

Betty Funk, principal of the Kikwit high school, had teachers asking to let them take home things like sewing machines and stoves from the home economics department, to prevent the government from taking them for other schools.

Eventually, teachers sold almost all of those precious items. At the same time, they started a girls' school within this mostly boys' high school (*"Coupe et couture cycle court"*). It offered a sewing pattern-making course, for junior high and two years for high school girls. Since they knew I was interested in an all-girls' school, they asked me to be the first principal.

"No," I said, reasoning that they had just sold all their sewing machines and had added this school. I was convinced they wanted ed me there to help replace everything that had been taken..

Kajiji was where the Lord had led me. He had blessed the efforts there. I felt no calling to return to Kikwit at this time.

Chapter 18

EVACUATION

A tropical downpour pounded noisily on my corrugated tin roof. I had just eaten breakfast and wanted to get my Kituba New Testament before walking to the mission church. Sunday school was to begin in half an hour, but I soon realized that no one would venture out with thunder rolling and lightning bouncing from tree to tree.

My second Sunday school class for the day was Doctor and Mrs. Buhr's three lovely daughters. At about 4:30, their mother Jan walked them to my home. During the Bible School hour, the youngest would sit on my lap while the other two girls huddled next to me, one on each side. These little ones needed to be taught in English in such a way that they could understand the Bible stories in terms of Zaire, but also in terms of their own Canadian culture.

After Sunday school, we held hands as we walked past the small homes of the Zairian workmen on our way to the mission. We headed for Helen and Elsie Fisher's home on the edge of the long plateau where the mission was built.

Stepping onto the verandah, which surrounded the entire house, we just had to stop and gaze at the mountains behind us. The sinking sun made the *nseki* trees and bushes seem taller than before. As the colorful rays of the sun spread from the mountains and over the valley below, Helen answered the door.

She too had to wonder at the sky turning from brilliant orange to burnt orchid to winter blue as we waited for others to join us for our evening Bible study and supper.

As we entered this unique, cool, stone building, mortared with adobe, showing every natural stone from this area, we again appreciated how its thick walls and elephant grass roof kept it cooler than our more modern corrugated roofs.

When Bible study was over, serious prayers took over. Soon one request outweighed all the others. Much unrest plagued the Zairian/Angolan border, about ten miles away. We might have to flee. Zaire hadn't recognized the Angolan government as yet.

"Get your suitcases packed just in case," we were told. Thus, we made ourselves ready to leave if necessary.

On Monday morning Dr. Buhr, who practiced at our mission hospital and taught at the nursing school, came to tell me that the Angolans had just destroyed a nearby river bridge in Zaire, between Mutetami and Kahemba.

"We almost evacuated today," he said, "but decided to wait a little longer. Word has come that the Angolans plan to first destroy several more bridges, then come to the mission to destroy the hospital."

I found it hard to understand why the Angolan government wanted to destroy this hospital. Many sick Angolans regularly crossed the border to receive medical help from us. No medical help could be found on their side for miles inland.

Our students had a few days of rest between semesters. Together with the medical students, we had spiritual emphasis week. On Tuesday, after I attended the special meeting, Dr. Buhr came walking by with his two daughters.

"I've called Missionary Aviation Fellowship to fly Jan and the girls out," he said to me. "You must also evacuate with them. You have no choice. We want only enough missionaries to stay who can escape in one vehicle. You must go."

"The kids in the high school will scatter," I said. "The school will stop. They want to get away from the border dispute, too."

"The school can't hinge on one person," Dr Buhr continued. "You have no choice. You are to fly out tomorrow with Jan, our daughters and Pastor Mubibo."

That evening, as I packed my dishes and cooking utensils, many questions kept popping into my head. The hospital and school didn't need four nurses and several students to hold down the fort. "Why can't some of them go and let me stay?"

When I asked Dr. Buhr this, he said: "They are all living at the mission, but you are living apart at Ecole Belle Vue."

"But what about Carry Johnson (a Christian Service teacher living in an apartment next to mine)?" I asked.

"He is a man."

Kasai, a worker, had been absent from Saturday through Tuesday. When he came on Wednesday, he wasn't surprised to find me packing. He said some villages close to the Angolan border had been forced to work for their enemies, the Angolans. If they refused, they were beaten.

These villagers obediently cut wood for their enemies across the border. The huge river that marked the border between Angola and Zaire hadn't always been the border. All of Kajiji had at one time belonged to Angola.

To leave on short notice wasn't easy. In my office, we had a duplicating machine used for the high school's legal forms, exams, and other papers. The office also had contained my personal effects, including many valuable books.

Knowing their poverty and their temptation to steal, I felt compelled to take the personal belongings out of the room. In that way, the principal of the high school could freely use the duplicating machine in my absence.

In my kitchen, I left only a broken set of dishes, hoping that when I returned they would still be there. My mind went back to my return from furlough in 1962. All my dishes had been stolen.

So many things needed attention before my taking off. I checked them off, one at a time. I had paid my garden helper through March 9. I hoped he would be able to keep my chickens alive and also look after the much-needed garden.

When it came to the material for school uniform skirts, there was just too much to leave behind. Why not let Zairian mission mothers buy yardage and reduce my inventory? In between packing, our friends came to buy the coveted skirt material.

I kept one ear tuned to the radio. When Kinshasa announced they had recognized Angola's government, I wondered if the border dispute might come to an abrupt end. Would I still have to evacuate?

As I continued packing, two missionary nurses invited me to their home for the evening meal. Then they took over some of the tasks yet to be done.

We expected to fly out early Thursday afternoon. The shortwave radio informed us that the small, one-motored Missionary Aviation Fellowship plane couldn't leave the airport because of a sudden tropical storm. Finally, it cleared up enough so that by 5:00 o'clock we could fly out.

But our final destination required a two hours' flight and sundown was only an hour away. Since the planes never fly after dark, the pilot called by shortwave and informed the Eidses at a nearby mission station we would be spending the night with them.

That evening, we joined them for supper. Then, a game of Scrabble took our minds off the crisis. (Were the Eidses ever good at the game!)

The next morning, as Jan and I stripped our beds, we heard a rattling sound. Jan quickly stepped into the next room and was aghast to find her youngest, Stephanie, sitting on the floor besides an empty tin cup with three sucked-on pills close by.

As a nurse, Jan recognized the pills as worm medicine. She knew that her daughter thought they were a chocolate-coated candy, called smarties. She called our hostess, asking her how many worm pills had been in the cup.

"Thirteen!" she answered, after checking the patient list.

Being a good missionary, with also many household duties to perform, she was not careless, but did not expect any children that day. She had taken the pills to her home so she could treat people quickly. She had taken us in, going out of her way to help in evacuating missionary neighbors.

Both nurses tried in vain to get Stephanie to throw up. We hurried to the plane, carrying our breakfast of pancakes in plastic bags. Then, we had a brainstorm. Why not try to contact the child's father, Dr. Buhr, at Kajiji, by shortwave? While they did this, Jan and I enjoyed a couple of swallows of coffee.

To our relief, Dr. Buhr said this type of worm medicine wasn't toxic. We thanked God for His goodness in providing protection for a lovely missionary's child. We again rushed to the airport, a cleared strip of land about three miles from the mission station.

Stephanie did manage to throw up some there.

We would fly to Kikwit as planned unless Stephanie became ill. If she seemed sick, we would fly just a little further and land at Vanga mission station, home of a good medical doctor and hospital. On the way, she seemed fine so we landed in Kikwit.

Seated at the table with friends, we all fixed our eyes on Stephanie. She was hyper, threw up some, but kept coming back for more to eat. The nurse decided she was a very sterile child, having had that many worm pills pass through her. Our good God loves the missionary children and stops to hear their simple prayers - and ours.

On Monday, I flew to the capital of Zaire, Kinshasa. Here I decided to make good use of my time, buying for both the school and myself. Kajiji stores had almost nothing to sell.

While having my devotions one evening, I heard the Lord speaking to me through Proverbs 2:21-22, "For the upright will live in the land and the blameless will remain in it. But the wicked will be cut off from the land, and the treacherous will be uprooted from it."

God had assured me I would soon return to Kajiji and continue in the mission work there. Later, we learned that the Angolans considered Kajiji a camp to train enemy soldiers. When they realized this was not the case, our mission was out of danger and I could go back inland.

Sewing was an informal class. When study hall wasn't in session next door, the girls were allowed to sing quietly while they kept time with their needles and sewing machines.

Citizen Pakisa Tshimika (center) talks with Nurse Lubi (left),Director of Public Health, and citizen Mukungula (right).

CHAPTER 19

A DOUBLE MIRACLE

Sewing was an informal class. When study hall wasn't in session next door, the girls could sing quietly while they kept time with their needles and sewing machines. Beautiful harmony came natural to them. Malu, (not her real name), taken in by singing the message of the Second Coming of Christ, said, "When He comes to get us, I'm not staying here. I'm going with Him!"

"Do you think He will take those who are always cheating on their exams?" I asked.

"I used to cheat, but I don't anymore!" she responded.

Some time previously, we had been challenged by Bible Emphasis week. Mr. Guy, a dedicated, French-speaking missionary from Switzerland, exhorted us not only to believe - for even Satan knows God exists - but also, in receiving Christ, to live a changed life. He taught songs with Biblical passages, still sung among them today.

Chapel, now held before the morning recess on the verandah beside Carry's front door and my side door, worked out just fine. Marching in, a class at a time, they quickly grabbed seats knowing that the last ones would have to stand. Different teachers took charge of chapel periods. When my turn came, I felt led to share a true story.

A tradesman, unfamiliar with the huge Zairian River in Kinshasa, wanted to show others he could swim across to Brazzaville. About one-third of the way across, crocodiles followed him. He hadn't seen them, but the people on the shore screamed at him to turn back.

He thought they were just afraid he didn't have the strength to swim across the rapid river. He kept on going, not knowing that he needed saving. The crocs got him. Satan, like those crocs, is after all of us. But many don't even realize they need rescuing.

After hearing the story, one pupil told me he now understood why he needed to be saved. He was one among many of our 200 students who had decided to follow Christ.

Earlier, one of the students said he wanted to be baptized. He added that all members of his family were heathens. I tried to explain that baptism wasn't the main issue. Later, I asked him whether he had trusted Christ.

"Yes," he replied.

When I asked him if he would pray in chapel, he hesitated. So I asked everyone to pray the Lord's prayer together. Later, I talked to him again. "If you're not real sure you have been born again," I said, "please come over and I will show you the way."

Several days later, he came to me and asked Christ into his heart and life. He knew that persecution would follow if he really lived for his Lord and Master - for him, and actually for all who name the name of Christ.

How could we have chapel services and Bible Emphasis Week when such activity had been forbidden? About a year and a half after the prohibition order, Mobutu Se-Se-Seko decided to rescind it. He noticed that the morality of Zairian youth had deteriorated so fast that he decided mission stations should be in charge of schools again. All schools could again teach God's precious Word as part of the school's curriculum. That miracle came straight from the hand of our loving Heavenly Father.

About two years after Pakisa's accident, all Kajiji missionaries met in Kinshasa for a church convention with Dr. Donald McGavran. One evening, Arlene Gerdes and I went to the post office and found a telegram that had been sent two weeks earlier.

Its message: Pakisa, along with Ann and Wes Heinrichs (Pakisa's adopted United States parents), were coming from Fresno, California. They would land at an airport about 20 miles from Kinshasa that very evening.

I offered to drive out to get them. That would have been out of the question if we were not sure a man would be in the car on the way home. Girls just do not drive that airport road alone at night.

Arlene and I took the mountainous country road out. When we

got to the airport, in order to park, I drove down the old driveway. A police officer stopped me, took my driver's license and escorted me into his office.

"Did I do something wrong?" I asked.

"Yes," he said, "you took Marshall Mobutu Se-Se-Seko's private pathway. It is open only to the leader of this country. I will send a copy of this infraction to your Embassy."

"Citizen, the sign was not clear to me," I said. "Have others done this too?"

"It is true," he replied. "We catch many in this mistake."

After talking a while, he returned my driver's license and let me go. Satan, the accuser of the brethren, tries to trick us into taking wrong paths. My advocate, Jesus Christ, has paid the penalty and pleads my case daily before the Throne of God.

Soon we saw smiling Pakisa on the airport runway, sitting up in a wheel chair manned by Wes, his American father. He could now sit up and even use his hands. The question still remained, will he ever walk again?

The next morning, they had reservations on Air Zaire for Kikwit. They wanted to stop there en route to Kajiji to see Pakisa's folks and friends. I drove them to the airport. When we arrived, the plane was just taking off - without them. Air Zaire had overbooked. On the way to the guest house, we went through town and stopped at Air Zaire travel agency for new arrangements.

"I'll stay in the car," I said. "This corner is known for thieves."

I locked all the doors. After a while, a teenager tried to unlock the back door without being seen. I managed to scare him away. Another young man soon played with the back tire. "Get out!" I shouted. He finally left after a policeman pointed his finger at him. (In Los Angeles, one sometimes gets shot by the thief!)

The next morning, we went to the open market. Pakisa met many of his friends there. People stared at the sight of a foreigner pushing a Zairian in a wheelchair. Pakisa introduced Wes and Ann Heinrichs to many of his friends.

"I want you to meet my American mother and father," he said. "They are also members of the Mennonite Brethren Church - but in Fresno, California. They took me in just as if I was their own son."

"When did you get here?" they asked.

"Just day before yesterday," he replied.

"Are you going back to white man's land?" they wanted to know.

"Yes, but first I will see my parents," he said, smiling. "Then, Wes and Ann are taking me to America by way of the Holy Land to see where our Lord Jesus Christ lived, died and rose from the dead for us."

"Go well, Pakisa!" they shouted.

"Stay well, Citizen Muntu," Pakisa answered.

While at Kinshasa, Pakisa gave his personal testimony in the English-speaking, interdenominational church. He explained how, after his car accident, he lay for weeks on end while hospital attendants came in many times a day to flex muscles in his legs, arms and fingers.

He told how donations from all over Fresno flowed in from people he had never met. His voice became husky as he leaned hard on the pulpit for support. He then took hold of one of his fingers from his right hand.

"When you move even one finger," he said, "can you not see God at work?"

People all over the audience wept, unashamed to show they were moved by the miracle God had done for Pakisa. Doctors had said he would never even be able to sit up again.

Several days later, after a picnic and ensuing prayer meeting, someone suddenly asked for attention.

"Please, everyone, be absolutely quiet," he said. "Do not move. Do not speak. Pakisa must not be distracted in any way. He must concentrate completely on every muscle he is to move."

With that, Pakisa stood up. He took one faltering step, with no one holding him. He took another, then another as he inched slowly across the room. We all held our breath, unable to believe our eyes. When he sat down, we all shouted out in unison: *"Pakisa, you are walking! You can walk!"* "But the doctor said you would never walk again," someone said. "Please explain!"

"God has worked a miracle in my body," he responded. "Praise the name of our Almighty God! Praise His name forever!"

After a short visit with his parents, Pakisa returned to California to complete his studies. He now walked with a cane. After receiving his Master's degree in Public Health at Loma Linda, he returned to Kajiji. Reaching many remote villages, sometimes even by helicopter, he helped villagers with medicine and gave them the precious Word of God.

After a number of years of service, he again returned to Loma Linda and gained his Doctorate in Public Health. In 1992, he and his wife Linda returned to Zaire, serving the Lord and His people as director of health and development for the Zaire Mennonite Brethren Church.

In 1997, he serves as Regional Secretary for Zaire and Angola, while his wife Linda is Zairian Team Leader.

When exam time came, all the students had more than a week of finals. Some of our students went almost wild as they realized they hadn't kept up with their studies.

Some bought fetishes, believing this would help them in the exams. They soon realized that these fetishes were powerless to make up for lack of study.

We arranged classrooms by crowding desks together into two of the four whitewashed rooms. Numbers, written with chalk on the desk tops, indicated where each student would be located. Two large charts, one for each room, listed all the students from the different classes, mixing them up so that no two students from a given class would sit side by side during exams.

On the day before the exam, the teachers had each exam approved by the principal. Then, they were kept under lock and key. The principal asked me to sleep in the same room with the exams, for fear of someone breaking into the duplicating room to steal a copy.

One day, a pupil came bursting in and grabbed the carbon that went under the stencil. He explained that his shoes needed shining. Instead of grabbing the carbon from him, the teacher simply rewrote the entire exam.

When teachers entered the classroom the following day, students sat in their respective places. We asked members of each class, in turn, to raise their hands, not only to give them their exam for that hour but also to see again if any were within eye-shot of their fellow classmates. We collected any scrap of paper they brought into the class, but at the same time gave them paper on which they could do any figuring needed for the exam.

Every teacher knew what period and which day they were to supervise. Their exams would be supervised by another. They remained in the room only long enough to answer pupils' questions as to how to mark their exam.

The exams at the end of each semester counted more than the entire year's work. Since each class had at least 21 subjects, almost every student flunked a course or more. After reviewing for an extra week, they could retake the exam if they had flunked three subjects or less.

Grade points were added up and report cards were handed over to the principal. All teachers met together with him to decide, class by class, pupil by pupil, who would pass, retake the year, or drop out of school. After handing back all school books, our vacation started.

Helen and I flew out of Kajiji to Kinshasa, glad to be on our way home. When we arrived at the guest house, we were told that Arn Prieb had gone to the government Education offices many times. Still they hadn't issued our tickets.

The next morning, Arn took us to the Education offices. Nurses, medical doctors and school teachers crowded around, also looking for their tickets to their respective countries. We made no visible progress that day, or the next day. We spent a whole week of precious vacation time going from one office to another.

One day, while waiting in our car outside a store, I met Dr. Fountain's wife, from the Vanga mission station. She said she had seen my name on a list. We hurriedly went down, only to be told that the tickets would be issued at another office. Helen and I lost no time going to the designated place where we finally received our tickets.

We went home with this truth ringing in our ears! Zaire wasn't saying, "Missionary go home!" Rather she was saying, " Missionary come back!" They needed high school teachers, Bible teachers to present graded Bible lessons, maintenance men and evangelists who could reach the unreached.

A visiting educational inspector had expressed a new interest in opening all-girls' schools, especially in the field of ("*Coupe et Couture Cycle Long*") pattern-making. How would we respond to the challenge?

PART THREE
GOD HAS DONE IT FOR ZAIRIAN WOMEN
1978–1987

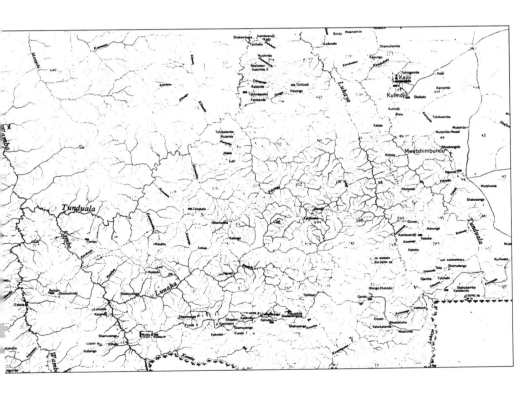

We Kajijiites invited all Mennonite Brethren missionaries to a spiritual retreat:
Back Row: Arn Prieb, Dr. Bob Buhr, Anna Goertzen, Dorothy Kopper, Carry Johnston, Jake Nickel.
Front Row: Helen Nickel, Murry Nickel, Reynold Nickel.

Diane Jost had taken sewing in high school and knew just how to make all those sewing samples.

CHAPTER 20
HELPING ONE ANOTHER

In the spring of 1978, a Zairian educator came to our mission at Ecole Belle Vue. Principal Tshinyama Aaron of the mixed secondary school received him. For some reason, they started talking about the Zairian Education Department's concern for their girls.

Two different permits had been recorded for the right to open an all-girls' school in this area. The visiting educator asked if we as a mission could possibly manage one. Principal Tshinyama knew that I had a number of sewing machines and an active food lab where the girls were already being taught basic nutrition. He asked me to apply.

"No," I said. "If you Zairians want this school, you will have to apply."

Thinking maybe this would become a reality, I decided to learn more about the pattern-making high school.

That same semester, Steve and Diane Deckert Jost wrote that they were planning to come to Kajiji to teach. Joy flooded my being, for we needed them to teach in whatever school developed.

When the principal heard about Diane's coming, he placed her name and mine on the application form he sent in for the pattern-making high school.

Ludima Short had opened that type of school for her mission at Nyanga station. In spite of not feeling up to par, I decided to go visit her school. If I didn't go now, I knew another opportunity might not present itself.

When I arrived at Nyanga, Ludima met me. There I saw Mr.

Rocke, who had been a fellow traveler on the Bastogne freighter in 1952. Mr. Eidse, the Bible translator from Kamiala, also was visiting Nyanga. We had a great time sharing stories of Jesus Christ helping us in our different tasks.

Next morning, in the high school classroom, I watched an advanced class measuring the human body. Then each member sketched it on a large sheet of paper. The procedure fascinated me. In another class, members showed various samples of their sewing exercises - different types of pockets, plackets and collars they had completed. Then, they duplicated the samples in intricate drawings to scale. Arrows showed the cut-down of different layers of material sewn together.

In the afternoon, I again followed Ludima to school where she gave me a copy of a course on pattern-making.

En route to Kikwit, we first flew to Kandala mission station. I had to wait there for an hour while the pilot flew Zairian pastors to their conference. This once well- established station had turned into ruins.

The *Jeunesse* (youth), called lions, wanted to destroy Nyanga, too, but some more adult-thinking Zairians stopped the rebels from doing so. Kandala Zairians wanted the missionaries to rebuild the station, but they refused because of how badly they had been treated. "Whatsoever a man sows, that will he also reap" (Galatians 6:7).

Later, I visited a Belgian Catholic-operated Sewing High School. To get there from Kikwit, I had to stick out my thumb for a commercial trucker to take me along. When we arrived in the small town, even though it was raining, the driver didn't risk taking me to the door of the Catholic school. His employer didn't want him to take any passengers along.

Umbrella in one hand and my suitcase in the other, I trudged along until I came to the convent. Since the rebellion of 1964-65, when Catholics and Protestants had been arrested and put together in small quarters, we found that we had much in common. Many lived and died together. We became friends instead of enemies. They welcomed me into their midst. The principal of the Sewing School even gave me samples of sewing exercises and let me observe her teaching.

That afternoon, I again went to class to observe commercial sewing. Each girl sat at her sewing machine. Placed in an assembly line, each girl knew what she had to do when another dress was handed to her.

The first girl sewed only the shoulders together. The next girl sewed the sides. Another saw that the skirt and blouse were sewed together. This quick, factory-like classroom completed many dresses in a short time.

I had gained a little insight into what I could be getting into if the school principal Aaron applied for became a reality. On my way home, I started drawing patterns, though I had never studied the subject in school.

When furlough time again arrived, it meant six weeks of visiting supporting churches, visiting my beloved family and attending a conference. My sister, Mrs. Frances Krause, always took me to get my wardrobe updated so I wouldn't present a spectacle in front of the churches I visited.

During the conference, Bill Wiebe and I discussed the privilege we again had to teach the Word of God in the classrooms. Then, I asked him if the Board of Foreign Missions/Services would allow me to act as principal. Principal Tshinyama had written to me that the school would become a reality in the fall.

Bill asked me who had applied for the school. I explained that it was Prefet Tshiyama. The state had asked the mission to take the school, and the Kikwit office had expressed a desire to have it.

Zairians who wanted the school asked me to be the principal. When the school passed inspection, the World Bank - through the Education Department in Kinshasa - would pay for its teachers. The students had to pay enough tuition to cover their expenses. Since I hadn't applied for this school, and since the Zairians wanted the school and had asked me to be the first principal, it would be fine.

"You went about this in the right way," he said.

At this time, Citizen Isaac Kilabi, Zairian Legal Representative of our mission before the Zairian Government, and my former head teacher at Kipungu, was in America. We talked together twice concerning this school. He said I should open the pattern-making High School.

When I arrived in Kinshasa, Missionary Arn Prieb knew nothing about the new school. Thus, I naturally thought the subject had been dropped. Passing through Kikwit on my way to Kajiji, the first Zairian I met informed me that I was to open the Pattern Making Sewing High School.

While Citizen Kilabi was in America, Citizen Matsitsa Charles took his place. He handed me an official letter stating that I had the right to start the school. The Education Office in Gungu sent me a letter giving me a number 127-770 of an official legal document stating that I should open the school. This wasn't my doing; it was a higher power at work. God was doing this!

To get a school accredited and teachers promised pay by the government takes a long time. Gungu had to report to Kinshasa; from there, final word would be given.

Returning to my "home sweet home" at Ecole Belle Vue, I put myself in high gear for the opening of the new all-girls' high school. Applications came in from prospective students, and soon we had 20 registered and attending students.

Diane Jost had taken sewing in high school and knew just how to make all those sewing samples. We two agreed on rules and regulations in the classroom. Without her, I couldn't have managed. The Lord had sent her and her husband to us.

Usually a high school in Zaire had only one major. All who attend must take all its subjects; there are no electives. That is why an all-girls' high school had been established. Girls could learn to be good housewives by sewing their families' clothes and earn a living by sewing for others or by teaching others to sew.

These 20 students also had to study math, history and geography in French (a foreign language to them). English also was a must, for they considered it a commercial language.

Later in the day, one could observe them busy measuring the body in minute detail and finishing a pattern they had drawn. Next, they cut out the garment and sewed it following the pattern of all the samples they had learned. Before receiving their high school certificate, they had to pass four days of finals given by the government.

Usually this type of school required that the girls stay in a dorm, because they needed practical experience in living in a semi-modern situation. We had no dorm in which to house them. We had 21 girls and a family of seven crammed into six bedrooms. The family stayed there because the wife served as dorm mother.

The girls studied the journeys of Paul in the book of Acts and also memorized the French Bible verses used in Campus Crusade's Four Spiritual Laws. Our goal was to establish Christ-centered homes for our Mennonite Brethren Churches in Zaire.

In 1978, the Kikwit office had registered 19,586 known church members. By 1979, their report showed 22,000. A few Baptist missionaries had turned over their mission stations to us.

"O, taste and see that the Lord is good" (Psalms. 34:8). After "tasting" all year, we missionaries at Kajiji and Ecole Belle Vue decided we needed a spiritual feast with our fellow missionaries as guests.

Invitations went out to all Mennonite Brethren workers in Zaire for almost a week of sharing and feasting. This meant looking for 30 to 40 beds. No hotels or motels existed in our area.

To complicate matters, two weeks before the date, I was called to Kikwit on business. All principals of the Mennonite Brethren schools were to be there no later than Tuesday. This was Saturday. It seemed likely I would be away for two weeks. How could I prepare for guests when I was away? It was impossible. The arrangements must be made before leaving.

My thoughts went wild. The double bed I slept in could serve as a place for two couples. How? Earlier, I had found out that box springs were just as comfortable as the innerspring mattress. The problem was to make the innerspring mattress stand up without the box springs.

Placing it on the floor wasn't a good idea, for just two months before, two scorpions and a centipede had been found in this very building. A plyboard was found, cut to size and placed over three bamboo poles, on top of the bedstead. The double bed for one couple was ready.

Cement blocks were placed in the empty apartment upon which the box springs were placed. Another couple's bed was ready. After still another couple slept for one night on their worn out coil springs and mattress, they asked for a plyboard to place between the coils and mattress. This did the trick. We used DDT to ward off mosquitoes and sand flies. Thus our guests would be comfortable.

From our corrugated roof, rain ran into rain barrels. The abundance of showers provided our "running water" for Ecole Belle Vue. Hot water for baths came from our kitchen, by filling a half barrel placed on the smoking, wood-burning stove. Thirteen guests came with kettles, buckets or pitchers for their portion, carrying the hot water to their separate bathrooms.

Since we had no electricity for nearly five years, and the collectors to recharge a car battery for solar lighting hadn't arrived, and with kerosene at a premium, our visitors were asked to bring candles.

The mission Kajiji, where the meeting was held, had electricity. After the evening services, we Ecole Belle Vuers picked up our flashlights or lanterns and walked the mile and a half to our lodging places. We lit our candles, had our devotions, blew out the flame and crawled into bed.

Food for this conference came from South Africa. All cooking and baking, done by Zairian-trained cooks in our kitchens, was supervised by all the women in turn.

Spiritual food was provided by Rev. Clark, our interdenominational church pastor from Kinshasa. This began with bread and water (nitty-gritty annoyances or the "little foxes that spoil the vines"). For dessert, he had ordered angels' food ("raised up into the heavenlies").

We parted knowing that now we could pray more effectively for each other. Some day, together with all our praying partners in Bakersfield, Heritage Bible, Rosedale Bible Church, and all our Zairian believers, we would be welcomed to that great feast of the slain lamb, to be with God for all eternity,

The first year of our school (called *Lycée Ditalenu*, "helping one another)" was all but history. School building plans had been accepted. The site was given and a few stones collected, but we needed to continue to pray for the finances. This included teachers' pay from the government. They had not yet recognized our school.

CHAPTER 21
TO BE OR NOT TO BE

When Citizen Aaron Tshinyama asked me to take the school, I told him we must have the use of the large room in the girls' dorm, then being used by the boys as a dining room.

Leading out the French doors to the south, an ample verandah narrowed itself as it skirted the length of a spacious front room. Even though it had two large picture windows, this overhang made it dark.

Dry season had arrived. All finals had been given, corrected and report cards handed out. Since this room was now empty, we decided It needed a bit of remodeling. Citizen Lubambu, the mason who had originally helped erect this building, was now called in again..

He did a real nice job and even volunteered to do a day's work for nothing. His eyes beamed when I walked to his home and presented him with a picture for his donated labor.

When my nephew and his family, Steven and Debby Siebert, Jason and Joshua came for a visit, they repaired many things. With them came a solar panel, donated by my brothers, sisters, Steven and Debby. Steven, through an interpreter, led the workers in their daily devotions. Their visit proved a great encouragement to me personally.

After one full year of school, we still had received no pay from the Zairian Education department. This had to be looked into, so I flew to Kikwit, headed eventually for Gungu. A friend took me to the truck barrier - a wide space in the road on the outskirts of Kikwit where trucks picked up passengers.

My nephew and family, Steven and Debby Siebert, Jason and Joshua's coming for a visit meant that many things were repaired. With them came a solar panel which meant light.

Some small stalls sold soft drinks, canned fish and hard-boiled eggs, good food for the truckers. My goal was to catch a ride to Gungu, where the legal registered number had been obtained for our school.

After waiting some time in vain for a ride, I saw some Zairians who recognized me. They directed me to a pastor's home, where they informed me that the Mennonite Economic Development Association truck would be going by way of Gungu.

By 12:30, I was on my way. Arriving at 7:30, I knocked at the door of a Belgian nun's mission home. They took me in without charge, treating me royally. We even discussed amicably the difference between Catholic and Protestant beliefs.

The next morning, I walked to the Education office in Gungu, just in time to join them in their flag salute. Then, they led me into rooms filled with legal documents - recorded numbers listing rights given to different schools, hospitals and dispensaries.

A clerk copied two numbers for me to check on when I got to Kinshasa. Hopes ran high that one of these would turn out to be the official number we needed. A helicopter ride had been promised me for my return to Kikwit. However, the Belgian sisters found an earlier ride back for me, so I didn't dare impose on them any longer.

While in Kikwit, I met the Commissar of the people, a representative of higher authority delegated for a special duty, Citizen Zangio. Talking over my problem with him, he asked me whether I could trust him with my legal papers.

When I asked the legal representative of our Mission what to do, he told me that the Commissar could get into offices that he himself couldn't penetrate. So he advised me to give Citizen Zangio the folder.

The Commissar's plan was to do all the needed research in Kikwit first, then meet me in Kinshasa to introduce me to the various offices there. A Missionary Aviation Fellowship plane came from a Nyanga retreat, flying by way of Kikwit to Kinshasa.

I hopped a ride to Kinshasa, where we landed at 5:45, only 15 minutes before sundown. That was cutting it a little close for a plane that didn't fly with instruments. The Lord was with us, and we arrived without incident.

On June 7, 1979, Tilly Wall left the field for America. Not yet 65, she hoped to come back to Zaire for another two years. However,

At Kanzombe the three-room dispensary was crowded with Zairians waiting for Tilly to examine.

Since Tilly Wall had delivered thousands of babies in the Kikwit area, she became a legend. Every time the Zairians saw a white lady driving a car, they would yell out, "Mama Wall."

her heart bothered her. My mind went back to a visit I had with her at Kikwit.

She had been in charge of our mission dispensary, Kinzombe. One day as we drove on our way to this clinic, we had to stop suddenly because of a washed-out bridge. After turning around, we headed back home to get a missionary friend to take us there.

He loaded two planks in the back of his pick-up and, when we got back to the river, he used them as a makeshift bridge. To get there was no problem, but now we knew we would have to find our own way back.

The three-room dispensary, crowded with Zairians, had Tilly doing the examining. Outside, a long line of people stood by an open window, waiting their turn to give a drop of blood mainly to test for malaria.

On the far north of this parcel stood the maternity ward, where many mothers had given birth. Citizeness Pangikani, a midwife and former student of mine, happily served these mothers by giving them the best care she knew how.

In the pharmacy, Citizeness Njoloko, also a former student of mine, sang while she counted out doses of worm and malaria pills. On our way home, we stopped at a grass hut where a dying cancer patient lived. He seemed full of joy - dying, yes, but sure of better times to come. He looked forward to his heavenly home, where he would meet his Master, the Lord Jesus Christ.

Then, Tilly and I walked on a path that led us ever deeper into the tropical forest. She had taken this trail hundreds of times to save child-bearing women's lives. Now we walked together, stopping just long enough to enjoy a picnic lunch under the tropical foliage of the dense jungle.

Because of the heavy rain that morning, slippery red mud hindered us most of the way. We managed to stay on our feet, reaching Tilly's home just before dark.

Since Tilly had delivered thousands of babies in the Kikwit area, she had become a legend. Every time the Zairians saw a white woman driving a car, they would yell out, "Mama Wall!" This tiny, but strong-willed, patient, loving midwife hardly weighed 100 pounds.

Now she was leaving us for a while. I was glad to have walked one time where she had often walked. It was hard to say goodbye. We all doubted that she would ever see the shores of Zaire again.

As we arrived at the airport, we were astounded to see the devastated building the Belgians had once furnished so lavishly. The fountain in the middle of the entrance no longer functioned. The ladies' room had been robbed of water tanks from its toilets.

Chairs in the waiting room had been stripped of their cushions. Greed and selfish reasoning no doubt had caused the deterioration. "If I do not take it, another will" had been the prevailing attitude. Only Christ can teach respect for public property.

When shopping time came around, to buy a year's supply for the interior, we found food in the Kinshasa stores exorbitant in price. A missionary couple, operating a company called Berklands, imported wholesale food and medicines for missionaries. We drove out to their storeroom, where I ordered cases of vegetables, meats, soap, sacks of flour, sugar and powdered milk. All this had to be shipped by truck into the interior, taking three days to reach Kajiji.

Next, I purchased such supplies as notebooks to sell to the students, and low-quality yardage which I bought at a cloth factory. It occurred to me that our pupils really couldn't afford to attend a school like this.

We next visited Zaire Protestant Relief Association, mainly supplied by the Mennonite Central Committee, to ask about food for the dorm girls. We always welcomed yardage, school bags and sewing kits donated by church people. After paying freight and customs, we had them loaded to be shipped along with the food order we had just placed.

We drove to Lemete on the outskirts of Kinshasa where the Commissar of the people, Citizen Zangio, lived. Our trip proved fruitless, for he wasn't home. We still had no registration number.

I soon found myself back at Ecole Belle Vue without having successfully completed my search for the right recorded number for our school to exist. Should I open the school another year without knowing the future or being assured of the right for the school's existence?

With one of my rare headaches, I was resting at noon when my house help called me. He told me the pastor was there to see me. He announced that the Commissar had come and needed guest rooms. After asking my house help to arrange for this, I again went in to rest.

Not long afterwards, a second knock came at my bedroom door. A fellow missionary handed me a copy of a telegram received by Arn Prieb in Kinshasa: FLYING TO NAIROBI SEPT. 1 KINSHASA OCT., NEED FIVE NIGHTS LODGING. EDWIN KOPPER

I had to sit down and reread the message. Was it possible that my own brother Ed would really stop here in Zaire to see me? He had no idea that I lived miles from the capital, Kinshasa, with no commercial flights going our way. Only Missionary Aviation Fellowship could fly him to see me here. Would they take the time to fly my brother to see me? If not, I decided to go to Kinshasa, no matter what or how.

Commissar Zangio called me for a talk. I asked the pastors and some elders to join me in this very important meeting. When he saw what I had done, he told me that I should decide whether the school was to be a lower level school or a four-year high school.

"This isn't my school," I said. "It is theirs."

Citizen Zangio explained that last year at Kahemba a Zairian had started a pattern-making school but hadn't finished out the year. He wanted to know if I could operate this school besides continuing with the one we had started last year. I told him this would be impossible. I couldn't handle two schools at the same time.

Then, I explained why I hadn't opened the school as yet. First, the number representing the permit to open the school was not right. Second, Citizeness Nkama from the head office in Kinshasa said that even Kahemba's school hadn't the right to start the four-year high school. Their permit only allowed for the lower level school. If they didn't open, we could operate under their number at Kahemba. They would, in turn, pay for the expenses of the past year.

Citizen Zangio admitted he had not gone to the office of Citizeness Nkama. He had gone to other offices instead. He said he would go to Kinshasa soon. Meanwhile, we should not open the school until he sent a message telling us what section we could open. He would send a message within 15 days.

Some days later, expecting guests, I baked all morning - bread, buns, sweet rolls and banana bread. After lunch, I went to the airstrip to meet the members of our mission staff from America, who were flying in that day. This was my chance to talk to the pilot, John Kliewer Jr., to make arrangements to fly my brother in. In my excitement, I failed to say hello to our guests. Upon hearing my request, John shook his head. "This is a hard one," he said. "I'll let you know."

By the time I finished talking to John, Henry Brucks, Vernon Wiebe and brother Defehr had already left the airstrip. I followed them as quickly as possible to welcome them and to apologize for not greeting them at the airstrip. That evening, the entire mission staff welcomed our guests with a potluck dinner. Each of our guests had a word to say.

The next day, I showed my guests the complicated steps the students had to learn in order to draw a pattern. I suggested that maybe we could find someone to study in Belgium to take Diane's place when she left. When the subject of overcrowded dorm space arose, I explained that the medical school anticipated building the school and dorm at the mission. Then they, in turn, would present us with their dorm space here. This would give us plenty of room for all our girls.

During the visit of the administrators, Citizen Zangio sent a message by short-wave telling me to open the higher level school, called *Cycle Long*. That meant it would be a four-year high school, including all the humanities, pattern-making, sewing, and drawing demanded for this section.

Even though he had given permission, I decided that this school wouldn't open its doors until our legal representative from our Mennonite Brethren office in Kikwit gave me the go-ahead.

It was suggested to me that maybe I should just forget school and entertain people, then give them the good news of salvation. This idea wasn't well received by the Zairians, who had great hopes for this school and for the future of the women.

A few days after our guests left, Citizen Funda, a college graduate who majored in English and was a former English student of mine, came to me with several pointed questions.

Do you think you have finished your task here? Who could take your place? What have you trained for? If you returned home now, would you say that the Zairians had chased you home? I pondered the questions carefully.

Every Sunday evening, we missionaries gathered in different homes for a meal, Bible study and prayer. I always looked forward to these times. One evening, Steve Jost suggested we read 2 Corinthians all the way through at one sitting sometime.

Later, while reading the book for myself, I felt the Lord speaking to me through 2 Corinthians 8:10-12: "...and I gave my opinion in this matter for this to your advantage, who were the first to begin a year ago not only to do this, but also to desire to do it. But now finish doing it also that just as there was the readiness to desire it so there may be also the completion of it by your ability. For if the readiness is present it is acceptable accordingly to what a man has, not according to what he does not have."

Lycée Ditalenu's pattern-making high school was started a year earlier. Just when I had given up hope for an all-girls' school, God dropped it into my lap. We started a higher-level sewing school by error.

What will Isaac Kilabi tell me to do? Am I hearing correctly? Will all this work out so that we can continue the school on a four-year high school level? For now, I determined to tell no man about the passage of Scripture I had read. I would be quiet, knowing that God is in control. He will work out His plan and will. I am in His hands.

That weekend, in anticipation of Ed's coming, my house help and I among other preparations made a big dinner for him. Then the message came by shortwave that my brother hadn't arrived. He wasn't on the plane approaching Kajiji.

Ed and his travel agent had used an out-of-date schedule for Air

Zaire. Someone at Kajiji handed me an up-to-date one. A plane from Nairobi was scheduled on the third, the day he was supposed to fly out of Kajiji.

On October 3, I flew out with John Kliewer Jr., arriving two and a half hours later. Upon arrival, Arn Prieb said, "I'm sorry you can't meet your brother."

"He will be on the plane tonight, the first flight out of Nairobi since the date he had set," I responded.

Martie took me to the Theology school which several of our members attended. Alf Schmidt, a teacher there, and his family drove me to the airport. The bulletin board showed nothing for Air Zaire at the hour given. At the information desk, a clerk told us that Air Zaire from Nairobi would be coming in at 10:30 that evening.

We soon found ourselves on the airport balcony overlooking the longest air-strip in the world. (Instead of making it double, side by side, they had mistakenly made it one long strip.). Finally, Air Zaire taxied up.

A bus drove up to the plane and brought its passengers close to the entrance for foreigners. I watched as they got out, one by one. No Ed. I waited just a little longer. The last one out was Ed. I shouted his name, though I knew he couldn't hear from the balcony. But praise the Lord, he had come!

Fairly flying down the steps, I waited at the entrance to the baggage room. I knew I couldn't get into the first room he had entered. At a ticket window, blacked out, only a slit could be seen at the bottom of it. Ed had to hand his passport to someone without seeing who it was. He couldn't speak any French. How would he manage?

I entered the luggage room. There he was, with Zairians pestering him, wanting to pick up his luggage. When I tapped him on the shoulder, he turned around. We flew into each other's arms.

"Am I ever glad to see you!" he said. "This is scary, coming to the airport without knowing French. Thankfully, I knew you would meet me."

All porters soon went on their way while we talked, standing close to the baggage belt, ready to grab Ed's luggage as it came out. He had already given someone five dollars to help him through customs. I told him not to change any more money, for I had more in their currency than I needed.

The next morning, Martha - from Kipungu days - and Margaret Dyck, doing translation work in Kinshasa, and I packed a picnic lunch and headed for the mission, Sona Bata. Ed just had to see a typical mission station, since he could not come to see me at Kajiji.

We visited their secondary school where two Peace Corps girls, one Jewish and the other Catholic, taught side by side with a missionary couple. Their classrooms also were overcrowded and furnished with typical double desks.

They too complained about lack of textbooks. Almost everything had to be written on the blackboard for the students to copy into their notebooks. Such conditions typified our mission schools as well, except for the Peace Corps teachers. Visiting their hospital and medical school, like Kajiji, the patients' relatives brought food to cook for the hospitalized loved ones.

The carpenters in their shop busily made furniture for their primary and high schools.

Kusemuka high school is far out in the bush. Teachers don't like living that far from the big city. From this place, however, they could hop a truck and get to Kinshasa in little more than an hour. To get from Kinshasa to Kajiji takes two to three days over land.

On the way out, we noticed larger villages than around Kajiji. Most of the huts were made of typical forest materials. On the outskirts of Kinshasa, I eagerly asked Martie to stop at an open market to buy palm nuts.

When we arrived home, I boiled them in salt water. The demonstration of how to eat them made Ed a little apprehensive. This oblong, orange-and-black nut, when put into the mouth, must be chewed getting all the straw off the nut, then sucked to get out all the rich palm oil from it. Ed tried only one, saying they were too oily. He was right, but their rich flavor enticed us to chew on straw in order to extract it.

After enjoying a lovely dinner together with Martie and Margaret, at last, Ed and I could talk.

My heart had been troubled with indecision. Now my brother, an ordained minister, just happened to come by when I needed him most. No, it didn't just happen. Our Heavenly Father worked it out that way. This was God's plan. I needed Ed's advice at that time.

We sat opposite each other, the table in between. At the end of my story, Ed placed his hands on mine and prayed. He asked Jesus Christ for a release of evil forces that hindered the work here in Zaire. He closed his prayer with these words, "May God have His way."

The next morning, since Ed was also a good carpenter, Arn asked for his advice on the roof problem he was having. Then, Arn showed us Mennonite Brethren Churches springing up in various parts of the city. After visiting our Mennonite Brethren bookroom and store, we saw the place where for so many years they had their radio studio.

At the ivory market, many vendors, speaking a few words of English, hung onto us. They wanted to sell everything from crude idols to well-sculptured animals and figures; from malachite beads to ivory ones; from rows of oil paintings to butterflies shaped into pictures. Most of the artists had been trained at the Belgian Art College in Kinshasa.

We spent the evening with the couples living at the theology school. The Hardy Schroeders were Kituba Bible translators, which Harold Fehderau had begun, while the Pete Bullers both taught in the theology school. The Kituba New Testament had been translated several times, but now Hartmut Schroeder worked on the Old Testament.

Each passage had to be clear in meaning, not only to the translator but to the Bantu mind as well. The Zairian translators, working side by side with Hardy, were Mwanga Givashi Jonas and Kikweta Mawa Jean.

It was now time to go to the airport for Ed's flight back to the States. Arn drove, going by way of Limete where the Commissar lived.

"Arn," I said, "I have to tell Citizen Zangio that I haven't opened the school yet this year. I want you to be a witness to our conversation."

"I don't want to get involved," Arn said.

"Neither do I," I responded, " but he has to know. Won't you go with me?"

"This evening I have time, but tomorrow I'm too busy."

"Can we stop in now," I asked, "since it is on the way to the airport?"

After knocking at the door, we three were invited into their ample front room. Citizen Commissar served us soft drinks.

"I haven't acted upon your shortwave message to open the school as yet," I said, "because I am waiting for our legal representative, Citizen Kilabi, to give his word. I am a missionary first, and he must tell me what to do."

"I will call him," the Commissar said.

"What about the number 832?" I asked.

"It is a rectified number," he replied.

As we got into the car and headed for the plane, Ed said, "I didn't understand a word of what was going on."

"I realize that, Ed," I said. "Let me explain. You have just been in the home of the greatest political leader of our area. He wants the school to function. He asked me to open it. He said my legal papers are in Kikwit. I am to ask his wife to give them to me."

At the airport, Arn helped Ed through customs and the ticket counter, since Ed knew neither French nor Kituba. We prayed together before he went into the waiting room. I thanked my brother for coming to me in the hour of my great need. I found it hard to say goodbye, but soon Ed was gone - behind doors we couldn't penetrate.

The day after Ed left, I decided to spend the weekend in Kinshasa. On Sunday evening, we attended the English interdenominational church service. Jim Schmidt, a former second-grade pupil from Ecole Belle Vue days, together with his lovely family, presented the evening program. Jim introduced his wife and family. She played and sang several numbers with Jim. Their three older children each held a microphone while they sang.

What greater joy can a teacher have than to see one of her former students praising the Lord? His father, the dentist, had been killed while in school at Kajiji in 1953. Jack, his brother, gave the flannelgraph story to the Congolese.

Later, Jack was killed while hiking in a cave that collapsed. His mother had been laid to rest beside her husband in Zaire just before Jim and family came out to help her. Now they were at

Nkara mission station serving the Lord.

On Monday morning, Arn took me to a truck stop. I sat down on my suitcase waiting for the most desirable ride to Kikwit. At noon, a beat-up truck that sounded as if it needed more than just oil, came up on its way to Kikwit.

After paying, an ex-school teacher turned trader and I climbed into the cab. The other passengers had to climb in the back, to sit on the cargo, or stand all the way.

The only paved road out of Kinshasa, in spite of a few chuck holes, wasn't all that bad. Even so, the truck soon stalled. With no garage between Kinshasa and Kikwit, the driver stopped another truck for tools and soon had it running again.

At 2:00 o'clock in the morning, our truck broke down again. We waited at the side of the road for an hour and a half before another truck came by. After paying again, I hopped in and finally arrived at our book room and guest house in Kikwit at 5:00 o'clock in the morning. I was now halfway home.

Matsitsa Charles, the legal representative substitute, signed a paper giving me the right to again open the school. I asked several other missionaries to join me in the office when I talked to the legal representative, Citizen Kilabi, of the Mission. Matsitsa Charles and Citizen Kilabi said that Citizen Zangio had already sent a shortwave message saying that I should open the school.

The Mennonite Brethren Education Office had already written to the Kinshasa Education Office stating that the sewing school at Kajiji would open again. They had, however, used the number 120 which meant that it would be the lower level sewing school. I went back to the office saying that I couldn't decide which school we would have but that they had used the number indicating which it was.

"Which shall it be?" I asked.

They then admitted that Kajiji had refused the lower-level school. They wanted a four-year high school or none at all. *Cycle Long* it shall be, just as the Lord had shown me in the 2 Corinthians 8:10-12 passage.

Thursday found me in Citizen Kegi's truck with his wife Citizeness Jolice beside me. She had been one of the women taking the three months' course with me at Kajiji. After Dr. Pauls had

Citizeness Jolice was one of the women taking the three month's course with me at Kajiji.

helped her physically, she had given birth to several more children. The first one after this they called *Dieu Donnée* ("God gave"). We scooted out of Kikwit on a back road, picking up more passengers. The truck, in bad condition, had a window on the passenger's side that could be rolled up or down only by pulling on the glass or by pushing it down. When it rained, a gunny sack was put over the window.

Before crossing a small, one-truck ferry, we stopped as the rules indicated we should. We got out of the truck, walked onto the ferry and crossed with the truck. When we reached the other side, the truck went off without us passengers. The driver had gone to pick up more passengers in a nearby village. He returned half an hour later.

Just before dark, we drove up to a Catholic mission station. These Belgian workers reminded me of my year's stay there. Some had recently visited Kajiji for medical reasons and knew our Dr. Buhr. Without my knowing it, some of the passengers strongly suggested that we spend the night here. It was almost dark and the truck's battery was very weak. The driver refused.

Soon after dark, the lights gave out. The passengers grumbled. They wanted to at least stop in a village. The driver couldn't go on for lack of light. All the men were asked to step off the truck and to sleep around a bonfire, while the women slept in the truck bed.

Before dawn, at about 3:00 o'clock, we again got into our places to try to drive on. The lights shone for only half an hour. We tried to shine ahead with a flashlight but soon had to give up.

At 6:30, we again bumped along on our way to Kimangala, one of our mission centers with a church and school. All passengers destined for Kajiji were to wait here until the truck went to Panzi mission station and back. I had been principal there in 1956-57.

After putting my things in the pastor's house, I waited. Surely, they would be back soon. By 5:30, they were nowhere to be seen. I had just purchased a cheap blanket in order to spend the night, when workers of OXFAM, an English charity organization working in Zaire to help different missions, drove up.

Believe it or not, on this isolated bush outpost where we hardly met another vehicle in a whole day, these folks were on their way to Kajiji. They offered me a ride. In two hours, I found myself thanking my Lord for His protection as I entered my own home at Ecole Belle Vue, Kajiji.

John Toews visits with Aaron Tshinyama, principal of Kusemuka's high school.

CHAPTER 22

NEW YEAR'S DAY

January 1st was always a great day for the Zairian Mennonite Brethren Church members at Kajiji. On that day, many flocked to the large T-shaped stone church building. Each member knew which of the three entrances he or she wanted to enter.

Young men in western clothes entered the front double doors leading to the center section. Mostly older Zairian men, some with canes - not only for the old and feeble, but special ones for a chief, or a préfèt, climbed up the red dirt step that led to the side door on the men's side. Latecomers squeezed into an already-filled bench, knowing there was always room for one more.

On the opposite side of this large whitewashed church, praying mothers entered on this New Year's Day. They too had an uneven step, formed by red mud with fiber of the manioc tuber pounded into it. Stepping onto this, they balanced themselves knowing that it had again changed its shape since the last pouring rain.

Most of the women came dressed for the occasion, with a baby tied to their backs. As each mother gingerly sat down at the edge of a bench, she slowly inched the cradle forward. When untied, the baby would either nurse or sleep in mother's lap while she participated in the service.

All who wished could participate by telling their story of how the Lord Jesus Christ had helped them in the past year. The pastor called for a song between testimonies. Tension mounted, for it seemed many wanted to talk at the same time. We heard Chokwe, Lunda, French, and the trade language, Kituba.

A designated speaker was now called on, but we felt bad that others who had wanted to give a word had to be cut off. Later, however, they were again given an opportunity to share their personal experience.

I told them about 2 Corinthians 8:10-12, how God had indicated to me we should open our pattern-making, sewing high school. Now, God had moved upon the Education Office in Kinshasa to issue the circular number of 833 for the school. This applied only to our *Lycée Ditalenu* at Kajiji, a four-year high school. This meant we could even keep the chosen name - "helping one another."

Reliving their experiences with them as they shared their stories convinced me that God was building His church in Zaire in spite of its shortcomings. Christ Jesus, who lives in their hearts, is alive forevermore.

"Shout for joy, O heavens, for the Lord has done it!"(Isaiah 44:23a).

CHAPTER 23

MISSION BOARD VISITORS

In 1980 Bill Wiebe, Peter Hamm and Arn Prieb flew to Kajiji to visit us. All Zairians were surprised to see Arn. He and his wife as missionaries had just recently said goodbye to them. Now, he came back as a member of the board of Mennonite Brethren Missions/Services.

When these guests visited *Lycée Ditalenu*, Diane Jost was teaching technical designing. They seemed to be in a hurry, but I showed them the storeroom with shelves put together from branches of a certain palm tree. The shelves were mostly filled with things from Zaire Protestant Relief Association, fed mainly by the Mennonite Central Committee.

Mennonite Churches in Canada and America sent sewing kits, including thread, measuring tapes, thimbles, needles, pins and scissors. Church mission circles made homemade blankets from pieces of new scraps of material which gave us our dorm blankets.

Mennonite Central Committee gathered remnant pieces of first quality yardage by the barrels full. We received other materials that were faulty. A huge bale of mattress material varied in quality, from very thin to a woven quality from which our dorm girls could sew mattresses. Even the thin pieces could be useful for dorm curtains and sewing samples.

Opening another barrel, we found a knitted beige material with the name "Winnie the Pooh" written all over it in red. Ribbed red material came with it, so we could make nice-looking gymnasium

Bill Wiebe, Matondo Tshimika and Jake Epp's *visit to Kajiji.*

Peter Hamm from the Mennonite Brethren Missions office and Ernie Doerksen from Kikwit helped Rev. D\ck from the United States and me to cut the ribbon. Henry H. Dick was former MBM/S president and pastor at Shafter and Reedley.

blouses for all our girls. Finding a picture of a bear, I was able to explain Winnie the Pooh to the girls.

At one time, we received old treadle sewing machines - of every make and kind. What a time we had not only assembling these machines, but also threading each one differently. Then came the task of getting them to sew properly. Sometimes, we spent hours working on the tension of each individual device.

After assembling one antique machine, we just couldn't seem to get it to sew. Finally, we decided to try to push the wheel back-

Palavsa Tshiantca and former English students of mine: Mrs. Therese Kulungu and her husband Pascal Kulungu. He now attends Fresno Pacific University. Their two children are Juliana and Cristelle.

wards. Presto, it sewed. How glad we were to hear that the Chinese government had donated sewing machines to all sewing schools in Zaire. Twenty machines would come our way.

When I got to Kinshasa to inquire about them, someone had already checked them out for us. I was glad I could put looking for them in the hands of George Klassen, our buyer in Kinshasa. I knew he would eventually trace down these precious new machines.

It was to this storeroom that I took my guests, explaining that if we served only our students, we had certain supplies that would serve our school for years to come. We found other school supplies more difficult to obtain.

For instance, I bought a certain ruler for pattern-making when passing through Belgium. French curves, pattern-making paper, extra bobbins and bolts of material were available from wholesale houses in Kinshasa or Kikwit. Each student had to pay an entrance fee to cover these costs, plus freight and customs.

On the following day, our guests came for a meal. Afterward, we went into my office which was in my home. Pointing to a graph from the Education Department in Kinshasa, I explained the different levels of schools in operation in Zaire. They asked whether this was a flunky school or a school with an accelerated program.

Pointing a second time to the graph, I showed them that it was an accelerated program. In fact, third year - our first year of high school - had 21 subjects. It provided all the humanities, plus the full home economics program: pattern-making, sewing, textile, and pattern drawing in place of a pattern book.

We missionaries constantly tried to work ourselves out of a job. "Let the Zairians do it as soon as they can" was our motto. Thus the question came up, "How many years will it be before this school could have a Zairian principal?"

"At present," I replied, " we have no one with a B.A., but maybe before long someone will show up with that qualification."

The church council met together with our board of mission guests. Among other things, they discussed how long they wanted me to stay.

"Until she is ready to retire," board members agreed. They expressed the earnest desire that this school would be a success. Our guests decided that they too wanted the school to continue.

With Diane and Steve Jost scheduled to leave at the end of the school year, who would take Diane's place? Her departure left me with one sewing teacher, and she who was not really qualified to teach in this school. I had to let her teach. No one else was available.

Now that we had our basic circular number from the government to operate the school on the higher level, would the Education Department recognize it and pay for our teachers and workers? Would the small number of students hinder the final outcome?

The Lord had showed me His will in the matter with words from 2 Corinthians 8:10-12. Citizen Zangio had said, "You can't drop the second grade girls." The Mission Board had said, "Go ahead." My only question: where are the qualified teachers?

God had worked out that passage of Scripture in detail. I knew He could work out our present problem - to His honor and glory.

Chapter 24

Cheating

We did not insist that all our teachers, workers and pupils be born-again believers in Jesus Christ. Good teachers, secretaries and pupils were hard to come by. Our school accepted all who had a record of good conduct on report cards presented to us.

Some other schools required that their pupils be believers and church members. That often made liars out of them. Furthermore, if we worked only with Christians, how would the church grow? In our schools, many students were Christians, but others were animists, fetishists and ancestral worshippers. Many believed in reincarnation.

All cultures have ways in which stealing or cheating is accomplished. Zairians too had sly tricks which they sometimes got away with. As the Bible declares, "...All have sinned and come short of the glory of God" (Romans 3:23).

Jean Rossing, an adventurous, dedicated girl, came to Zaire to teach on a two-year contract. An idealist, young, well-trained, she lacked experience in the devious ways of some people. We old-timers warned her about certain pitfalls but soon found out she needed to experience them herself.

During my first days of supervising exams in the grade school at Kipungu, all pupils had carried their slates into the classroom to work out problems. As they entered the classroom, I would inspect the slates but failed to look on the wooden frame around the slate where some had written answers.

Another time, a pupil seated close to a window had placed the answers on the window sill. While we checked arms and legs for concealed writings, and pockets for hidden notes, we didn't catch everything.

Jean, supervising the mixed high school finals, had the doctor's wife from Haiti come into the room. What made the visitor look up to the ceiling? She had seen many of the students constantly looking up. Following their gaze, she saw to her utter dismay that the formulas needed to solve their problems had been written on the whitewashed ceiling.

At dinner time that evening, we talked about the problem. "How could I have prepared you for this?" I asked.

"You couldn't have," Jean said. "I wouldn't have believed you."

My mind went back to a fellow missionary's experience. She had taken the precaution of placing her exams in a room other than her front room. Some students knocked at her door seeking spiritual help, they said. While she prayed for them, another student sneaked through the unlocked door and snatched a copy of the exam. Discovery of this ploy nullified the exam, of course.

Steve and Diane Deckert Jost, my neighbors, and I often compared notes. One day, Diane told me that the watchman for the sewing school, together with her (Diane's) cook, had sold copies of exams taken from her house.

In the non-Christian world of Zaire, they hold the view that stealing from another tribe or from someone who has much more than they do isn't sin. So, stealing was common. However, they always tried to do it without being suspected.

When they wanted a certain thing, they would "misplace" it to see whether it would be missed. When not missed, they would take it home. One April Fool's Day, which they called April fish, some Zairians played a joke on one of my servants. They told him I had asked them to tell him to bring back everything he had taken from my home. To my knowledge, he hadn't taken anything.

Another time, I placed two library books on the secretary's desk for him to put the library cards back into the books. A little later, he insisted that the two books were missing.

"I'll look for them," I said.

The following Saturday, while looking for some old stencils stashed away on a high shelf I hadn't looked at in years, I was

The inscription on the church wall says, "BE HOLY, JESUS IS COM-ING SOON."

astonished to find one of the books. No doubt the other one had been hidden as well.

On Sunday, January 17, 1980, I went to Sunday school a little late. After the class session, many people excitedly waited to enter the church. Something was in the air; I wasn't sure what. We went in early and I sat in the back as usual, so that my Zairian friends would listen to the message instead of watching my pale face. The two side wings of the T-shaped building were already filled up. The middle section was filling up fast. Special choir numbers were presented, as everyone swayed to the music.

Suddenly the pastor was standing in front of the audience with a known thief, Luvunu (not his real name). He asked the man to share his testimony. Luvunu admitted he had stolen many things from missionaries, from pastor Tshimika and others as well. While taking refuge in Angola for two months, he had been warned that if he continued in life like this he would go to hell and burn forever.

Now, acknowledging Christ as his personal Saviour, he came

back to ask our pardon. He wanted to go from house to house to ask for forgiveness. The pastor added that many young people had followed in his footsteps. He asked them to come now to straighten out their lives.

Next came time for the morning offering - a special one called *Sisani* (contest). Letting Zairians take charge of their own Sunday services called for change, but was necessary to enable the church to become truly indigenous.

Three baskets, placed on the table in front of the pulpit, had been designated for offering from specific groups: (1) grown men; (2) married women; (3) young people and children. The idea: to see which group would give the most on this special *Sisani Sunday*.

The songs they sang had a special purpose, indicating which group should go forward next to place their offerings in the appropriate basket. Soon the audience was on the move, swaying to the music in their unique style.

Young men had dressed up in their best Zairian outfits. Older men varied in their dress from a loin cloth and cane to a well-tailored suit. Women dressed in their Sunday's best with baby on their backs came not only with their money but also with produce from their own gardens: onions, potatoes, manioc, peanuts and corn - to be auctioned off after the service.

Suddenly, I noticed some of our girls from the sewing school going out of the church time after time, reappearing, then marching up to the front repeatedly. When I asked about this, they explained they had gone out to find smaller change in exchange for their larger piece of money, giving them more opportunities to go up front with their offerings.

An usher handed me a note. I was to thank God for the offering. As I began to pray, I thanked God for Luvunu's confession, and thanked Him for those who gave. Then I asked God to forgive those who gave with unclean hearts.

I knew that many school children had stolen pens or notebooks from each other. Medicine had been taken from the dispensary. Some had even cheated on their exams.

" Please, Holy Spirit," I prayed, "cleanse us from sin - from stealing, from cheating, in Jesus' Name, Amen."

As I sat down, the congregation's reaction echoed in the church. I knew that God's Spirit was doing His convicting work in many hearts and lives.

Sala-Nsaka was a plump, jolly girl - fun to be with. Her father, a tradesman, presented me with the necessary report card for her to enter into our sewing, pattern-making high school. Her junior high certificate indicated a 68 per cent grade. It seemed too good to be true. Most of our students entered with an average of only 52 percent. Fifty percent was considered passing.

My only argument against her entering was that she belonged to another mission. They had plenty of sewing, pattern-making schools within their church schools. Upon further examination of her report card, it was evident that it had been tampered with. Somehow, it must have gotten soaked. The eighth grade certificate looked authentic, but I was told that even these could be bought.

"Do you want a leopard skin?" her father asked me.

"They are forbidden, aren't they?" I responded

"Yes, but if you contact your embassy, maybe they could help you," he said.

"I am a missionary," I reminded him, "and I don't want to do anything that is forbidden."

"What about carvings?" he asked cryptically. "Are you going to Europe this summer?"

"I am going to America whether the government pays for it or not," I replied.

"How much will it cost?" he asked.

"A thousand or two of American dollars," I said.

"I only have her and one son in junior high and a little girl," Sala-nsaka's father continued. "She means a lot to me. I want her to go on to Europe to study."

"Europe or America can be very lonesome," I reminded him. "It isn't heaven."

I went on to tell him he should let her get all the education she possibly could here in Africa before going abroad. "I'm not sure she would pass," I said.

At the end of the first semester, he returned to check on how she was doing. As we talked, the professor of African sociology walked in.

"Please check Sala-Nsaka's grades," I asked him. "Her father wants to see them."

After checking the first two quarters she had flunked, but had passed the mid-semester exam.

Other teachers came and reported that Sala-Nsaka was flunking. I called in the dorm mother. She said that Sala-Nsaka didn't study. She pulled lots of pranks on her friends, like locking them in their dorm rooms and not letting them out.

"Sala-Nsaka," I said to her, "you are fun to live with. Joking is fun. Now, however, your father's money can't buy intelligence and put it into your head. You must decide just what you want to do with your life."

We had six days of school a week; however, Wednesday and Saturday afternoons were free. Students from Kusemuka high school would sometimes come over to read or to play games on those free afternoons.

One student informed me that after high school he wanted to go to the Seminary in Kinshasa. Anna Goertzen had helped him and the other students learn many Bible verses, which gave them a good foundation. This created a desire within him. I suggested he talk to his pastor.

Another asked questions about salvation. In response, I showed him the Four Spiritual Laws. He again came back with questions. We continued to study the last part of the Laws booklet. He prayed the sinner's prayer, confessing his sins and asking Christ to come into his heart and life.

Another group of fellows came over asking whether it was right to pay in order to pass. I said it was wrong. They too studied the Four Spiritual Laws. Sensing their confusion and lack of assurance, I told them to re-study what we had gone over and, if they still were interested, to come back. One came back while the other went on vacation.

When two others came over I said, "If you have a spiritual question, I'll listen. Otherwise, I'm too busy, for I must fly to Kinshasa Wednesday."

They asked how they could be saved. They too were shown the

way. When I thought they had gone, they came back and asked, "Is Christ really coming back to this earth?" I invited them to my home. We studied Acts 1 and other passages dealing with the subject.

Others blamed us for their falling into the sin of stealing. They said we hadn't given them proper work. I reminded them we couldn't solve their economic problems. We would teach them so they could help themselves. If they wanted to work, they could cut poles, get tall grass for roofs or cut wood for fires. Other than that, I had no work for them.

After high school, many students went right into teaching. Others proceeded to Kikwit for teacher's training. Some of these associated themselves with a group of Christians in a lively spiritual revival. They had come back to Kajiji and continued with their youth meetings.

About this time, Citizen Malesu, a member of this group, came for a visit. His face was aglow.

Citizen Malesu said, "You taught us the Word of God. When I followed the Lord in baptism, you took a picture of me." "It wan't me," I assured him. "The Lord has done it. He prompted me to show you the picture of your baptism. Now the same Lord is working through you. Praise His Holy Name!"

"You taught us the Word of God," he said. "When I followed the Lord in baptism, you took a picture of me. You kept on showing me this picture. Because you reminded me of my commitment, I kept on faithfully with the Lord.

"Yesterday afternoon, we had our young people's service. Seven young people came forward to receive the Lord Jesus Christ. It is because of you that we are able to lead others to Christ."

"It wasn't me," I said. "The Lord did it. Someone led me to Christ. I showed you the way, in turn. He prompted me to show you the picture as a reminder of your commitment. Now the same Lord is working through you. Praise His holy Name!"

On the last night of the year, this group of young people had an all-night watch service. Citizen Pakisa Tshimika gave his message at 2:30 a.m. on New Year's Day 1981. They finished at 6 o'clock.

Ever so often, we saw professors, students and medical workers cutting grass or helping to clean up Kajiji - not because they were told to, but as a witness for their Lord and Master. We praise Him for their spirit of servanthood.

CHAPTER 25

MUD MORTAR AND MANIOC FIBER

Seated at my dining room table, having finished my lunch, I glanced out the window. I saw the usual tall eucalyptus trees which missionary kids had climbed since 1952. Now sturdy and full-grown, these trees no longer bend with the weight of a child.

Under them walked the principal of the mixed high school, Kusemuka, Citizen Funda, carrying a heavy pole he had just cut from the forest. He placed it close to my garden. Knowing we needed volunteers to get the building project started, he became an example and got other volunteers interested in bringing materials needed from the forest.

In 1976, he had asked me four pertinent questions about God's continuing call on my life. Now, I could see that God was continuing his call on Citizen Funda's life as well.

When I hired government paid workers for the school, I told the watchmen, "You will be working. Don't expect to just walk around. There will be plenty to do. If you do not want to work, do not apply for this position."

It was for a shelter to protect mud-drying bricks that Citizen Funda had brought a cut pole. We would erect a grass roof on them. In preparation for making hand-made bricks, a barrel was placed close to the wall-less shelter.

Watchmen walked with a bamboo pole over their shoulders, dangling water buckets at both ends. Down the steep mountain-

Cement hand-made bricks were now being made by pressing them into a mold, then gingerly placing them under the grass roof to dry.

side they went, to and from a river. Other government paid workers dug a red-dirt pit, filling wheelbarrows full and dumping the red dirt next to the water barrel.

Another barrel sat on four stones over a hot fire where manioc peels were being heated to add to the red dirt. These peelings come from the tuber all Zairians eat as their staple food. Mixing cooked manioc fiber with the red dirt formed hard, durable bricks for our new classroom. Brick formers pounded this mixture into the mold, then released them under the straw-roofed shelter to dry.

Meanwhile, the medical school applied to an English firm for money to build a medical school and dorm at the mission station a mile and a half from Ecole Belle Vue. Believing this would be accomplished, they gave up one of their manioc storerooms. It became another classroom.

Soon, eager seventh-graders entered, among whom was Kasongo Lunda Umba, niece of the great Lunda Chief. She soon showed that she wasn't only of a Chieftain's line but was also almost always at the head of her class in conduct and academic achievement.

With some of her friends, she entered because the government demanded that all high schools add a junior high. During an informal sewing class, these motivated girls talked among themselves.

"We sure have chosen the right section," one said. "Isn't it great to learn how to sew?" Kasongo Lunda Umba heartily agreed.

When we received the 20 sewing machines from the Chinese government, a workman and I uncrated them and readied the nine

Soon eager seventh-graders entered. "We sure have chosen the right section," one girl said. "Isn't it great to learn how to sew?"

hand-turned ones for the classroom.

Later, we tackled the treadle machines. Reading the directions and looking for the right screws for each part, we suddenly discovered that most of the body bolts were missing. Since George Klassen, his wife and family were in Kinshasa to pick up groceries and run other errands for us, I asked him to try to find the storeroom where the machines had been stashed. George made numerous trips to the place, but never found the man or the missing screws.

Not even the Singer Sewing Machine parts store had all the bolts. We had to give up for the moment and concentrate on other necessary work. The treadle machines were placed in a storeroom until a remedy could be found.

Soon the school year was at an end. We needed to prepare for next school year, which meant adding eighth grade. That explained why the mud bricks were drying underneath the shelter. By building with these, we added a school room with three thousand dried bricks onto the renovated storeroom, at little expense.

My sister and her husband, Alice and Art Newfield, had given me some tithe money. That paid for hand-sawed planks bought from the sawyers in the forest. When the boards were somewhat dry, our carpenters made windows and doors for the classroom.

Since money was scarce, I scrounged around to buy elephant grass to form the roof. After getting a coat of mud plaster and whitewash the eighth-grade classroom was all ready for use.

Our enrollment jumped from 73 to 92. These girls not only received a rounded education, but with it studied the Word of God. To me, that is what missionary life is all about.

Kafusa, a former student now teaching.

CHAPTER 26

FORCED INTO IT

Three years after the pattern-making Sewing High School began, we had five girls ready to enter their final year. We had neither classroom space for them nor a technical teacher qualified for this crucial year. What should we do? We applied for them to enter different high schools. Mukelengi High School hesitated, but upon recommendation of Citizeness Nkama from the Education Office in Kinshasa, the principal of that school accepted all five.

Our girls really applied themselves. Finally, the last days of that school year came. All five were ready for their final exams with the state. After taking the exams, in the first days of July, they had to wait until the first of September to know whether they would receive their high school certificates.

To our surprise, the Kinshasa newspaper announced that all five had made it. That was indeed very unusual. Even if only three of them had made it, that would have been a high rate of success. That September, all five girls came to me asking for a teaching position.

"Yes," I told them, "there will be a place for all five of you."

Third grade had 24 students, too many for one teacher to handle in sewing. I assigned Citizeness Jimo and Professor Manzaka as team teachers.

My chief head of the sewing high school, Citizeness Nkama, gave me a good suggestion. It led me to the University of the sewing, pattern-making school in Kinshasa, on the same ground as the high school of the same section. They received me royally.

One special secretary informed me that many of their faithful

Belgian teachers, who had been with them from the beginning, now considered retiring. The University of Kinshasa was asking them to write out their courses of study to be duplicated for all of Zaire's sewing, pattern-making schools.

Each time one course of study was finished, they let me pick it up, as gifts from the Belgian government. Knowing that all state finals would be taken from these courses gave me great hope for our students. If the teachers did their job faithfully and the students applied themselves, I knew our students had just as much chance of passing as any other students.

My secretary and I spent years recopying the many courses, then duplicating them on our Gestetner.

I asked Citizeness Nkama just how serious it was that we hadn't opened sixth year as yet.

"Do not open it until you have qualified teachers," she said.

For that reason, for the second year in a row we sent our finalists to other high schools. Now our parents' committee, together with the Kikwit Education Office, insisted that we open sixth year regardless.

In the meantime, application had been sent to CIDA, a Canadian organization, for building funds. On May 18, 1983, word came by shortwave that CIDA had agreed to donate $20,000 for our school project.

We had received word a little earlier that the Portage Avenue Mennonite Brethren Church Mission Circle, in Winnipeg, Canada, had donated $8,000.00 for the same project. We praised our heavenly Father for this great breakthrough. "And He put a new song in my mouth, a song of praise to our God. Many will see and fear, And will trust in the Lord," (Psalms 40:3).

Local masons were hired and soon dug the foundation. Cement, handmade bricks, made by pressing them into a mold, were gingerly placed under the grass roof to dry. Our dream of a six-classroom school, one-third of our ultimate goal, had begun.

While walls of the high school building went up, we waited for the window frames. They were being made in Kinshasa at our carpenter's school, run by Rob Neufeld. The 500 percent devaluation of Zaire money raised building costs considerably.

Before I left for home on a short furlough in July of 1984, the parents' committee asked me what I had in mind for the sixth grade for the next school year. I told them I would look for teachers.

While in Kinshasa on my way home, I went to the University pattern-making, sewing school. Students had just finished their last sewing exam - making a dress for themselves. One by one, they modeled them for us. I was impressed. When I talked to them about Kajiji and the need for teachers, some expressed interest. When diamonds were mentioned, their interest increased.

On my way back, I again made contact with them. Even though one had signed up for our pattern-making school, no one came. At another parents' committee meeting, they made it very clear: they expected me to open the sixth year, regardless of classroom space or a needed teacher. My reaction: I opposed the idea - until a remedy could be found.

When school again opened, I still didn't know how to handle the sixth-year students. When I heard that Professor Kasombo, a former student of ours and last year's teacher, was coming back, it looked more hopeful that we could handle it. We had to get these students in school. Others had to come back as teachers or this school would die.

One valuable teacher, Citizeness Mushika, was scheduled to arrive late. Her house was waiting for her. Maybe we could let our sixth graders meet in her home for the first week.

We needed desks and tables for sewing, but neither was available. What could we do to have them ready overnight? Improvising is a familiar word for missionaries. Looking around in a crowded storeroom, I noticed some old, upright, treadle sewing machines that didn't work. Putting plyboard over two of these formed a temporary table, suitable for two students.

Then, my eyes caught sight of packing boxes that had been made into cupboards. I asked the carpenters to cut another strip of plyboard to place over these two crates, as another temporary table. *Voila!* That temporarily solved our table problem.

Two-by-fours were attached to another plyboard for legs, then painted to serve as a portable blackboard. We had solved the problem for one week. That gave us very little time to erect another classroom.

My attention was drawn to the lovely, large verandah right outside the third-grade classroom. French doors separated it from them. It was really the back part of the neighbors' home. They were now houseparents for medical students. Their front-room window faced the verandah. Could this nice roof be converted for our sixth grade?

Workers chopped holes into the cement floor to imbed poles from the forest. Next, they nailed ever handy plyboards to them, forming a small, makeshift classroom on the back verandah. In this way, we neither blocked the French doors nor the kitchen exit. With permission from the pastor's family, we pasted paper over their window so that light would still come in but their privacy would be protected.

Shortly after I assigned teachers to the class, all préfets (principals) of high schools were called to our Mennonite Brethren Education Office in Kikwit. This meant a possible two-day trip by truck. To tell the truth, I was glad to get away for a while.

As we passed over the ferry, on our way from Kajiji to Kahemba, I recalled an earlier trip with missionaries John and Sophie Esau. At that time, as we approached the ferry, we noticed that the river lifted the ferry very high in its waters.

It was in the middle of rainy season. The runways were mostly hidden in this swift, unpredictable river. As usual, the ferry was chained to stumps implanted in the ground. As the rules demanded, I got off the pickup - but Sophie didn't.

As the couple tried to board the ferry, the stumps holding the chains leaned over and came unattached. That allowed the ferry to be pushed away by the force of the pickup. As they plunged part way into the rushing river, I screamed. John quickly put the truck into reverse and backed up on solid ground.

He quickly got out his winch, hooked the ferry to his pickup and inched it up onto the ferry.

Now, in our present situation, we crossed without difficulty. Soon we found ourselves in Kahemba, looking for transportation from there to Kikwit. A land rover was all ready to take this trip. The driver placed me in the back, three of us to a seat sitting sideways. We faced three others on the opposite side, our knees touching and even overlapping.

I climbed out, offering to wait for another way. He then placed me in the middle in the front seat. Springs from the damaged seat hit me in the back. Again, I decided to climb out and wait. He then, reluctantly, let me sit in front next to the window. I accepted.

When we were ready to go, to our surprise the driver assembled a group to push us off. Driving along the narrow, one-way paths, we went quite a while without any trouble. When we thought we had it made, however, the land rover (carry-all) suddenly stopped dead between Kahemba and Mukoso. A truck came by and took us to Mukoso village, a cluster of mud buildings, to wait for the land rover.

After some hours, I decided to check out the local bush motel. It wasn't a comforting sight. Its grass roof and mud walls looked as if they had seen better days. But since I had no other choice, I rented one of its four rooms.

Confronted with a bare bamboo bed, I got out my bed roll and air mattress and made myself quite comfortable.

On a Coca-Cola crate, a single candle furnished light. The red dirt floor hadn't been watered down to discourage invading jiggers, eager to build a nest in human tissue. The room had no ceiling. A bamboo pole, hung across one corner and attached to the rafters, served as a clothes closet.

Two low bamboo stools provided the only other furnishings. The innkeepers brought me about four inches of water in a bucket to wash up. This primitive motel somehow brought to mind Jesus leaving Heaven's glory to be born in a stable.

When we arrived, crowds of villagers thronged the area. A celebration was in process: the installation of a new village chief. The old chief had been in a car accident. Seemingly, he came out of it all right. Very shortly afterward, however, he fell over dead.

Zaire was so partitioned off that no Protestant group overlapped, save in the larger cities. We all found that in our mission territories we each had plenty of responsibility without infringing on the area of another.

Mukoso was in Baptist territory. When their minister heard I was there, he walked over with his little girl and handed me some small, green mangos. I thanked him for his thoughtfulness. When I peeled one and tried it, I found it deliciously sweet - as sweet to me as fellowship with a member of God's invisible church.

The next morning, Zairians pushed the land-rover from 6:00 o'clock to 9:15. The driver finally found a way to start his vehicle - by letting it coast on a steep mountain a block off the main road.

A handsome, yellow-clad chauffeur-helper sat beside me. Soon he took off his jacket and dabbed himself with perfume. He filled the idle hours by smoking and drinking beer. At every stop, he bathed, even washing out his socks, handkerchief and underwear in streams along the way to Kikwit. Married, he and his wife expected their first baby.

The driver, a Zairian from Kahemba, had divorced his wife with eight children. He leisurely drove along, sometimes turning up his short Roman nose as others overtook and passed us. Having traveled the road often, he knew each turn and did a good job of missing at least some of the hundreds of bumps on this unpaved path of a road.

However, he was breaking the law. His insurance covered just so many people. He had overloaded again. He hadn't learned that too much weight causes overloaded vehicles to break down.

"Please," he begged me, "when we get to Kikwit, tell the police officer this is a mission vehicle."

I explained that I would tell them he had helped me, but I wouldn't tell them a lie.

After leaving Mukoso, we traveled until 10:30 that morning, then stopped for a Zairian bake-out. The passengers built a fire and placed a deer on a stick to roast. Everyone went to the river to bathe. Taking an hour for this provided just part of the day's fun. A salted pork sandwich and some more of the tasty mangos comprised my lunch.

At Gungu, a small town with simple village huts, the travelers and driver went into a Zairian cafe, hardly more than a lean-to, and bought their luku. Nzila, principal of a pedagogy school at Kajiji, and I bought soft drinks. We had to gulp them down, for the storekeeper insisted we return the bottles.

Finding another hill he could later coast down, the driver stopped again near a large river. Now everybody ate the luku they had bought at Gungu. The driver wanted to kill time, hoping the police would be off duty when we arrived in Kikwit. Eventually, he again piled in the passengers, even adding more people along the way. Again, we coasted down the hill and were on our way.

A pickup that had also stayed overnight in Mukoso now passed us. It had also been overloaded with passengers. We soon found them by the side of the road, changing a tire. Further on, as we came to a turn-off, the vehicle just stopped. This time we were out of gas.

While we were filling the tank, the pickup passed us again. I noticed that one of its passengers was the clerk from our Mennonite Brethren bookroom.

"Please," the driver begged again, "say that this is a mission vehicle." Again, I refused.

After arriving at our guest house in Kikwit, I was enjoying the evening meal when the Mennonite Brethren bookroom clerk thoughtfully sent a message. They should go after me; the vehicle I was in had broken down.

He hadn't noticed that we were just out of gas and the driver filled the tank with available gas he had on hand.

Our Zairian brethren felt responsible for us when we traveled together. Truly such fellowship as brothers and sisters in Christ must have honored the Lord even as it blessed our own personal lives as His servants.

CHAPTER 27

A SCRAP OF PAPER

As the doors of *Lycée Ditalenu* opened for the sixth year, things looked a little more promising. Our nine teachers and six workers, with two in the office, proved a great help. All received their pay from the Zairian Education Department.

Meanwhile, the six-room school building progressed very slowly, due to the builder's prime interest in the medical building he had been assigned to construct. Crude individual desks and teachers' tables served each classroom. Some rooms had useful long tables which doubled as school desks and sewing tables.

School met in different places. The seventh and eighth grades had their renovated two-room brick school building. The main large room of the girl's dorm, renovated some years before, became the sewing room for third-year pupils (first-year high).

Next to it was the fourth grade. To the left was a wing of dorm rooms, a large kitchen and a dining room turned over to us by the medical staff. The kitchen was now a classroom, while the spacious adjoining dining room served as another. We looked forward to some day having all these scattered students under not more than two roofs.

A week's supply of food continued to be given on a designated day each week to a faithful worker named Citizen Tshilenga, so that he could supervise the cook and the feeding program for the girls' dorm.

Although we had mutual respect for each other, I couldn't get very far in telling him about his need for Christ Jesus. At one point he showed disrespect for me. His manner softened when I explained that I wasn't getting double pay; only the mission board salary was mine to keep. That which the Zairian Government paid me for my teaching was given to the mission board.

One day, Citizen Tshilenga came up complaining about his arm. Gradually, it became worse, but he kept on working for a while. His four-year-old son often accompanied him to work. The boy and I became friends. He would sit on my lap while his father poured palm oil from a greasy barrel for the greens and meat sauces, or when the manioc tubers were piled into a tub to be weighed.

Increasingly, the Zairian government had to cut down its expenses. Decreasing foreign funds, used to run their education system, caused them to lay off all unnecessary help. Almost all secretaries and ordinary workmen had to go. The parents' committee had to find a solution to the dorm problem. As long as we had a school dorm, we had to have someone looking after our student residents.

For the most part, we managed in the office by having a part-time teacher as acting secretary. A new sewing school teacher gave us renewed hope and encouragement. We felt that the graduates would profit from this great addition. If the sixth-graders worked hard in applying themselves, they too could succeed.

Even though the French word for *souche* means a scrap of paper, to all the high school finalists in Zaire it means something much more than that. It means collected data that the Education Department inspects to decide whether a student can take the final high school exams. If they pass, the state gives them their high school certificate.

This particular year, I decided to stay at Kajiji, Ecole Belle Vue, until someone would bring the *souches* to us. Since the airplane was scheduled to come our way on February 16, 1985, I arranged to have the *souches* picked up as part of their mail service. I would have the girls sign them at the airstrip. Then, I had reservations to fly out with them.

On Tuesday, the pilot flew out. The plane, due to land at Kajiji at 10:00 o'clock, arrived at 11:15. Four girls, Uzzana, Katesha, Misambu and Tshingoma, waited for me at the public health center, located a block from the airstrip. At a table in the reception room, the girls filled out as much as they could and signed the documents for me. Since all information about their schooling was in the folder I had with me, I knew I could finish the rest when I got to Kikwit.

What an interesting trip! Everyone seemed to be transporting a pet, including a kitten, a puppy that snuggled up to me, and a pig's *oui, oui* (French *yes*). After picking up passengers at several bush air-strips, we finally landed at Kikwit.

I finished my business with the Education office, giving the required envelope to put the *souches* in, and leaving a package of typing paper for their office work. Then, I flew back to my picturesque home at Ecole Belle Vue, Kajiji.

Now, I had to concentrate on orienting the candidates for their finals at Shamusenga, a Catholic mission station.

Meanwhile, Tshilenga's shoulder became worse. The mission doctors could not find the cause of his problem. When Katy Penner, a missionary nurse and medical teacher, had to be sent to Vanga for medical help, we decided to send Citizen Tshilenga along with her.

When we welcomed him home a while later, we heard the dreaded word "cancer." It had been diagnosed late. I prayed that someone would be able to win him for Christ.

John Kliewer, Jr., a pilot for Missionary Aviation Fellowship, was flying in hopefully with a new passport and visa forms for me to fill out.

CHAPTER 28

THE DELAYED FINALS

"But this wife of mine, Tshingoma, a citizeness of Zaire, is not smart," her husband said. "She will never get her high school diploma. She has no learning ability."

"Oh, yes," I responded. "There is good hope for her. Please pay for her debt at school, and do find money for her transportation and food while she takes her state finals."

"There is no money. Why should she eat my money?"

"Find it. She is doing good work in high school. Her sewing is much better than some of the other students. Please make an effort. We must leave Friday. This is already Monday."

"If she goes, I will take her."

Four high school girls from our pattern making sewing school were asked to find the money to finish off their debts at the school.

When the Belgians had Congo as their colony, they saw the need for schools. Since they did not have enough teachers to fill these positions, they decided to pay for the teachers and principals who existed in their colony.

They started with the Catholic schools. Later, they offered the same to the Protestant schools. No money was given either to operate the schools or to build them. That is why students even today must pay for all materials used in their particular schools. They even had to pay for transportation to the Catholic Mission Center, where the state gave all graduates of the area their finals.

I walked to the sixth-grade classroom to discuss plans with my students there.

"We must bring the necessary food along that we will need for our stay there," I reminded the girls. "We must also pay for the trip down there. Uzzana, you still owe me Z.200,00. When will you pay this, and when will you pay for the trip and the food while at Shamusenga?"

"My aunt at Kahemba will help me," Uzzana responded. "Trust me."

"Katesha, you have paid a good part of yours," I said. "How will you finish off this debt?"

"I-I-I- believe you sh-sh-shall see the rest by phonie (short-wave)," she stuttered. "The m- m- mouth of our pastor from K- K-Kinshasa will arrive and help with this."

"The rest of you girls are dismissed," I told them. "Tshingoma, how about you? I must talk to you about your debt."

All the girls except Tshingoma walked out with their books on their heads. I turned to Tshingoma.

"You still have quite a debt at school," I reminded her. "You must write your finals. Who can help you?"

"Only one person must pay for me," she replied. "It is my husband. He does not believe that I will get my certificate."

"Tshingoma, I will go talk to him," I promised. "He is working in the office at the health center, isn't he?"

"Yes," she said. "He works mornings only."

Tshingoma's husband, a young, immature man of 20, was not ready to be a father in about five months. He dressed like his peers, who all copied western style clothes. He had only a part-time job.

From Lycée Ditalenu, I walked the mile and a half to the mission station where the church, hospital, maternity ward, dispensary, nurses school, public health office, a primary school and an airstrip were located. Both Ecole Belle Vue and the mission station were built on the edge of a long plateau.

As I walked, I noticed many paths leading down the steep, grassy mountainside. Zairians with heavy loads on their heads took paths without any difficulty. They led them to gardens, villages, streams, forests and hunting grounds.

As I passed the primary school, children recited their times tables (multiplication tables) in loud, certain voices, using the French numbers.

When I entered the public health office, Citizen Mushete greeted me politely, shaking my right hand while holding his right elbow with his left.

After some lively conversation, he asked, "Why are you always bothering me? Explain again why you think she can pass."

"Mushete," I said, "take a look at her report card. She has been studying hard. Half the final grade is taken from her report card of this year. She has covered all the technical material we received from the University of Kinshasa. They take all finals from these courses of study. She did well on the exams we gave her on these subjects."

"All right!" he responded rather vigorously. "You have convinced me. I will see what I can do. We will see each other tomorrow."

After shaking hands again, I left.

On Thursday, Tshingoma came to the school office to pay a part of the amount she owed.

"Tshingoma," I asked, "who finally paid this for you?"

"My father went to see my husband. He said, 'If you do not pay, there will be trouble.' In Zaire, this is no idle threat. He became afraid. He paid."

Early Friday morning, sixth-grade high school students from the surrounding villages walked to Kajiji with their préfets in order not to miss their ride to Shamusenga. The principals had corresponded with one another in order to arrange the much-needed ride for their students and themselves.

As names were called of those who had paid, they climbed into the back of the deep, large truck bed. When they were all in, they resembled clothes packed tightly in a large tin trunk.

Two other principals and I climbed into the front seat. Some small children, placed in our laps, would be shielded from the dry season dust and cinders.

Just before we left, the local pastor asked God's protection on each of us. It was no formality. We needed such protection, for outside of the big cities in Zaire, there were only a few paved roads. Others were only trails.

When we neared the ferry, the driver honked his horn to let the men who worked there know that we were coming. All of us got off the truck to wash up. When the ferry operator came, he said, "I do not know which approach to the ferry is best. The water has gone down. What do you think?"

I looked at the two approaches and both looked dangerous to me. Along the lower one, water reached well over its borders. The higher approach was so high above the low water line that we would have to drive down to get on the ferry. I told the driver of the truck to choose. He had to drive, not me.

"I think the lower is better," the driver said. "We will try to drive up by this path."

"How about putting your planks in front of the wheels leading up to the ferry?" I asked the drivers helper.

"Aaa (yes in Kituba), good!" he exclaimed. "We will try that."

They brought out their planks and put them in the road, covering up some of the deepest ruts, now filled with water. The ferry operator directed the driver.

The front wheels lined up just fine, but the back ones were not quite on the planks. Once the plank tipped up and almost stopped the truck, but finally the back wheels hit the runners of the ferry and the truck was on.

While crossing the river, we watched for the crocodiles and hippopotamuses that frequented at night, but we saw neither. After everyone was back on the truck, the students sang lustily in part harmony, songs in French, English, Chokwe, Lunda, Kituba and Lingala.

The truck came to a halt right in front of a bamboo barricade. We parked off the roadway. A soldier came to the truck, looking under and in back of the driver's seat.

"Where are you going?" he asked.

"We are going to Shamusenga to take finals," the driver replied.

"Show me the list of your students," the soldier said as he pointed to Professor Munda. "Who is he?" he asked.

"He is a teacher from Lycée Ditalenu's pattern-making high school," he said. "He came along to see his relatives."

"Show me your things," he ordered.

Professor Munda took his things and entered the bamboo shelter. Even though he was only five feet four inches tall, he had to stoop to get in.

"You women, you are not students," the soldier said. "Come with your things. We must look."

"We have no diamonds," they assured him. "We came to see our parents."

After about half an hour, the driver paid the small fee, then made sure all had boarded the truck.

"Citizen Kisalu!" the commander called out. "Let the students go."

The soldier clicked his heels together and saluted, then opened the bamboo barricade. We gave a sigh of relief, glad to again be on our way. After two hours on a rough truck ride, we reached the Catholic Mission Station, Shamusenga.

That Saturday, in June of 1985, 250 students stood at attention around the door of the exam room, waiting for pre-exam orientation.

Typically, the students from the different high schools and from the different majors were mixed to prevent them from cheating.

Each student received a number, marking the seat they would occupy during all four days of finals. After the students found their seats, the instructor gave them instructions for filling out their forms. The orientation given on Saturday stood them in good stead on Monday morning.

When Monday morning came at last, Misambu, Uzzana, Katshai and Tshingoma dressed with care. Each hair was braided in place. No two heads were alike. Katesha had Tshingoma do her hair in eight tiny rows of French braids on the top of her head.

Rounded to outline her smooth forehead,the rows ran straight back over the top of her head to the back of her neck. At the sides, she had a part running from both sides of the eight rows to her ears. From this part, branch-like braids led sideways to her neck. The ends, then braided together, formed curl-like earrings at the tip of her oblong ear lobes.

Uzzana had her hair squared off into about 50 bunches. Each square, tied together and fuzzed out, looked like dandelions ready to blow away in the dry season wind. Her hair was quite short because of the Zairian rules on high school girls' hair.

While in school, the girls had to fix their hair like the boys'. This was to prevent a lot of time spent on their hair, to decrease flirting with their fantastic hair styles, and to save the money they would have to pay for black string used in tying their hair.

Misambu had her hair braided, starting from a central point at the right side of her head. They were half-circles, finely braided French style, curved, leading to the back of her head. The ends were tied together to form curlicues, from the back top of her head to the neck.

Girls comprised a minority among those hoping to get high school certificates. The high school students didn't wear their required uniform, blue skirt and white blouse, because the inspector didn't demand it. Instead, they proudly displayed the dresses they wore, for they had sewed them in their classes.

Their skirts were three tiers of ruffles, gathered in to fit their slim waists. The dresses had a set-in sleeve with two three-inch tucks, like pleats, protruding from the shoulder. About two inches from the border of the sleeve, they inserted a ribbon forming a ruffled effect. Their medium-low neckline was sculpted with a rounded collar. As the Zairian students stood in a circle, they sang "*The Zairoise*," their national anthem. Our girls took their places, each at a separate table. I went to the inspector.

"Citizen Inspector," I asked, " may I give these things to the pattern-making, sewing high school girls?"

He looked longingly at these tools. "Yes," he said, "you may. After you give those things, you understand that you must leave the examination room."

I gave each student a French curve, a graded metric ruler, an eraser, a pencil sharpener and pattern paper. They would facilitate the meticulous sketches they had to draw. I talked to each student, quietly reassuring them in a low voice.

"Misambu," I said, "do not even pretend to look at your neighbor. You do not want to be dismissed from this exam room."

"Katshai, think before you answer," I suggested. "Do not hurry."

"Tshingoma, you can do it," I assured her. "Think positively."

"Uzzana," I said, "I have confidence in you."

I walked briskly to the nuns' home for breakfast. On the way, I noticed that the other principals had gathered at the home of the local principal. They enjoyed a banana, sweetened coffee and a bun. They stayed as close to the examination room as they dared.

The inspector had asked us all to leave the mission grounds altogether, but that seemed unreasonable. When anyone left the examination room, he or she was questioned as to the types of problems or questions presented.

They wanted to find out if these exams were a true review of what they had their instructors teach. They always hoped for better results than the year before. Their reputation as préfet (principal) depended on the number of their students who passed.

In passing, I greeted some of the latecomers, but felt I must hurry on my way, for the sisters were waiting breakfast for me. Following the footpath, I cut across a large expanse of green grass mingled with trees which were still green, because we were only into the third week of dry season.

At breakfast, I started to tell the sisters about the 250 students crowded under the makeshift shelter, when there came a knock at the door. A Zairian principal called to me.

"Mademoiselle Kopper," he said, "you must go right now to the examination center. The inspector is calling for you."

I left the table without breakfast. I met our pattern-making students on the path leading to the girl's dorm. They wept.

"Our exams didn't come," they said. "We cannot take our state exams. Mademoiselle, please go and see what is wrong!"

I entered the exam room, where the inspector sat at the desk. Zairian surveyors walked up and down the aisles to be sure no students were cheating. I approached the inspector.

"Citizen Inspector, you called for me?" I asked.

"Yes, Mademoiselle Kopper," he said, "look at this list of exams that were sent in this banded, tin trunk. The exams for your students are not here. They sent exams for stewardesses instead of yours. We must let the Education Office know right away. I hope they will have a way to send them immediately, but how?"

"How about the Catholic father sending a message by short wave?" I suggested. "Should we send it to Kinshasa and Kikwit?"

"Yes," he said, "let us have faith that they will see a way to send them, either by plane or by truck."

Both the Protestant mission, Kamiala, about five kilometers on the other side of Kahemba, and the Catholic father sent shortwave messages to the different places. All now knew of our dilemma.

The other students kept on writing. Most Zairian high schools were geared to meet the future needs of the man more than the woman. Many a husband or boyfriend has gone off to the big city to get a job, leaving his village wife or girlfriend behind because she "just would not fit in." We started the school in the bush in order to stop that trend. We wanted the Zairian man to be proud of his country wife.

I wanted her to be happy with her husband and children, with a solid Christian foundation. This would do away with superstitions, fears, witchcraft, and idol worship that had been known to destroy and kill.

Our girls fixed and refixed their hair. I called them in to have devotions. I counseled them to study.

"But Mademoiselle," Katesha said, "we have already prepared a long time ago."

Sympathetically, I turned to her. "I know you have," I said. "Have faith, the exams will come."

Uzzana, her pale face not even looking up, said, "Maybe our government does not even know we exist. Maybe they do not count our school as good."

"Uzzana, look at me," I said. "You know that is not true. Remember when our secondary school inspector came to Kajiji? He made a thorough inspection of the office. He left me a copy of the report. I was very pleased with the marks he gave us.

"A letter from the Education Department in Kinshasa also verifies our listing there. They even sent us the number under which we are listed. We are an official school. If we are not, would they keep on paying all our teachers?

"They accepted all our applications for these finals. Uzzana, the finals will come. Have faith in God. Did we not just pray and tell God all about this? We are His children. Have faith. Jesus will stand by us. He will never leave us nor forsake us."

On Thursday, after their exams, other students packed up and left for home. Somehow, I knew the exams would eventually come, but how long would we have to wait?

On Friday morning before breakfast, the inspector sent a message. "The exams for the sewing, pattern-making high school are here," it said. "Come to Kahemba. I am no longer going to stay at Shamusenga to give these exams. Relocate at Kahemba."

Our girls put their few belongings on their heads and walked the 17 kilometers to Kahemba. They waved freely, and with joy, to the mission people who lived on the south side. Some stopped them, asking where they were going.

"Our finals have come," they said. "We can take our finals. We can't stop to talk now. Pray for us."

The way was an unpaved, dusty, dirt road with a few large trees on the side, but the trees were mostly stumps trying to grow in spite of being burnt every year.

Upon arrival at Kahemba, they passed the large open market. They headed right down main street, then cut down towards the residential section where the high school was located.

No patterns were sold in Zaire. All people had their clothes sewn by a seamstress. If a Zairian girl could graduate from a pattern-making, sewing high school, she could earn her own living, for the Zairian woman must help earn the living for the family. She could either teach the first two grades of technical subjects in high school, or she could sew for her family and others.

The exam room, a run-down shell of a stone building, had a dirt floor and home-made desks. At least, the shelter had a good roof over them preventing the hot tropical sun from beating down upon them while writing their exams. This could not be said of the lean-to, temporary shelter where the others had written their finals.

When the girls walked into the exam room, not a hair was out of place. "*Petrou* (beautiful)," said the inspector.

In the course of the four hours of exams that morning, the inspector looked over Uzzana's shoulder as she meticulously drew the fly of a pair of men's pants to scale, with the cut down and arrows to show the different layers of material. He marveled.

That afternoon, they again wrote for four hours. This meant, of course, that they wrote exams for eight hours that first day.

The local administrator called to us to join his wife and children for the evening meal. They lived in a semi-modern brick home, about a block from school. They also invited the general inspector and the visiting inspector who was giving the exams.

In Zaire, at a big dinner, the usual way was to place everyone according to their respective walks in life. All inspectors would be placed together. The principals would be next. Then the teachers. The wife and children would wait until all were served. Then, they would eat what was left.

Here, however, they broke the rules, and we all tore a bite of luku from a large ball, dipped it into one dish of meat sauce and enjoyed every bite even though we ate without any plates, knife, spoon or fork.

"Where are you going for the night?" I asked Katesha after we had eaten.

"The g-g-general inspector is a r-r-relative of mine," she said. "They gave me a p-p-place to sleep."

We were already walking down the path when I asked the teacher, "Where do you and your baby want to spend the night?"

"My child and Misambu and I want to see a motel room. Can we take this path and look at the motel over there?"

After looking it over, they decided to take it. "Mademoiselle préfet," they said, "let us walk you home."

"What about the food that is left?" they asked upon entering the fenced-in home of the sisters. "Can we divide it among ourselves?"

"Yes, but there is not much left," I responded. "There is a little bit of manioc flour, a few cans of sardines, a few caterpillars and palm oil."

"Mademoiselle," the teacher said, "what do you think? Would the sisters let me take a small kerosene tornado lantern? I need it to look after this baby of mine."

"I will ask them," I said.

They left with the food and kerosene lantern on their heads. Misambu carried the one-year-old tied to her back. Uzzana and Tshingoma walked to Uzzana's aunt's home. The rest went to find their rented room.

The sisters led me to their guest room. I slept well, knowing our students would get a full opportunity to prove their knowledge.

The next morning, we arrived refreshed and ready for the day's exams. After writing all morning, to our dismay the inspector wanted the girls to resume the exams in the afternoon. I refused. I approached him in front of the general inspector.

"Citizen inspector," I said, "these girls are tired. They have the right to take four days for these exams. Please stay and let them finish on Sunday morning."

Wrinkling his forehead while placing one leg on a broken bench, he said, "I want to visit my sister in the village before I go back to Kikwit. She is tormented. Since my folks died, she has been trying to contact them. I don't know how to help her."

I couldn't give up. My girls needed rest. Their minds needed a change before writing again.

"What would it take to induce you to stay until after the exams on Sunday morning?" I asked, "You will still have time to stop and visit your sister on your way to Kikwit."

He wanted more money. He knew he had me.

"I cannot pay for another night's lodging in this motel. If you pay, I will stay." Since night lodging, according to American standards, costs only peanuts in Zaire, that is what I did.

When the finals ended, to our surprise Mushete, Tshingoma's husband, was there to take her home. He was now proud that his wife had taken the finals. We said goodbye, knowing that the results would be written in the Kinshasa newspaper in about two months' time.

In the first days of September, news of the finals reached us. Only 15 out of the 250 students who had taken the exams at Shamusenga had passed. Three out of our four girls received their certificates.

When Misambu came to get her certificate, she had traveled a long way by truck. She wore a long, Zairian, two-piece dress and a matching scarf, artfully folded into pleats around her head. She now teaches at another pattern-making high school, helping others not only to sew, draw and make a living, but also providing a positive influence on all whom she meets.

The Lord is building His church. These women are doing their part, glorifying their Lord and taking their rightful place in their homes and communities.

Tshingoma's husband came over to pay the rest of his wife's debt and to pick up her certificate. "Thanks much for making my wife take those exams," he said with a smile. "Thanks to God and to you also!"

CHAPTER 29
CIGARETTE WINDSHIELD WIPER

The Education Department of Kinshasa really demanded the impossible of all principals with a sixth-grade graduating class. The same frustrations plagued us every year. The *souches,* legal forms that every applicant had to fill out to take his or her high school state exams, forms we asked our Kikwit friends in the Education Office to send us, hadn't arrived.

Citizen Pakisa, the Public Health Director, found the forms in Kikwit all sold out. Citizen Kabeya, found the forms still depleted in Kahemba. He left a note saying he was on his way to Gungu to buy some forms. He expected to be back Saturday or Sunday.

After the church service, the four sixth-grade girls came over and related all kinds of stories. I couldn't blame them. If I had been in their shoes, I too would be upset. All the other principals had already presented the *souches* to the Education committee.

On Monday, March 21,1986, I walked to the mission to get information by shortwave from Kikwit. The church short-wave message from Citizen Pakisa's brother said there were now *souches* at Kahemba. A carryall was leaving that day for that small settlement.

The carryall picked me up at 9:45. We drove the eight miles to the commercial center and waited close to the new open market. I found I had some time to visit the open market and look up a vendor to whom I had owed a small debt. He couldn't be found.

Back at the place where I had left the land rover, it was gone. I walked up the street to where the stores ended and sat down on the roots of a beautifully shaped mango tree. There a breeze helped a few clouds to hide the sun. Not sure what else to do, I sat and waited...and waited.

Much later, the vehicle drove up.

When it started to rain, the driver informed us that his windshield wipers didn't work. A little later, he stopped in the middle of a one-way trail, took out some cigarettes and, crushing them, spread the leaves all over the windshield. The tobacco absorbed the bulk of the downpour, while he continued to drive on.

The carryall leaked in several places. My right side was getting wet. The rubber padding around the door had gone. In front of me, vents to let in air, also let in rain. I opened my umbrella a little to ward off the rain to my right and in front.

At Kahemba, again I joined the Catholic sisters around their table - a real treat. I welcomed a steaming cup of tea and Belgian-type pie made of shortbread with jam on it.Having no mode of transportation at my disposal, and since it was still raining, I took the afternoon off to read.

The next morning, I walked to the Education Office to look for *souches*. None had been sent for us. They suggested that I ask at the high school where our girls had taken their exams last year. The manager called me by name into his outer office.

He explained that the principal had gone to Gungu to present his school's *souches*. He knew of no extra *souches*. They had received enough for three schools but not for us. All hope to find them here had vanished. I had to rely upon Citizen Kabeya eventually to bring them to me.

I walked to the edge of their large open market where taxis were parked. I had hoped for a ride back to Kajiji that afternoon. One chauffeur said they were going that way, I arranged for them to pick me up at the sisters' home, but it didn't work out.

I tried to walk back to the taxi stand with my baggage, umbrella and food, plus a back-pack, but the load was too much for me. A kind student offered to help me with my things. When I reached the taxi stand, he refused to take pay for it.

I stayed around the taxi stop until it became obvious that no vehicles were leaving for Kajiji that evening. Starting to walk back with all my things, I met the same student who again offered to help me. He knew just where I was going and even the room I was staying in. This time, he reluctantly took 100 Zaires and a Christian tract.

What a joy it was, during my stay in the area, to meet some of my former students by chance. Muadiya, who received her government high school certificate and had taught for me for a while, had married and now expected their first child.

About 6:00 o'clock, a former student asked me to walk with him to meet part of his family. After he confided some of his problems, I suggested that he talk to his pastor.

After walking back to my room, we sat outside and reviewed the Four Spiritual Laws he had read while at Ecole Belle Vue. He was now a diamond smuggler, illegally going in and out of Angola. I reminded him that he had more brains than that and insisted he could make his living another way. He finally realized the danger in such a work, and we prayed the sinner's prayer together.

The next morning, he was there again. We talked for a while. At 8:00 o'clock, I walked back to the taxi stand without my baggage. From my perch on a bench, shaded with a leaky grass roof, surrounded by a bamboo-like fence, I found life very interesting.

This open market was much larger than the one at Kulindji. The mud-and-stick lean-tos and bamboo shelters with roofs of grass, palm branches and occasional corrugated tin, all looked to be in some stage of disrepair.

Many people loitered near the bench where I sat, in front of a tumble-down store. Periodically, some stopped to buy fried fish or chicken being barbecued in a dusty, vacant lot. The yelling of taxi helpers calling out their destinations filled the air.

There were diamond smugglers leaving for the border town of Shanafaha. One man they called pastor, who traveled between Kinshasa and Angola, sold gas in the alley between open market sheds.

Others stopped to chat, having nothing else to do. Occasionally we had theological discussions. Some asked pertinent questions. One wanted to study to be a medical doctor. Even though I could not get the souches, all had not been lost. I could witness for my Savior and Lord.

I met an official school director coming from Kikwit. He had heard that Citizen Kabeya was in a broken-down truck, 40 kilometers from Kahemba, and was going to go there and see what he could find out.

One woman I met at the open market looked almost frightening. The garment thrown over her fat body looked like a negligee, something very few in Zaire could afford. She wore a *pan* (wrap-around piece of cloth) over it for a skirt.

"She is my big sister," some men said.

She looks like a harlot to me, I thought, but I didn't say anything.

Later on, she came back with just a *pan* wrapped around her. She had had a bath, probably at a nearby river. To my surprise, when we loaded up to go to Kajiji, this hefty lady also boarded. She sat next to me in the front seat. She overlapped my shoulders, but I felt surprisingly comfortable. She helped keep me warm, despite a broken window just in back of me.

These Zairian women kept up a stream of conversation. I hardly had an opportunity to say anything. She knew Lingala and French, but not Kituba, our trade language. Of her six children, three lived abroad, two were in Belgium, one in America. Her husband worked in auto-financing in Kinshasa.

We headed for the sisters' home. After saying goodbye - the Belgian way, with kisses on both cheeks - we took off.

It started to rain. The road became a running stream.We rocked from one side to another, as the driver tried to dodge some of the worst, washed-out ruts and potholes.

To find the village where the ferry workers lived proved quite an ordeal. After spending an hour stumbling in the dark, the driver and his helper found the village where they lived and managed to persuade them to come out into the rain.

At the ferry, I knew we would have to wade into the water to enter. Being experienced at this, I decided to keep my shoes on, for fear of dropping them into the swollen river. With my flashlight guiding each step, I went in, shoes and all, stepping on stones covered with water. Eventually, I reached the ferry without mishap and stood on planks next to the carryall.

The gangplanks were pulled up by hand pulleys. Doing this in the dark wasn't pleasant, but it did have the taste of adventure. After everyone else got off, we arrived at Ecole Belle Vue in front of my home. Wet, dirty and hungry, I ate some homemade breakfast rolls and a banana, then I went to bed, knowing I had tried my best to get those elusive *souches* for my girls.

CHAPTER 30

"NO" WAS THE ANSWER

As I walked to the bush mission station airport, some Zairians, mostly students, followed me.

"I didn't come to this sewing, pattern-making high school with my baby just to be turned away from the final exams," Mambu screamed. "I must have my high school diploma."

I faced a quandary. As principal, I couldn't go to Kikwit to get the final legal papers for our graduating class required by the Zairian Education Department. Since Principal Ngunza planned to pick up the forms for his school, he agreed to bring some along for me.

The forms asked that pupils state the year and name of each school attended from sixth grade through high school. Dates and names had to correspond with their report cards. Each student had to sign her report.

Since Principal Ngunza helped his graduating class fill out their forms, I asked him to please help my students with theirs. I had an hour before the Missionary Aviation Fellowship flight to Kikwit.

After finishing my report, I walked into my front room where the principal helped our girls. He had already gone.

"Now I will check to see if you have filled it out correctly," I said to Mambu.

"MMmmmmm," she muttered. I knew something was wrong. Her friend Kamba looked as if something big was brewing.

Upon checking the dates of their last years of high school, I noticed that they had changed dates to cover up the year before. In 1983-84, the girls had flunked. It was their fault, for they refused to study. Later, we asked them why.

"*Kambangist* (diamond smugglers going into Angola) like us. If we flunk, we won't need to teach. They will marry us."

This time, they were determined to pass high school. They wanted to teach and make a living by sewing. In 1984-85, both girls were out of school. Mambu became desperately ill. Kamba married and had her baby. Her husband attended our carpenter's school in Kinshasa.

The Education Department of Zaire has a rule that students cannot repeat one given year of high school more than once. If, on this report, there is a missing year, the authorities automatically assume that the student had gone to another school and flunked, therefore left it blank. This was the reason for changing dates. I had previously cleared it with an inspector, however. He assured me it would be all right. I refused to sign their cover-up.

When I started to erase the lies, Kamba called for her brother, Lulendo. He had the air of an educated teacher, for he had been to college. To admit that he was aiming to repeat the last year the third time was below his dignity. He knew, however, that this was strictly against Zairian rules. He hoped for a cover-up to overrule his case.

Lulendo tried to shame me out of erasing the false dates. I refused.

"Haven't you ever sinned?" he asked me.

"Yes," I said, "I'm not perfect."

"Is this a greater sin than those others?" he persisted.

"I refuse to sign a lie," I answered.

Soon a Zairian pastor appeared outside. Dressed in his clerical collar, he wanted to impress us that he was also the legal representative for the mission to the government for our Southern field. He tried to appear as if he just happened to pass by. He looked around, not saying a word.

The bush mission station airport at Kajiji is about two miles from my home. While walking to meet a plane, the two students and Lulendo harassed me all the way.

"You said you came from America to help these girls of Zaire," Lulendo said. "This isn't helping them. If they can't take their finals, you will pay for all their school expenses."

If I had not been an expatriate and a Christian, I would have

Doctor Roger, Joan and son Jonah Fast.

Son Nathaneal Fast held the umbrella while the pilot filled the Missionary Aviation Fellowship plane with gas.

worried about his cursing me.

"This is all your fault," Mambu said, almost shouting.

"But I spoke to the inspector at Kahemba," I explained again, as politely as possible. "He assured me that all is well. You will take your exams."

In passing the church, I noticed that two Zairians pushed the large gasoline barrel back over the rough footpath leading from the airport. The pilot and workers had already pumped gas with a hand pump to fill the one tank on the Missionary Aviation Fellowship plane.

We arrived at the airport, where no building or sign stood to indicate the location of the lonely airstrip in the middle of a forest. An occasional government official came from Kulindji to check out passengers coming and going.

Mambu, breathing hard with indignation, tried to dissuade me. "When the inspector at Kikwit sees the missing year, he will reject our applications. You must sign these filled-out forms as they are. You know erasures are also against the rules."

"But that is why you did it secretly, so that I would have to sign," I responded. "Isn't that the truth? I refuse."

I quickly grabbed the mail bag that had just arrived by plane. Heading for the cab of the mission pick-up, I sorted the incoming mail looking for my letters.

The airstrip attendant forbade the villagers to cross the airport runway on the east side, for the one-engine plane would be heading in that direction soon after take off. Just before boarding the one-engine plane, I took a minute to try to reason with them once more.

"You know," I said, "I can't fly to Kikwit, pick up new forms, fly here to let you sign them, turn around and fly back to Kikwit to again present them, then fly to finish out the school year. Who can pay for all of this? You also know that the deadline to present these papers is tomorrow."

It was a relief to board the plane. Strapping myself into the co-pilot's seat of the four-passenger plane, I looked over my shoulder to see who the other passengers were. A medical worker and a sick patient needed to get to the hospital at Vanga.

Just before take-off, I saw villagers from the hospital and a group of first-year medical students at the side of the airstrip. Medical students held their long knives like grass-cutters. As soon as the plane took off, they would cut the fast-growing grass that covered the landing strip.

In two hours, we arrived at Kikwit. After greeting my fellow missionary friends who worked there, I asked them for a black felt pen, a black Bic, a good eraser and a ruler. I spent the evening making the dates correspond to their authentic report cards, not allowing any cover-up.

Thanks to good paper and honest intentions, the finished corrected documents really didn't show the erasures. My friends and I prayed that these truthful reports would be accepted.

The next morning, upon arrival at the inspector's temporary headquarters, the head inspector glanced at the report of one of my pupils.

"Why are you not at Gungu?" he asked. "You know that all principals from Kajiji are to go there for this important inspection."

Placing my left hand over my right elbow to indicate the sincerity of not having a dagger in my left hand while shaking his right hand, I shook his hand with respect.

"The Missionary Aviation Fellowship plane refused to fly me to Gungu," I said. "They agreed, however, to fly me here. Since there are neither buses nor trains going to that isolated village, and since today is the last day to present these reports, could you possibly inspect them here?"

Looking at my graying hair, he asked me, "Are you the préfet of the Kajiji pattern-making, sewing high school? Isn't that close to Kulindji and close to the Angolan border? How many expatriates are there at that isolated mission station?"

Before I could answer, he looked at another principal's report but called upon one of the inspectors to look over my students' applications for the final exams.

I kept on praying. After paying the specified amount for each student, and after giving him a picture for each application, they all passed. I felt like shouting, with David, "I will give thanks to the Lord with all my heart" (Psalms 8:1). My missionary friends' prayers, our students' prayers and mine had been answered.

Upon returning to my students, I rejoiced that they settled down and again began to study for their finals. I didn't feel at ease, however. What if the government Education Department decided to go over all this again? What if they found the missing year for these two students? I knew what I must do.

Two medical doctors must verify that these girls were ill, explaining why they were not in school last year. Our mission doctors filled out the required legal papers stating each case. Then, I sent them with a letter asking them to please place these into their folders. I felt relieved for having told the truth, never wavering on this point. God gave me strength to be a testimony in an hour of crisis.

Meanwhile, Citizen Tshilenga wasn't improving. He had recently remarried and was the father of a small baby. He had received regular chemotherapy, and 11 blood transfusions which temporarily strengthened him.

When he was at Vanga Mission Station, Dr. Fountain and others tried to lead him to our Christ. He would not listen to them, but when Citizen Kaseka, a faithful medical worker at Kajiji, talked to him, he finally trusted Jesus Christ as his Savior and Lord.

A week later, while being seen by the doctor and nurses at Kajiji, he started to gasp for air. While they gave him his twelfth blood transfusion, he died. Loud wailing from the girls' dorm meant each had to out-do the other in expressing their grief. Typically, the one not wailing would be blamed for Tshilenga's death.

After dark, our professors came to me saying that the mourners needed another pressure lamp. I joined them and walked to the dead man's home on the west side of the mission station. On the way, some of our teachers stopped to enter the church to pick up a bench. They placed it close to the large bonfire friends had built in the middle of their yard.

Friends had already constructed a shelter of palm branches over poles cut from the forest. Citizen Tshilenga's body still lay on a bamboo bed. A number of women sat close to his body. Men gathered a little farther away.

Pastor Tshimika sat close to one of Citizen Tshilenga's sons. The young man broke into a mournful chant. Among other things we could decipher, we heard him say, "You should have died after your oldest son had finished secondary school."

After this, other family members took up the chant. "He died like a dog one-half *kupolad* (rotten)." Others picked up the mournful chant. The men's church choir sang songs in between their chants. Tears streamed down the faces of others who did not wail loudly.

On Friday, the day of the funeral, I again met the mourners. Most of them had stayed up with the body all night. When I sat down, Tshilenga's four-year-old son crawled on my lap. I hugged the lonely child and again fell in love with him. How could I comfort him? His father had gone to glory.

Citizen Tshilenga's brother happened to be Citizeness Kabey's husband. A faithful woman, she had taken care of the girl's dorm for many years. This delightful couple took Citizen Tshilenga's children in, including the four-year-old.

Meanwhile, Tshilenga's body had been covered with a Zairian flag. Having served his country in battle, he merited a military funeral. Ladies sitting closest to the body kept busy chasing away flies. After his body had been placed in a home-made casket, everyone followed the pallbearers into the large church.

Thinking of Tshilenga's short Christian life, only a week, reminded me of the comforting words of our dying Saviour to the thief on the cross: "Today shalt thou be with Me in paradise!" (Luke 23:43).

Principal Kabeya, in charge of the mixed high school, Citizen Ngila, director of the pedagogy school, and the director of the primary school and I sat in my front room trying to figure out the monies sent to pay all teachers in the region. It had come from the World Bank to the Kinshasa Education Office, then was sent to our Mennonite Brethren Education office in Kikwit. It was brought to us by a faithful, trustworthy teacher.

As we were discussing just how to get this money to the bush schools, several students knocked on my door. They told me that students from other high schools had just arrived with their principals for their French dissertation final.

They claimed that these other schools, together with our finalists here at Ecole Belle Vue, should take it here, for our mission station had now been named as a secondary final exam post.

Earlier, the medical students had moved into their new dorm, leaving the old one here at Ecole Belle Vue for us. This included a huge kitchen, where we later had our food lab, and a large dining room.

The school inspectors and principals of the various high schools decided that since the kitchen and dining area were the largest two rooms available, and they were attached, this final exam in French essay should be given here.

The rooms were made ready on a Saturday afternoon. School desks were brought in from various classrooms. In this essay, it was virtually impossible to cheat. So it didn't matter that the students would be placed close together.

On Sunday morning, all the finalists reported on the grass in front of the building. It was my responsibility to provide Sunday breakfast to the principals who came with their students, the inspectors and the police who looked after the students.

With eight at the table, I served a continental breakfast, with bananas.

At the appointed time, hundreds of students waited outside the exam rooms. The inspector read off the names of each student eligible to take part. Before all were settled in their appointed seats, the inspector handed an envelope to Mambu, the representative of our students. She would verify that the envelope had not been tampered with. Then, he opened it and read the four different topics they would choose from for the dissertation.

The students started writing at 10:00 o'clock. The inspectors made their rounds, just to make sure nobody cheated. Upon looking over the shoulder of one of my students, the inspector told me later that she was the first girl he had seen who could write a French sentence without making a mistake.

Inspector de Pool sat there in front of the students sipping a drink to keep cool. The primary inspector kept busy at a typewriter, composing a request asking for the right of one of his schools to open a fourth grade.

Citizeness Nsumbombo, the sixth-grade teacher, sewed all day, making the sample garment that the students of the graduating class would copy. She also kept occupied repairing sewing machines so that the students wouldn't be hindered from finishing their two finals in sewing the next day.

Four and a half hours later, students came out of the exam rooms, exhausted but happy that at least one exam had been completed.

After collecting all their papers, the inspector sealed them in a large envelope and then sealed it the second time with wax. This was done in front of the students as witnesses. Now, this precious package would be sent to the Education Office in Kinshasa to be corrected.

The students from other high schools went home, but the inspectors stayed. The next day, our girls faced a whole day of sewing for their two different final exams.

On Monday morning, our four finalists waited patiently to enter the sewing classroom. The inspector must see that all was in order before they could start. Second period had come and still the sixth grade hadn't been able to start sewing. I felt sorry for them and brought them buns and bananas to cheer them up a bit.

While ringing the bell for the third period, I noticed that the inspector had finally come. The exams could get under way. After seating each girl in her corner, to discourage cheating, the proctor called them to the teacher's table to look at the finished garment they were to copy. No directions on how to proceed were given them. This was all part of the final exam in sewing.

A blouse for a 3-year-old had been chosen for this exercise. It had an inserted pocket and an unusual enclosure at the neck. After each student examined it, the girls went back to pick up the pieces of this already cut-out blouse. They knew they would not be leaving the exam room until they had finished sewing this complicated blouse.

The teacher and the state inspector watched them while they sewed at their own speed. They finished around 3:00 o'clock. When the blouses had been graded, two girls had passed but two had not. The two who had not passed were very near to 50 per cent, so even now they could possibly pass when the other finals to be given in June would be averaged in.

Tuesday found these students back in class. In the remaining school days, their teachers brushed up on all points in their English, Math, French, pattern-making, and others that they thought might be on the finals still ahead at the Shamusenga mission station.

When the next exam time came in mid-June, we hired a big cattle truck to haul all the registered sixth-grade finalists for their exams at Shamusenga. Students from nearby high schools walked to Kajiji for their ride. A few of the passengers sat on top of the lug-

gage, while others had to stand for lack of space. Another principal and I sat in the cab.

As we bounced along the one-way dirt trail through the stump
forest of half-burnt trees, the students sang songs in harmony
using all the different languages they knew. Once, we got stuck in
the sand. As in similar situations, the chauffeur-helper jumped out
and pulled out two long planks of wood. After placing them under
the wheels of the big truck, he threw the truck into four-wheel-
drive and let out the clutch.

Slowly, we gained traction and momentum. The two chauffeur-
helpers quickly replaced the planks, then ran to catch up with the
truck and climbed aboard without stopping it.

The ferry was a flat, wooden platform built upon two row boats.
It was just large enough to hold one truck and its passengers. It
was the beginning of dry season, and the river was low. The ferry
could not float in close to the shore. So we had to wade into the
water to walk up the runners and into it.

We stood on the sides of the truck, holding on to the railing of
the ferry. The workers pulled on the chain, slowly hauling the
barge and its cargo across the swift, deep river, while we watched
other Zairians as they rowed dug-out canoes and bamboo rafts.

Reaching Shamusenga after about two more hours of travel, our
girls were shown the crude girls' dorm they would live in for the
duration of the finals.

On Monday morning, a police officer from Kahemba arrived.
The appointed inspector for the center came from the big city, carrying a banded tin trunk in which the final exams were kept. All
finalists watched as they chopped off the bands and a student verified that no one had tampered with the contents. Then, for four
days these students wrote their final examinations upon which
their futures so greatly depended.

These exams to gain their high school diploma seem overdone,
but for these Zairians their teachers say it is a good thing. One
Zairian said when the state does away with this, it will be a sad day
for us. It keeps both teachers and students on the alert.

After a lifetime of "exams" on this earth, will I eventually win a
crown to place at my Lord's feet?

CHAPTER 31

A CITY OF REFUGE

When the last student had left for dry season vacation, I had to begin preparation for the next school year. Thus, all would be in order for the incoming principal to take over. I also had to think of an orientation trip home with Margaret Dyck.

The unassembled treadle sewing machines that the Chinese government had given us haunted me. Before leaving Zaire for good, I just had to get all ten of the sewing machines properly assembled. So I flew off to Kinshasa to look for necessary parts.

When I arrived at the capital city, our mission chauffeur was given to me for my final shopping. He and I searched for the right screws in every open market we could find. I did find some that fit fine. I ended up wiring some parts together with baling wire. Now, our students could use all 10 treadle sewing machines given to us by the Chinese.

After the dry season, in the last week of August, the Kinshasa newspaper announced the names of students who would receive their government high school diploma. Under Lycée Ditalenu's pattern-making, sewing high school, Mambu and Kamba's names indicated-they would be receiving their high school diploma. God had honored my truthfulness and given these two girls wisdom and strength to persevere.

Meanwhile, a well-dressed, dignified, older man walked past my home. I could not remember seeing him at the mission before.

"This man just recently came from a small village," my house help told me. "He has moved to this larger center because he is now old and therefore is blamed for all ills, including deaths, that befell his village. Younger ones in his village asked, 'How else had this person survived to live this long?'"

Soon after I came to the Belgian Congo, we missionaries had been invited to join our Congolese friends at a political meeting. The sector chief called about eight older people, detained in a primitive jail, to stand in front of us.

These graying senior citizens hobbled up to obey orders. We looked at their wrinkled faces and were surprised and appalled to see that someone had woven green grass into mocking, eye-glass frames they were forced to wear.

"These are the ones who are eating your children," the keeper of the jail said.

I asked Pastor Tshimika Sr., about the attitudes of villagers towards the elderly. He said part of his work was to warn older people not to complain about having no one to gather wood for their fires or water for cooking. That was to prevent their being blamed for deaths in the villages.

An older pastor, Citizen Lumeya Sr., told me he shaved his head in order to try to cover up his gray hair. I asked the pastor who came to the mission station and for what reasons.

Some disagreeable citizens couldn't get along with their village relatives. They escaped them by coming here. Others came because they found employment here. Many found this convenient because there were classes of higher education for their children.

Many came for the right reasons: to hear the Word of God, to grow spiritually and to have fellowship with other believers. Others, like this fellow, came for a refuge. They were old and didn't want to be blamed for the misfortunes of their village.

On Thursday, February 3, 1987, I invited Pastor Muyeshi and his wife, who planted a church at Kulindgi, the commercial center, to my home. They played a vital role in leading some of the 35,000 precious members of our Zairian Mennonite Brethren church to the Lord Jesus Christ.

I also invited Mama and Papa Kamanda to my luku dinner. Seated around the table, I asked them to tell me their conversion experience; also, some of the fables shared around their campfires to help correct someone who isn't living right.

Now Kamanda was retired. He admitted that before he was a Christian he had killed many a person. Citizens from Kamanda's village wanted him to become chief. He refused, saying this would draw him into witchcraft. "I am a Christian now," he said. "I am staying close to Pastor Muyeshi."

Citizen Muyeshi, pastor of the church of Kulindji, about five miles from Ecole Belle Vue, Kaji-ji.

Citizen Kamanda, a grandfather, still strong and healthy, talked about many things. When I arrived in 1952, it was Kamanda who had learned to keep the water ram working. This German-made water system ran without any sort of fuel.

The force of the water pushed a piston up and down, causing the water to run into a pipe leading up the steep mountainside. It filled a large tank which supplied us with running water for years. Kamanda constantly shoveled out collected sand which would stop water from running.

Now retired, Kamanda admitted that he had killed many people before becoming a Christian.

"A chief in a village had to have killed someone before he became chief," he explained. "The muscles of the dead whom he had killed were braided into a bracelet. After he became chief, he again had to be covered with human blood by killing someone else.

If this pattern isn't followed, Zairians without God believe this *ndoki* would backfire upon him.

"The one who has a *ndoki* is believed to have power to send a crocodile or a snake to kill his victim. The idea behind eating human flesh is to gain the wisdom of the dead person. If a teacher died, part of his flesh was sent to another fetisher in secret to eat. The receiver must either pay the high price for the human meat or kill someone with like credentials to send flesh back to the first sender.

"When a friend of the one marked to be killed tells him, he either runs for his life or calls the chief of the village and elders. They discuss this for a long time. If the intended victim pays the price that the enemy bought the flesh for, he finds himself free and out of danger."

The citizens from Kamanda's village wanted him to become chief. He refused, because this would draw him into witchcraft.

"I am a Christian now," he said. "I am staying close to Pastor Muyeshi."

Now, in 1987, Chief Shamulele of Shauyanga village had been very ill and lay unconscious for three days. When he regained consciousness, he said, "I have seen God. God told me that I couldn't possibly be accepted by Him because I had been too wicked."

When he was told that God could and would forgive even him, he said, "I'm waiting for my so-called Christian brethren to change their behavior, to quit dealing with *ndoki power*."

When they listened, the chief also became a child of God. He told his children not to live as he had. "Follow the Lord Jesus Christ," he said.

That experience had a great influence on all who lived in the village. Almost all of them turned to our loving, merciful God and His Son Jesus Christ, who paid in full for their redemption.

One Zairian told me that since they saw that the chief's evil power didn't prevent him from getting ill and dying, many are turning to the one who gives life eternal. *If only I had known more of these things at the beginning of my ministry.*

Truly our mission stations are like the cities of refuge spoken of in the Old Testament, for the Word of Life is given out freely. "And the cities which you shall give to the Levites shall be the six cities of refuge."

CHAPTER 32

ASKING THE QUESTION OF THE YEAR

On October 15, 1986, all directors of schools who had a graduating class were called to Kahemba. From Kajiji and Ecole Belle Vue, we walked five miles to a small, commercial center called Kulindji and caught a ride with a big commercial truck.

After paying our fares, we rode along on one-way trails and log-covered bridges spanning rivers. We crossed the last river on a cable ferry pulled by hand to arrive at Kahemba.

We presented all the report cards of our students from sixth-grade primary school through high school. Each girl I presented was cleared for the finals.

The following Saturday, we found ourselves seated in the same truck riding to a distant city called Gungu. A meeting was called to study why we had such a low percentage of students passing.

The road between Kahemba and Gungu resembled a washboard. Road workers had buried logs across the road, thinking this would prevent washouts and repair the road, in a way. I wondered how often I have put logs in my pathway instead of asking for guidance from the Lord Jesus Christ.

We arrived around 11:00 p. m. A Zairian Catholic sister and I stepped off the truck at the Catholic mission in Gungu where the important meeting was to take place. With our backpacks on, a bedroll in one hand and a flashlight in the other, we stumbled around until we found the home of a Zairian sister.

She had only one bedroom. Three of her nieces slept in her washroom. That first night, I put my bedroll on top of my air mattress on her front-room, cement floor and slept well.

On the next day, Sunday, I was led to our Mennonite Brethren Zairian pastor, his wife and family. They invited me to stay with them, giving me a private room with a bamboo bed.

At our principals' workshop, we had three days of solid meetings. The Education officials and school inspectors gave the instructions. They elaborated on all the different duties, plus documents and yearly reports we had to complete.

School inspectors decided one reason so few students passed the finals was because the principals slipped in former flunkies who had not been attending classes, falsifying their reports, hoping after so may tries they would finally make it.

In one session on discipline, the speaker explained among other things that all unmarried mothers must be put out of school. This idea upset me, as I reflected that it takes two to cause her to become a mother. Usually after each lecture there was time for questions. This day we had run out of time.

The last day and the last session came at last. With the same speaker on the platform, I arose and asked for the privilege of asking two questions.

"To put out all girl mothers is fine, but what about the boy fathers?" I asked.

You would have thought an explosion had taken place. Everyone started talking at once. In the audience were only four women. I knew that my time in Zaire was up in 1987, so I had no fear of asking questions that might help the women even though it made me unpopular with the authorities.

"You asked the question of the year," one principal said to me later.

But now, the speaker answered that we should deal with the father the same way as with the girl, but he was harder to detect.

Then, I asked, "How can we prevent our girls from being tempted even at the center where the final state exams are given?"

The few missionaries who attended had been asked to eat with the inspectors. All other principals ate at another place. It was interesting to see them and study this group of Zairians. They were the ones who had the job once a year of supervising all state-given exams at the different centers. My question seemed a direct threat to them.

I felt like Ezekiel 33:9. might be applicable to the tense situation. "But if you warn a wicked man to turn from his ways, and he does not turn from his ways, he will die in his iniquity; but you have delivered your soul."

A Zairian sister told me that a Belgian medical doctor just a few blocks up the street had invited us over right after the last session. After visiting for some time with this lovely family, I accepted their invitation to stay for the evening meal. I didn't feel like eating with the inspectors that evening, after the question I had asked.

Later, when one of the inspectors visited us at Ecole Belle Vue, he asked me about that second question.

"I was told that at Shamusenga mission station, some important monsieurs with cars had driven up to where our girls were staying while taking the exams," I said. "I knew nothing about it at the time, but they had tempted our girls."

"Oh," he said, "I have no car, so it couldn't have been me!"

Zairians, in their culture, do not go out on dates. To them that indicates sexual involvement. One day a student of mine walked

On inauguration day, never was I so proud of any group of girls and teachers as when Citizen Professor Mbeni directed us in the song he composed for this occasion.

THIS SIGN IN MY OFFICE WAS MY MOTTO:
The main thing is not to be happy,
but to make others happy.
Not to be loved, but to love,
and to be a blessing to others
"Shout for joy, O heavens, for the Lord has done it!" (Isaiah 44:23.
He worked miracles that we could have this school and building.
Praise the wonderful, matchless Name of out Triune God!

to Kulindji with one of my teachers. The three of us were called in
for questioning by a state official who happened to be related to
the girl involved. Even an innocent walk can be misinterpreted.

When I lived in the dorm, I set aside one afternoon a week for
boys interested in or engaged to a girl. They could come to the
dorm and visit in our front room. I believed they should learn to
be friends before thinking about marriage.

CHAPTER 33

HE HAS DONE IT

Lycée Ditalenu's six classrooms had been under construction for two years. The laying of the foundation and the raising of the walls had been supervised by David Klassen. He had completed his main project, the medical school and dorm, but did not find time to complete our building before he and his wife and family left Zaire.

Walking into the doorless, roofless and windowless building, we looked at the north wall. An open, slanting, center partition, giving the effect of venetian blinds instead of solid bricks, had been built in instead of windows for good ventilation. Thieves couldn't break in here.

When I examined Kusemuka Mennonite Brethren High School's building, about two blocks from our school, I noticed that all windows on the hidden south side had no glass. They had been stolen. I didn't want this to happen to Lycée Ditalenu's school.

If a window would be stolen or broken, they would certainly also take some of our precious sewing machines. How could I install large glass windows on the south side, that had been made by our missionary Rob Neufeld's students in our Mennonite Brethren carpenters' school at Kinshasa?

At our Kikwit Mennonite Brethren High School, called Mbandu, I inspected it for ideas. Where there were bars at the windows, the glass remained intact. This gave me a clue for Lycee Ditalenu.

Our window frames, at least four inches wide, were made of wood. The original plan was that all this excess wood would be on the inside and that the glass would be more or less flush with the walls.

I had the carpenters drill holes into the frames to insert building iron for bars. Then, I placed the glass on the inside, leaving the bars on the outside of the window. I then slanted the windows so that the tops were even with the wall, while at the bottom they were almost two inches further in. No rain would stand for any length of time on these wooden window frames.

After the corrugated roofing was nailed on, George, our watchman, had brush in hand painting old oil on the rafters to make them termite proof, before the plyboard and laths became our ceilings.

Selling all our excess building materials, including some much desired paint, I managed to get enough money together to buy cement to finish the floors of all the classrooms. In place of the paint, whitewash covered the classrooms inside and out.

One classroom had to be converted into an office, secretariat, and store room. An unusual cubby-hole cupboard, formerly used by our missionaries' children to sort laundry, was cut down to the height that we needed and carried over by a group of strong Zairian men. It served as a room divider and a place to put school supplies for each teacher.

Professor Kamwimba, a former student of mine, after gaining further training in Kikwit, came back as a professor. He, together with other teachers, helped me in all of the renovation.

It was now January 21, six days away from the inauguration of our new school building. Even though we couldn't possibly finish all the details by that date, we couldn't put off the big event because the medical staff and teachers would have their new medical school and dorm dedication at the same time. Members of the Mennonite Brethren Missions/Services would be here for the occasion.

Students and teachers, excited over the prospect, wanted to do their best to prepare the grounds and schoolrooms for this great ceremony.

All students washed windows and removed whitewash spots from their classroom floors. Two to a desk, they carried them from their former classrooms over the path to their new, clean classrooms. The treadle zigzag sewing machines came next, and students placed them next to cement benches, under the large glass windows in the south wall.

On Tuesday, school went only for three periods. Then, the students helped in the clean-up. They had brought grass cutters, short handled hoes and rakes. That helped make quick work of the clean-up.

Kasongo Lunda Umba and friends gathered large stones to divide the walkways, placing some around the flag pole as well. Umba rejoiced to see that the double sink donated by the Mission Circle of Bakersfield Mennonite Brethren Church (now called Heritage Bible Church) had been placed in their classroom. Five ironing boards had been attached to the back wall where charcoal irons waited to be used. Double plyboard blackboards dominated the front of the classrooms.

On Saturday, the teachers finished placing stones around the flagpole. Since all the rooms lay in a straight line, paths from all six rooms led to the small circle around the flagpole. In between each path had been planted either grass or flowers. Poinsettias filled one area completely. They grew well and bloomed profusely.

Our teachers wrote the words "Lycée Ditalenu" with small stones in the circle surrounding the flagpole and covered the stones with whitewash. Earlier, a link fence had been nailed to forest poles surrounding the immediate school grounds. Consequently, from then on the students couldn't sneak around the sides of the building to run off.

On Saturday evening, I served coffee to our helpful teachers, carpenters and sentinels. They went home tired but happy, knowing they had all contributed to the inauguration of the new school building.

A few tasks remained unfinished. There were still cupboards missing; teacher's chairs needed to be attached to their desks or they would "walk away." Nevertheless, for the inauguration, we would get by.

In my office, I placed the French world globe I had purchased in Belgium on my way back from furlough. Since my bags were full, I had put it in my backpack and had carried the "whole world" on my back to Zaire. Yes, the whole world is a mission field. I hoped to encircle it with my prayers.

Displays of pattern-making, sewing, textiles - including fiber the students had pounded from a certain cactus plant - would be explained. Our pupils were highly motivated, proud of their work and rightfully so.

Others marveled when they saw the intricate drawings of a garment that had been sewn, showing even the different layers of material with appropriate arrows for the cut-down. Bible lessons brought out the real aim of this new school.

On Sunday morning, we made sure that the students who would explain their school displays knew just what to say. Benches from the classrooms had been placed outside the immediate school grounds. They filled up fast.

An interested audience joined in when the students sang their national anthem while raising the flag to the beat of the patriotic song. It was done to perfection.

Never was I more proud of any group of girls and teachers than when Citizen Professor Mbeni directed us in the song he had composed. In it, he praised God and asked His guiding hand concerning the future. In this French song, the second verse went like this:

We are now placing in your beloved hands
Lycée Ditalenu our beloved school,
May God's blessings be on this place,
For glorifying God by His matchless grace .

Standing in front of our audience, I officially welcomed them. In a beautiful French, one of our technical teachers shared the history of the school. Citizen Kusangila, the legal representative from Kikwit for our mission before the Zairian Government, gave a meaningful message from God.

We had invited the Sector Chief from Kulindji (where the government office was located) to cut the ribbon. He sent one of his office workers. In the midst of this procession of earnest prayers and praise to our Lord Jesus Christ, we called on him to cut the ribbon. Peter Hamm, from the home office, Ernie Doerksen from Kikwit, Rev. Dyck from the United States, and I walked forward for this ceremony. Then, the Zairian cut the ribbon in the name of his ancestors.

Brother Hamm prayed a touching dedicatory prayer. I wish it could have been in French or Kituba, for only a few of us could understand it, but all felt the Spirit of the living God in that place.

"Shout for joy, O heavens, for the Lord has done it!" (Isaiah 44:23). God worked miracles so that we could have this school and building. We praise His matchless Name.

CHAPTER 34

AU REVOIR BUT NOT GOOD BYE

After 39 years of service in Zaire, how does one say good-bye? In my case, I knew that the Lord had released me from overseas duties in Zaire. I told the Education committee that I was not going to be principal the next year.

That position involved many associated details: school library, school supplies including courses which had been typed and duplicated with the Gestetner, books, rulers, French curves and pencils. Marking sewing machines, indicating which belonged to the mission and which to the school, demanded genuine honesty.

Turning over the responsibility meant explaining office procedures, taking inventory, signing as to its authenticity, and distributing copies to various offices. It was better equipped than most Zairian schools, therefore presented a greater temptation.

At home, after work, I kept busy sorting, packing, selling, eliminating, having friends in for dinner, farewell speeches, embracing, tears and exchanging Bible verses. In a goodbye speech to the church, I asked forgiveness for losing my cool a time or two. Yes, I was far from perfect. For that attribute, I will have to wait until I get to heaven.

At a dinner given for my workers, George Nkozi cried like a baby. "Who will look after me as you did?" he said.

Kasongo Lunda Umba begged me, "Can't you stay until the end of this school year? I was among the first sixth-grade students to enter this school. The Lord willing, I will be graduating this year."

When the final day came, I brought a rugby football to chapel that

As I looked down for the last time, while swooping over the airstrip, one person stood out in my mind. That was Kasongo Lunda Umba, the great Lunda chief's daughter, and her request, "Can't you stay until the end of this school year?"

"You had better also say good-bye to Nkoshi George. He is heart-broken."

morning as a final gift to the student body. It was impossible for me to stay, but for a couple of minutes tears streamed down my face.

My last suitcase had been sent ahead to the airstrip. Now, I had to walk quickly to the airport to catch the Missionary Aviation Fellowship plane. It was scheduled to leave as soon as the pilot filled it with gas. Workmen had already pushed barrels of aviation gas to the airstrip from the mission storeroom.

Walking down the path, my dog - already handed over to a new owner - tore loose from his rope and followed me, jumping up and down, trying to say goodbye. Some of my Zairian students followed me along the 2-mile stretch, in tears.

As we reached the airstrip, some of my students, unable to hold back the tears, were wailing. I too broke into tears, lacking words to express my grief at this necessary separation. Or was it final?

Just before I boarded the plane, a friend said, "You had better also say good-bye to George Nkosi. He is heart broken."

After saying *au revoir*, I strapped myself into the seat. A hundred different incidents raced through my mind. Who would have thought that I could learn two foreign languages and teach in a third? Certainly not me.

Who helped me meet some of the many needs of the Zairian

Reaching the airstrip, more of my students, not able to hold back the tears, were wailing. I too broke into tears, lacking words to express my grief at this necessary separation.

woman? It all seemed like a dream. I knew that it wasn't in my strength that I accomplished it, for I found my answer in Isaiah 44:23, "Shout for joy, O heavens, for the Lord has done it."

Looking down for the last time as we swooped over the airstrip, one person stood out in my mind. Kasongo-Lunda Umba. "Can't you stay until the end of this school year?" she had asked me.

She and her father had invited me to a great event. Her uncle, the great Lunda Chief, had died. Her own father was to be installed as Chief in his place. I just had to find a way to attend that great historical event.

Drums in ordinary life are their Morse code. Messages are sent to distant villages in this way. On installation day, drums beat out the invitation to join them in the great installation service.

CHAPTER 35

THE HEAD LUNDA CHIEF'S INSTALLATION

Most people think being a missionary in Zaire, Africa, is a great sacrifice. On the contrary, it is a great privilege. Living for Christ to help the whole person in that part of the world gave me an insight into customs and let me observe another lifestyle that few foreigners can understand.

In September of 1985, for example, I was invited to attend an installation service of Citizen Kasongo Lunda to become the head Lunda Chief. The Lunda Chiefs date back to about 1600, when Kubinda Ilunda a Luba founded the Lunda empire. Lunda means friendship, but joining them was not always voluntary. They, however, integrated the conquered chiefs into their empire. Although these conquered chiefs had to pay tribute, they were given a share in this system.

Through the seventeenth century, this process continued. The head Lunda Chief formed the Mwant Yav King of Vipers headquarters, 100 kilometers east of the Kasai river. This location gave them access to wealth by controlling the end of major trade routes inland.

From 1884 to 1904, King Leopold II of the Belgians ruled Congo, which is as large as the United States east of the Mississippi. In that period, a son of a paramount chief of the Lunda tribe was disinherited; therefore, he emigrated and formed the Chokwe tribe. In 1885, the Chokwes successfully invaded the Lundas and turned the tables on them.

When the Belgians took Congo as their colony in 1908, even though the Lundas had not been in power for 30 years, they looked for someone in authority among the Lundas. District Commissioner Gosem deliberately organized the native administration system around Muteba's authority.

In 1923, the Mwaant Yav had been explicitly denied any direct executive authority outside of Kapanga territory. Since the Nzofu village, home of the head Lunda Chief and his family, is in Kwango territory, this law made the Lunda Chief of great importance. He was then chief of all the Lundas in the Kwango and in Angola.

Since we were invited to attend, the great question was, what gift would be appropriate for such a one of this honored position? We had to choose something already available at the mission station.

On the morning of September 7, 1985, at 7:00 a.m. Helen and I excitedly threw our sleeping bags, a basket of food, and drinking water into the back of the four-wheel-drive public health jeep. We climbed in, ready for the five-hour 130-kilometer drive over crude dirt trails leading to the Nzofu village. This unique village, close to the Angolan border, housed only the chief's wives and his closest relatives.

It was not raining, although the sky looked threatening. Later, we heard the Chief-to-be had worked some kind of magic to keep the rain from his village for the great celebration. Other villages all around him had rain, but not Chief Nzofu's village. We know that Satan can also work miracles, but to keep away rain?

Since it was only September, the usually tall elephant grass stood about knee high, and green. It made the country look like a park, with tropical blooming trees, ferns and blooming orchids. Coming close to small villages, we had to watch carefully to dodge village goats, pigs, chickens and barkless basengi dogs.

Many of our students came from these small, traditional huts that had dirt floors and grass roofs. They entered a new world as they studied advanced math, trigonometry and chemistry (usually without a lab.)

"Helen," I said, "look! There is Medicine Mountain. It is the highest mountain to our left. Shannon Lake where the Shannons built a vacation hut, is at its feet. I hear that you know the history of this lake."

"Yes," Helen responded. "The old story is that they believed the first white man came up from that lake. To the Congolese, he was a bleached-out ghost who lived under the lake. They would not go near it to bathe or to soak their manioc.

"Now, however, since they saw that it didn't hurt us, and we had a good time on the bamboo raft, they decided that it would not kill them either. Today, they not only soak their toxic manioc on its shores, but they also enjoy bathing in it."

"What about Medicine Mountain?" I asked.

"When we wanted to climb it," Helen said, "the Chief nearest it insisted that we, accompanied by their guide, follow their rituals."

As the mountain grew smaller behind us, my thoughts turned to Nzofo village.

"Did you bring the gift along for the Chief-to-be?" I asked.

"Yes, do you think we chose wisely?" she responded.

"We will most likely see by his reaction to it," I assured her.

At 9:30, we stopped beside an old wooden bridge. The aroma of coffee poured by Pakisa's wife Linda made Helen and me hurry to the river to wash our hands. While eating a bun and drinking our coffee, Helen and I started walking. We asked the driver to meet us on the other side of the bridge. All passengers felt that if the logs or planks in the bridge had been hollowed out by termites, our walking across would lighten the load for the jeep.

We soon arrived at our mission outpost, Shawiyanga. We saw the palm trees under which were built the inexpensive temporary village school, its dorms and teachers' houses. Outside walls of the school had been lined with bamboo to protect the building from washing away in the tropical storms.

Right across the street stood the home of the pastor and the church building. This neat outpost made us realize that the school principal, Citizen Fima, teachers, pastor and the Chief had interested the people in educating their children.

The next post was Kapinipini. Our mission outpost boasted of a junior high, a church and a primary school. We met the principal of the junior high. After a hearty greeting, he showed us the small, grass-roofed hut where we would spend the night. Taking our sleeping bags, food baskets and towels, we followed him, having to duck as we entered the low hut through a bamboo doorway.

Principal Fima and Dorothy Kopper

Principal Santu Thoka opened the bamboo shutters. This brought a ray of light into the dark entrance room. Seeing the bamboo shelves that lined the wall, a small bamboo counter in front, and the uneven dirt floor, which spoke of many feet, made me think that this had been a small school store.

In the bedroom, there was hardly any walking space between the two bamboo beds. The mud-plastered walls had crumbled, so we could see daylight through the cracks. The beds looked as if they had been used before, so we dared not put our sleeping bags on them before we sprayed for ticks, as a precaution against tick fever. For the moment, we decided to leave our sleeping bags on the shelves in the entryway.

We knew that we would risk not only scorpions and centipedes, but also the inevitable chigger. Cathy Esau, the daughter of John and Agnes, said it well: "The bare-footed prodigal son will get chiggers."

At last, we entered the great Nzofu village. First, we saw a bamboo fence made from branches of one of the 200 genders of the palm tree. The fence marked the boundary of this small village. The village of the great head Lunda Chief featured houses of red mud and other natural materials, like an African picture book.

Its quaint traditional huts, with bamboo shutters and doors, had new roofs made from the long elephant grass. All were complete but one, whose thick roof was neatly trimmed on one side, but long and shaggy on the other.

Right across from where we parked stood a medium-sized tree with about 40 polka-dotted, guinea fowl roosting among its green branches and leaves. As far as our eyes could see, the whole yard had been meticulously swept clean of any paper, weed and blade of grass.

Sitting in the shade of an overhanging grass roof, we started to relax when we answered a call to partake of an authentic Zairian dinner. After walking to the newly erected dining hall, we stood in line to be served.

By the door, a portable basin of water with a bar of soap allowed us to wash our hands. On all four walls, an opening between the four-foot-high bamboo wall and the grass roof caught every breeze, a welcome relief in the tropics.

As we passed by, they served us generous portions of luku. The rich meat sauce they served with large pieces of beef had a special flavor that only their tasty orange palm oil can give. We savored each piece of the luku, dipping it into the meat sauce and almost licking the plate clean.

Outside we met many of the invited guests. My pupil, the Chief's daughter, Kasongo Lunda Umba, named after her father Kasongo Lunda, introduced me to two of her sisters. She was a member of our Mennonite Brethren Church and sang in the school choir.

"Bon jour, Umba!" I greeted her. "It is a pleasure to be here. I see all of you have worked hard to be able to welcome so many people here. I hear the top ruler of Zaire, Mobutu Se-Se Seko Marshal, has also sent a large delegation including the governor from Kinshasa. You must be proud that your uncle chose your father for this position."

"Yes," Umba replied. "He did choose him over his own son."

Custom ordains that the Lunda aristocrats choose a king from the sons of dead kings, born in the purple. This means authentically related to the chiefly line by blood.

"You remember him, do you not?" she asked me. "He often has come to Kajiji to talk to you about my schooling. He paid for me. He often traveled with me to protect me."

"Your father will be in charge of all the Lundas in the Bandundu and in Angola as well, will he not?" I responded.

"Oui," she said. "There are many in Angola, that war-torn country, as well as here in Zaire. My father, however, can no longer go back to Angola, because of an accident. If he goes there, his life is in danger."

Later, a messenger from the big chief came. "Would you like to say something to the next head Lunda Chief?" he asked me.

"Helen," I called, "did you hear what he is asking us? He wants to know if we want to talk to the next Mfumu."

Helen had gone to the jeep to rest, but this brought her right to her feet. "We would consider that a great honor," she said.

"When does he want us to see him?" I asked the messenger.

"Can you come now?" he replied. "I will show you the path."

Before we realized what had happened, Pastor Shawakela, legal representative Kasombo, Helen and I were led down the neat path to his nicely whitewashed home.

Also built with materials from the forest, the home had been well kept. Because of its small windows, our eyes had to get accustomed to the darkness.

When soft drinks appeared before us, the Chief-to-be politely declined to drink with us. Custom demanded that if he had a drink in our presence, we would have to close our eyes and bow our heads until he clapped his hands, signifying he had finished.

Citizen Kasongo Lunda, seated on a grass mat next to the wall, could not be seen directly by us. Behind him hung five animal skins on the wall. In one corner lay a large elephant tusk, other horns of animals and objects from the forest of special significance to him as a chief.

He appeared to be about 40 years old. His muscular body showed he had been no loafer. In the dry season, he and his friends would walk miles to the grasslands where game hid in the elephant grass. They used bows and arrows or guns (some homemade) to shoot the trapped animals encircled by a wall of fire.

Well qualified by his extensive social experiences, the Chief-to-be had attended school and lived in Angola until 1970. He knew the trade languages of Zaire, as well as Portuguese, French, Lunda and Chokwe. He could understand many more.

Although traditional in some ways, he a Lunda, had adjusted to modern life. Citizen Pakisa, a Chokway and the Public Health Director, would sit next to him. They even ate and drank together, forgetting tribal customs.

"Do you have something you want to tell me?" he asked.

"Yes," I said. "Thank you for allowing your lovely daughter to attend our school. First in her grade, she studied diligently."

"I have heard good things about you and your school," citizen Kasongo Lunda said. "Thanks much for opening the school for us."

His gracious word of thanks reminded me of the Psalmist David, who said: "The Most High is ruler over the realm of mankind, and bestows it on whom He wishes and sets over it the lowliest of men!"

Kasonga Lunda Umba gives Mademoiselle Principal a guinea fowl.

"Chief," I said, "it is God who sets you up to be Chief of the Lunda tribe. Each of us must do our part, our best where God places us."

"Umba, come here," Citizen Kasongo Lunda said to his daughter. She came kneeling before her father.

"Give Mademoiselle Principal a guinea fowl."

When we stood outside, Citizeness Umba gave me the white polka-dotted guinea fowl I had been admiring all morning. My arms went around this special Zairian Christian Chieftain's daughter, and I kissed her on both cheeks - the French way.

The next great Lunda chief had given us the appropriate gift, something with blood. If he had given us an egg, that would have been an insult. This was a special gift. Since I was able to express my deepest thoughts on the sovereignty of our King of Kings, I felt we had chosen an appropriate gift for this great Head Chief.

We also had given him something with blood. Just as they settle tribal affairs by killing an animal and having a feast, God asks us to settle our affairs with Him by accepting the gift offering of His Son's blood, shed for our sins.

We prayed that he might read about the great provision of eternal life, heed its message and live forever as he read about it in the Kituba New Testament, Chokwe Bible and beautiful French Bible we gave him.

Feeling exhilarated, I wanted to witness more. "Why do we not wait and see what they will do tonight?" I suggested to Citizen Kasombo. "I am curious to see their preparations for tomorrow's great event."

"Ve! Ve! Children of God cannot stay here tonight," he warned. "Many chiefs are here. Many evil things will be done tonight to give power to this new Lunda Chief. We must not stay. We cannot stay. We will go to our mission outpost at Kapinipini."

We heard whisperings among lesser chiefs of gifts they had brought for their leader. Bracelets *the price of human blood,* to give (*ndoki*) evil power, would allow him to reign with fear, not only to gain the respect from the spirit world of his ancestors, but from his great Lunda tribe as well.

Upon arriving at Kapinipini, we received royal treatment from the principal's wife. She brought us a bowl of luku and greens (*sakasak*) she had raised in her own garden. The next day, they served us monkey meat spiced with palm fat and hot red peppers. That helped to cover the undesirable taste of this meat.

Before crawling into our sleeping bags that evening, we sprayed the bamboo beds and mats against ticks and fleas.

At Nzofu village the next morning, the people said, "It won't be long until they put Chief Nzofu on the leopard's skin." Drums already beat out the invitation to join them in the great installation service. We walked up to the royal fence, inside the village.

Inside the fence stood the chief's house, the houses of his wives, the royal kitchen, and a shed in which certain ceremonial objects of the Chief stayed. The fence was a traditional shape and design.

As we looked on, waiting to see the Chief come out of his home, suddenly behind me a delegation of all the dignitaries sent by the head ruler of all Zaire, Mobutu Sese-Seko Marshal, marched up. Standing directly in their path, I was embarrassed but not frightened. Quickly stepping out of the way, I saw an amused smile on the Governor's face.

Lesser chiefs from the villages wore their colorful beaded hats. Medicine men had their skull caps, and fetishes around their necks, arms and ankles. In sharp contrast, the dignitaries wore authentic well-tailored suits, called abacos, without a tie but with their type of scarf.

Now the drums' rhythm changed to an entrance march. Soon, we witnessed stirrings at the other end of the yard. The one to be installed came out of a small, mud-and-stick hut on the shoulders of a Zairian.

He wore his beaded red, white and blue Chieftain's hat with pride. The white star on top of a knob protruded from the middle of it with another star on its tip. Two bead-covered knobs, at the back and front, adorned the rounded pill-shaped hat. This unusual head-piece also featured two colorful, striped, beaded horns, attached on each side.

Over the front and down the back of his body was a raffia, a striped piece of Zairian woven cloth. It was thrown over a full, dark-flowered loin cloth. Men standing guard next to him wore no clothes on the upper part of their black skin. From the waist down, they wore colorful loin cloths richly folded over with an abundance of material.

The chief to be and his entourage had their separate shelter. Over the erected bamboo poles had been draped many women's colorful skirt cloths. All the village chiefs, after being introduced, nodded with their multicolored hats or came forward to give their speeches in the language of their choice. It was like the biblical tower of Babel.

Dignitaries climaxed their speeches giving the chief power in the name of Zaire and their ancestors. Only one speaker, Citizen Zangio Kampew, Commisar of the people, proudly said that he presented him with this power in the name of Zaire, and in the name of our Triune God.

The women now danced, shuffling their feet in a way that soon hid their feet in the dust. It was a dance reserved only for this occasion.

When the previous Lunda Chief died, the different emblems of power, taken as tradition dictated, had been hidden by Citizen Kakwata. He alone had power to bestow them on the new tribal chief. He came forth dancing in a white loin cloth with an off-white shirt, fuzzy tassels hanging from his sleeves.

As he danced, Kakwata came ever closer to the Chief-to-be. In his path was a huge leopard skin. At the tip of its tail was placed a four-foot ivory tusk. Meanwhile, Citizen Kasongo Lunda sat on his grass mat, ready to accept the tokens of his new mission.

A poem tried to capture the excitement of the historical moment:

> The bearer of their emblems of power
> was topped with feathers fitly fitting
> over his entire head,
> sticking straight out like quills of a porcupine.
>
> Drummers beat to the steps of this carrier,
> left toe forward, shuffled to the left,
> Right foot forward, shuffled to the right.
> Sugar cane, sharp knife, chain and bracelet,
>
> Two steps forward and one step back,
> hidden from all when Lunda's Chief died.
> Cherished chosen symbols of challenge
> to check and chide his children in Zaire.
>
> Drummers frenzied beat as he danced closer,
> over the ivory tusk unto the leopard's skin.
> Two steps forward and one step back.
> beat the drum as his feet just flew.
>
> Left foot straight forward shuffle to the left,
> Right foot forward shuffled to the right,
> dancing forward power placed on him,
> Raising their Chief from straw to leopard's skin,
> Loyally leading all Lundas to him.
>
> In their political rallies, the Zairians cheer by crying:
>
> Live the Republic of Zaire!
> Live Mobutu Se-Se Seko!
> Live the district of Kwango!
> Live the village of Nzofu!
> Live the new Lunda Chief!

Others now entered the courtyard, some dancing, throwing dirt in the air. Finally, we could see nothing but dust, sifting around the

The one to be installed came out of a small mud-and-stick hut on the shoulders of a Zairian.

Two steps forward and one step back, beat the drum as his feet just flew.

The bearer of their emblems of power was topped with feathers aptly fitting over his entire head, sticking out like quills of a porcupine.

Raising their Chief from straw to leopard's skin, loyally leading all Lundas to him.

many villagers.

After the judges and others signed official papers, they exhorted Lunda's chief to stay within the rules of the Zairian government. They now lifted Chief Kasongo Lunda to his feet. He stepped on the leopard's skin and danced to the beat of the drums, as he announced new names he had taken. Mwant Tshend, Mashind, Mfumu a Nsangu Katend wa Mutshadi, meaning: He is the second or youngest king (chief) and can go anywhere.

One of our gifts to him, the French Bible, he gave to his daughter Kasongo Lunda Umba for use in the classroom - to study and teach how God's children will some day go to the greatest "installation" of all, the coronation of His Majesty, our Sovereign Lord, to crown Him King of Kings and Lord of Lords!

THE END

POSTSCRIPT

5/21/97 American On-line update from Zaire states as follows:
Since Mobutu Sese Seko has been forced to leave Zaire for good,
Kabila has presented Zaire with a new flag and going back to the
name of The Democratic Republic of the Congo.

We as former missionaries to that country, praise God that from
1912 to 1997 even though some have lost their lives through tropical diseases and some have had to evacuate a number of times, no
missionary has been martyred for their faith.

Dr. Pakisa Tshimika and Linda, his wife (Dr. Pakisa is the regional secretary for the MB work in Congo and Angola) quoted II Kings
6: 15-17 which refers to guardian angels in a recent communication:

"This past weekend, especially Saturday was very tense for all
inhabitants of Kinshasa. I checked our Mennonite Brethren office
in Kitambo area. Stores there were either looted or burnt by Mobutu's soldiers on Saturday and Sunday, but our offices were not
affected." As he gathered information, there were no reports of
death or damage among the Zairian Mennonite Brethren Christians nor of the Mennonite Central Committee or Inger Mennonite
Mission staffs.

Pakisa continues: "We had the worst gun fires we ever heard in
our lives this past Saturday. Four of our neighbors were looted
completely by Mobutu's soldiers. We could hear how their doors
and windows were being destroyed, children and mothers scream-
ing while the soldiers went on pillaging without pity. They stopped
by our gate a couple of times but each time they left to pillage
another house next to ours. Later on, a guard from next door
informed us about how four soldiers had stopped by to ask information regarding us. They knew that missionaries lived in the

house but wanted to know if we were still there. He informed them that we had left due to insecurity in Kinshasa. Without asking any more questions, they left. Many angels were watching over us. My prayer during the whole night was that God would confuse any soldier who might want to enter our house. Your prayers did more than you might ever know."An army officer told Dr. Pakisa not to go anywhere as the order had gone out to kill 5 more people in the area. Fortunately the angels were still watching over Dr. Pakisa and his family and an organization called SIAMA was able to arrange passage for Linda and their two daughters all the way to Kansas. All of our missionaries are out of the country, but what about our 75,000 Mennonite Brethren Christians left in Zaire? This is a terrible time for all of them. They need God to grant them courage, wisdom and leadership power.

So PRAY! PRAY!

Appendix A

Missionaries serving in Belgian Congo pictured at front of book.

Row 1: Mr. William Baerg, Mrs. Margaret Baerg, Miss Nettie Berg, Mr. Henry Brucks, Mrs. Elsie Brucks, Miss Susie Brucks, Mr. Henry Derksen, Mrs. Helen Derksen, Miss Margaret Dyck.

Row 2: Mr. Ernest Dyck, Mrs. Lydia Dyck, Mr. Ivan Elrich, Mrs. Alma Elrich, Mr. Siegfried Epp, Mr. Abram Esau, Mrs. Sarah Esau, Mr. John Esau, Mrs. Agnes Esau.

Row 3: Mr. George Faul, Mrs. Gretchen Faul, Mr. Harold Fehderau, Mrs. Nancy Fehderau, Miss Elsie Fischer, Mr. Irvin Friesen, Mrs. Lydia Friesen, Miss Erna Funk, Miss Arlene Gerdes.

Row 4: Miss Anna Goertzen, Miss Elsie Guenther, Mr. Ben Klassen, Mrs. Anna Klassen, Mr. John Kliewer, Mrs. Ruth Kliewer, Miss Dorothy Kopper, Mr. Robert Kroeker, Mrs. Wanda Kroeker.

Row 5: Mr. Harold Kruger, Mrs. Susan Kruger, Miss Daisy Martens, Mr. Leslie Ortman, Mrs. Hope Ortman, Miss Katy Penner, Miss Sarah Peters, Mr. Arnold Prieb, Mrs. Rose Prieb.

Row 6: Mr. Walter Sawatsky, Mrs. Irma Sawatsky, Mr. Alfred Schmidt, Mrs. Viola Schmidt, Mr. Ernest Schmidt, Mrs. Leona Schmidt, Mr. Clyde Shannon, Mrs. Elizabeth Shannon, Miss Helen Toews.

Row 7: Miss Mary Toews, Mr. Vernon Vogt, Mrs. Mildred Vogt, Mr. Arthur Wiebe, Mrs. Ella Wiebe, Mr. Orville Wiebe, Mrs. Ruby Wiebe, Miss Mathilda Wall, Miss Katherine Wiens.

Row 8: Miss Kathryn Willems, Miss Martha Willems. *At Home:* Mr. Frank Buschman, Mrs. Clara Buschman, Miss Anna Enns, Mrs. Martha Janzen, Mr. Theodor Martens, Mrs. Frieda Martens.